COAST

MICHAEL COULTER

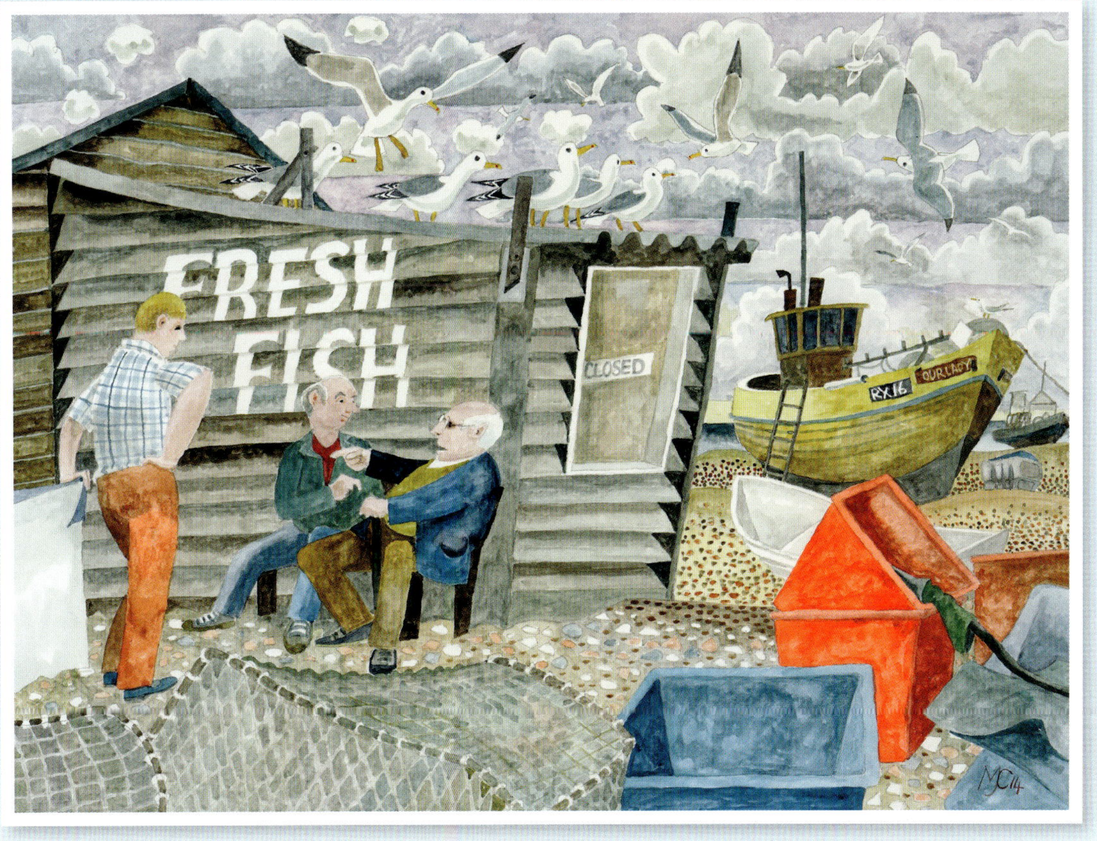

MADE IN NORFOLK BY MASCOT MEDIA

Published in Great Britain in 2018
by Mascot Media, Norfolk, UK.
Email: mascot_media@btinternet.com
www.mascotmedia.co.uk

A CIP catalogue record for this book is available from the British Library.

ISBN: 978-1-9164783-0-5

www.michaelcoulter.org

Written by Alan Marshall & Michael Coulter.
Designed by Alan Marshall.
Edited by Marion Scott Marshall.

Printed by Swallowtail Print, Drayton Industrial Park, Taverham Road, Drayton, Norwich, Norfolk NR8 6RL.
Email: contact@swallowtailprint.co.uk
www.swallowtailprint.co.uk

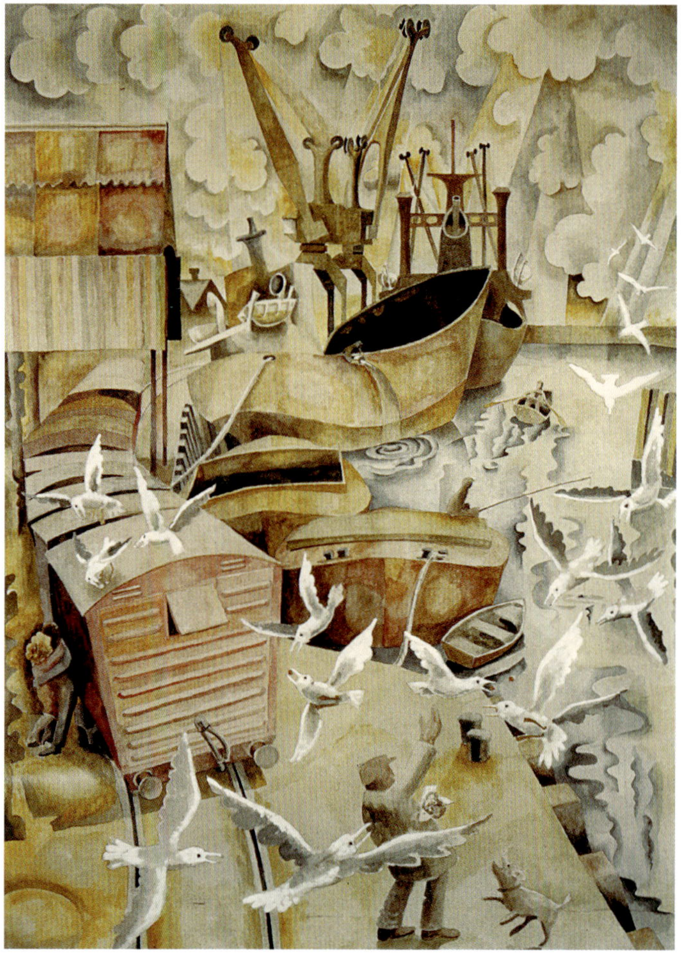

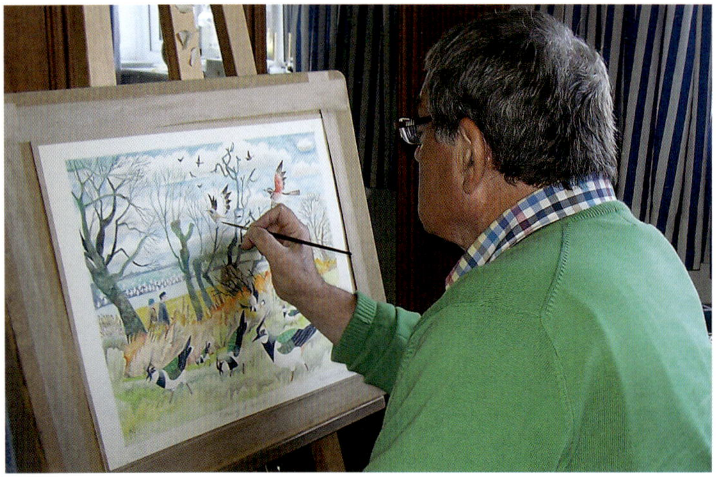

Front cover: 'Beach Scene with an Anchor' (2018)
Title page: 'Conversations and Gulls' (2014)
Above: 'Sunday Dock' (1980)
Left: Michael Coulter at work in his studio
Facing page: detail from 'Waders' (2017) – see full image on page 31
Page 4: 'Divers near Wreck' (1989)
Page 5: 'Harvest House from the Beach' (left) and 'Thursday by the Sea' (right). Both Felixstowe, dated 1990 and 2013 respectively
Page 6: 'Waldringfield' (1991)
Page 7: Deben bookmark commissioned by Deben Decorative and Fine Arts Society

CONTENTS

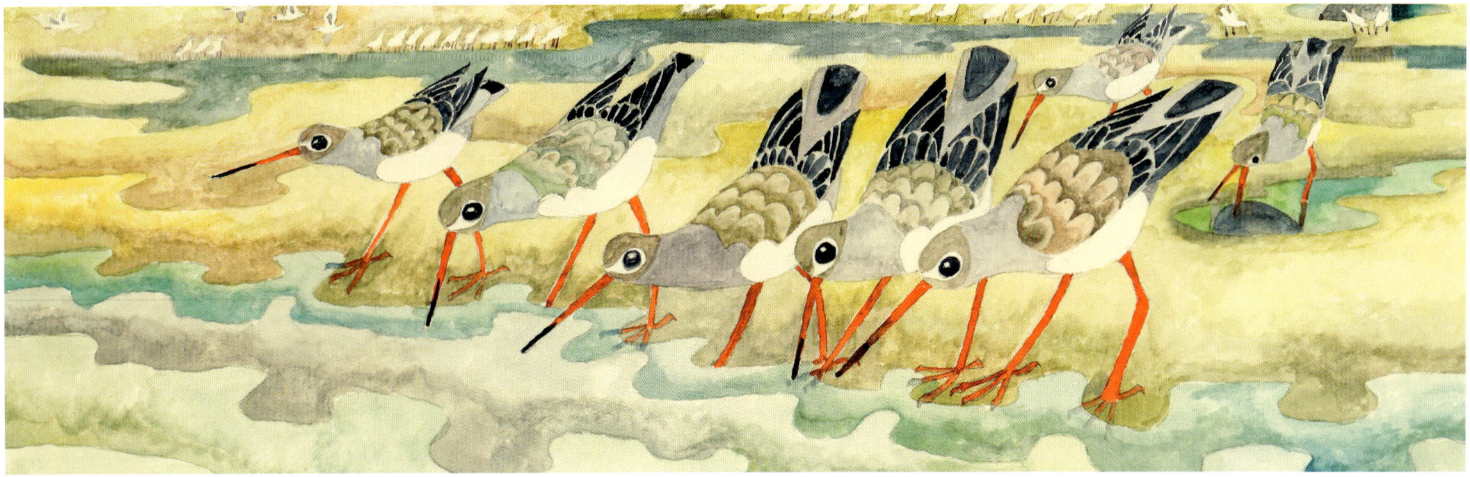

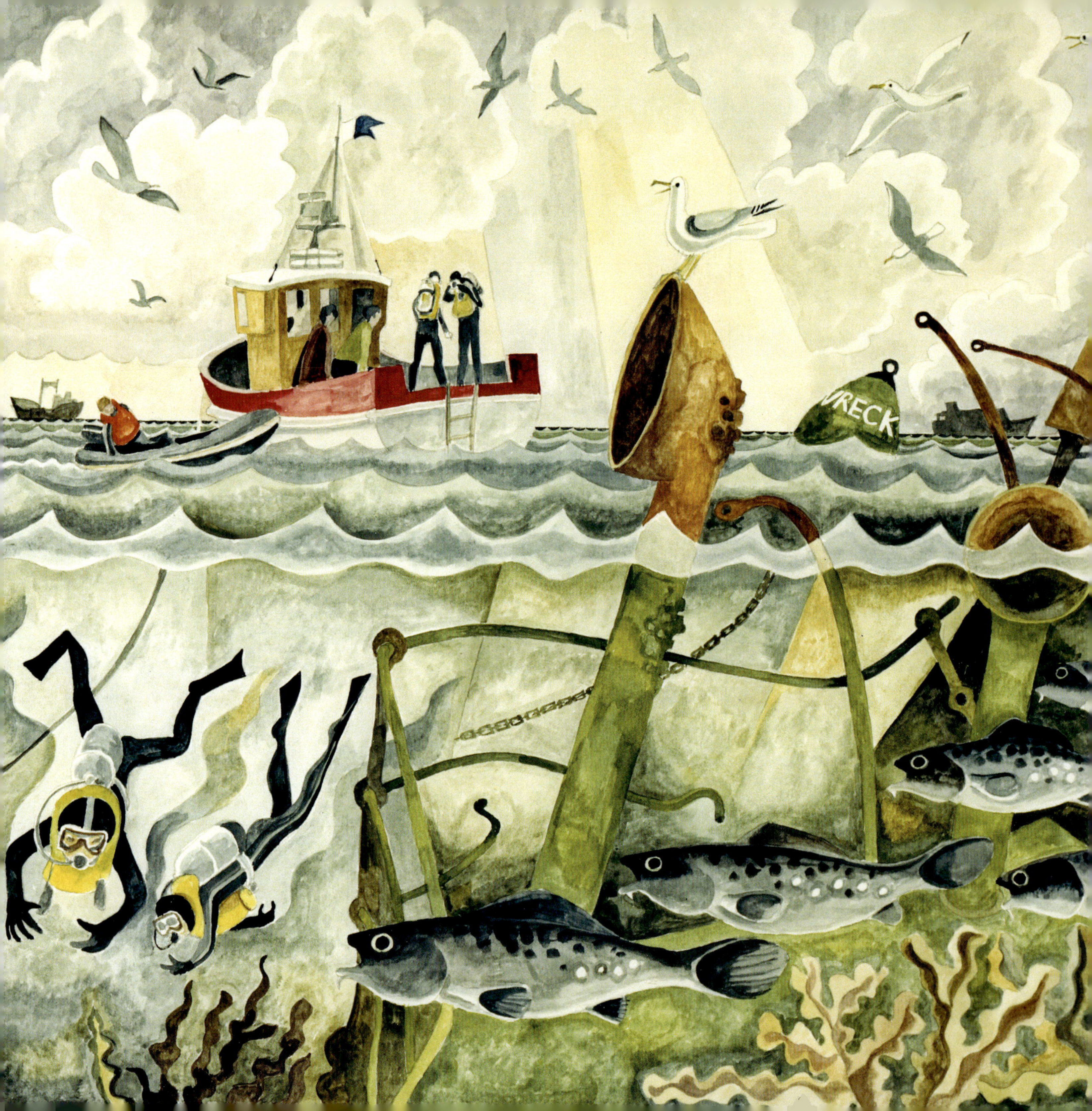
RECK

SHIFTING SANDS

ALAN MARSHALL

Michael Coulter has been painting the seaside for more than three decades. During this period the sands of time have brought change both to the subject and to the artist's work. Early influences Ravilious, Bawden and Burra shaped his output in the 1970s and 1980s, becoming absorbed gradually into his own distinctive style in the 1990s as his inspiration and output soared in the wake of his recently ended teaching career.

Two of his watercolour paintings below merge coastal landscapes of 1990 and 2013. This is hardly a seamless transition, as the artist's style has developed, his colour palette has been transformed and the scenes themselves mark the passing of time. Some of the elements have survived the process, with beach huts still adorning the promenades of many seaside towns. Deckchairs are nowadays a rarity, but the gulls are still with us. Michael may today prefer to populate his paintings with birds rather than people, but his snapshots of family fun have a similar charm and appeal.

This book deliberately overlaps very little with our earlier title, ***Coulter's Countryside*** (Mascot Media, 2012), partly because this author and publisher always planned to tackle another element of the artist's portfolio and create a book celebrating the joys of coastal Britain. This volume does unapologetically head inland on occasion, capturing tidal inlets and waterways that represent (at least to the artist) an extension of the coast. We should be forgiven therefore for including Michael's home town of Woodbridge, some 13 kilometres from the sea, or the occasional diversion along the Rivers Orwell, Stour and Deben.

While Shropshire-born, and certainly no son of the sea, the artist has lived in Suffolk since the late 1960s, having moved down south to teach art at Woolverstone School near Ipswich. It is therefore no great surprise that his adopted county provides the settings for a large body of work taking us from the 1980s to the present day. Excursions are made over the borders, both north and south, to take in the coastal landscape of Norfolk and Suffolk. Much of East Anglia is therefore captured in these pages before the artist roams farther afield.

Heading south and west, Michael offers a smattering of Sussex and Kent scenes before reaching Dorset and a large portfolio of its glorious coast strip that he describes as "Suffolk

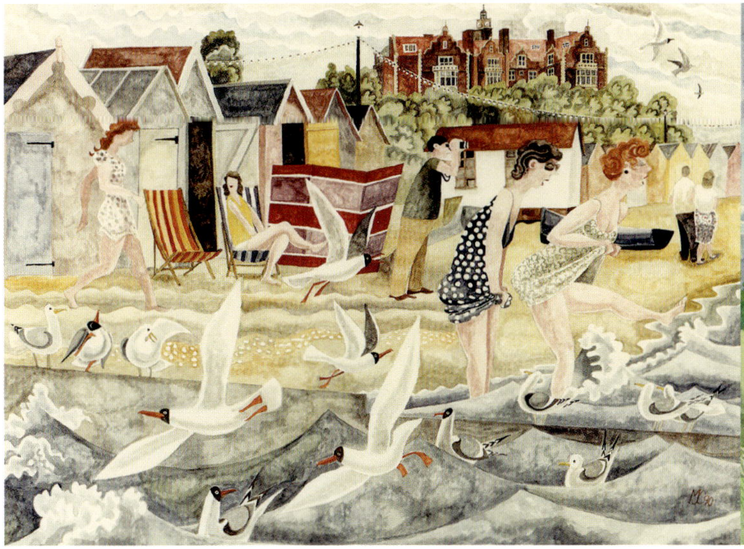

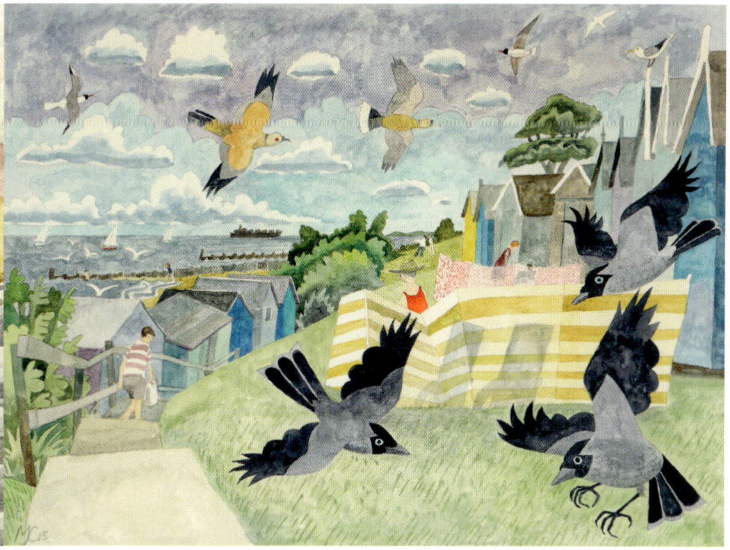

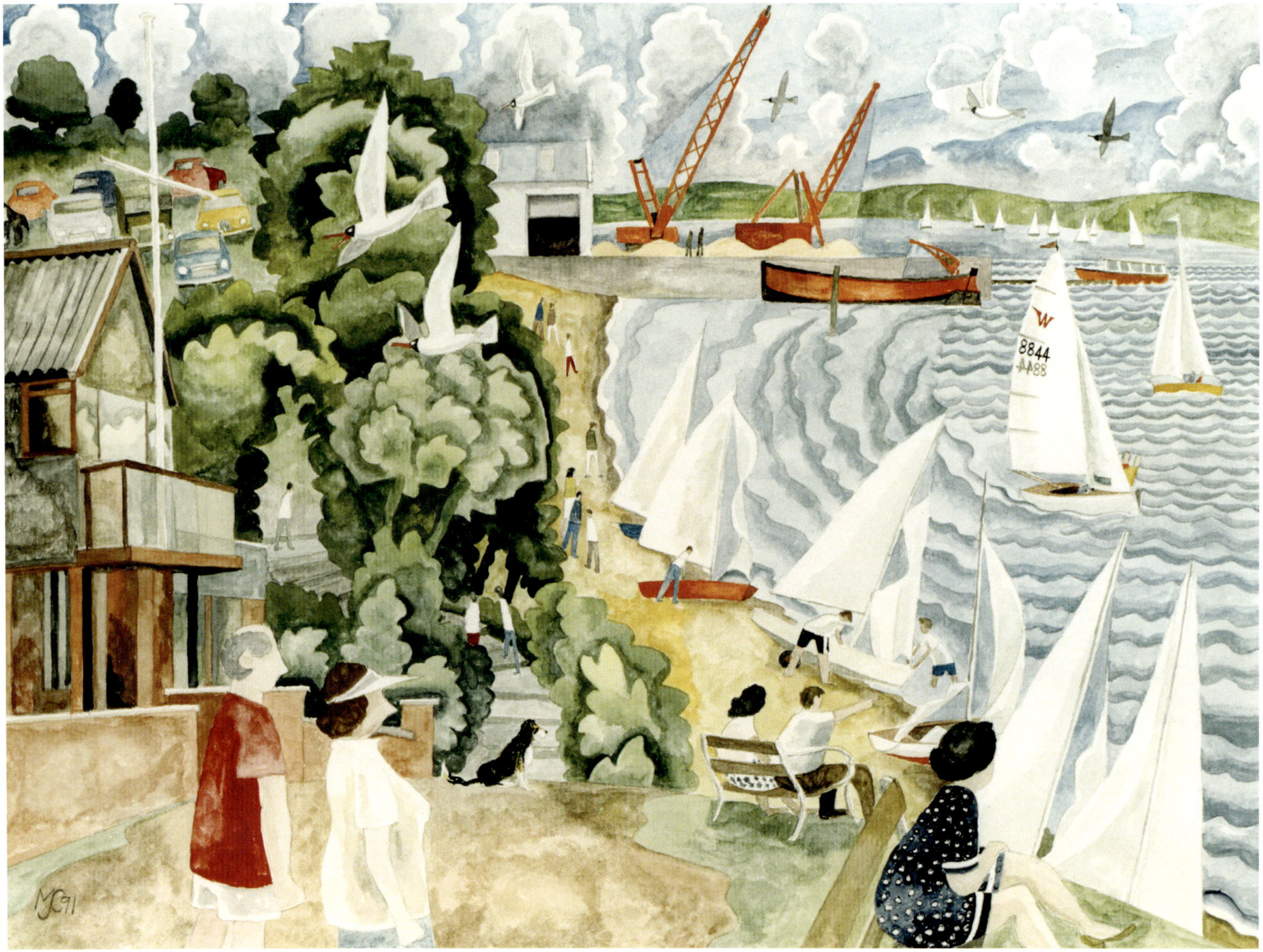
W
8844
MJC91

with hills". Painting and exhibiting in the county represented a very pleasant interlude for the artist in the 1980s and 1990s, providing literally a change of scene as his teaching career ended and his art gained momentum. We then continue west and visit the very tip of the UK at the Scillies, popping briefly into Irish waters to complete the tour.

While reports of the death of the British seaside resort have been exaggerated, it clearly isn't in rude health. There may be a number of spots seemingly unaffected by the malaise that swept along the coast following the upturn in 'foreign' holidays, but far more have never recovered from the changing tastes of the British public that favoured unbroken sunshine over piers and picture postcards.

As well as cheap flights that lured families off the promenades and pebbles, and on to the concourses and runways, Britain's seaside has been forced to contend with vanishing rail routes and spiralling train fares – where lines and stations survived Beeching, nationalisation and privatisation.

Water and beach quality has been variable, to say the least, and the country's elderly hotel, guest house and B&B stock has struggled to compete with newbuild resort accommodation in Europe and the rest of the world. Britain's roads struggle to keep traffic moving to and from the coast; fuel has become increasingly expensive; and the incidental costs of parking, snacks and entrance fees keep rising.

There have been signs that popularity is recovering, helped by flight delays and airport queues, higher taxation for air travel, fears over the UK's relationship with the EU and scare stories resulting from natural disasters and terrorism-related threats. So-called 'staycations' have been on the rise and there is no doubt that the long, hot summer of 2018 will have helped show off the nation's seaside at its best.

The changes in the British coastline reflect decades of neglect and prolonged national austerity. Resorts have had to contend with the high cost of maintaining structures such as pleasure piers; improved health, safety and hygiene requirements; modernisation

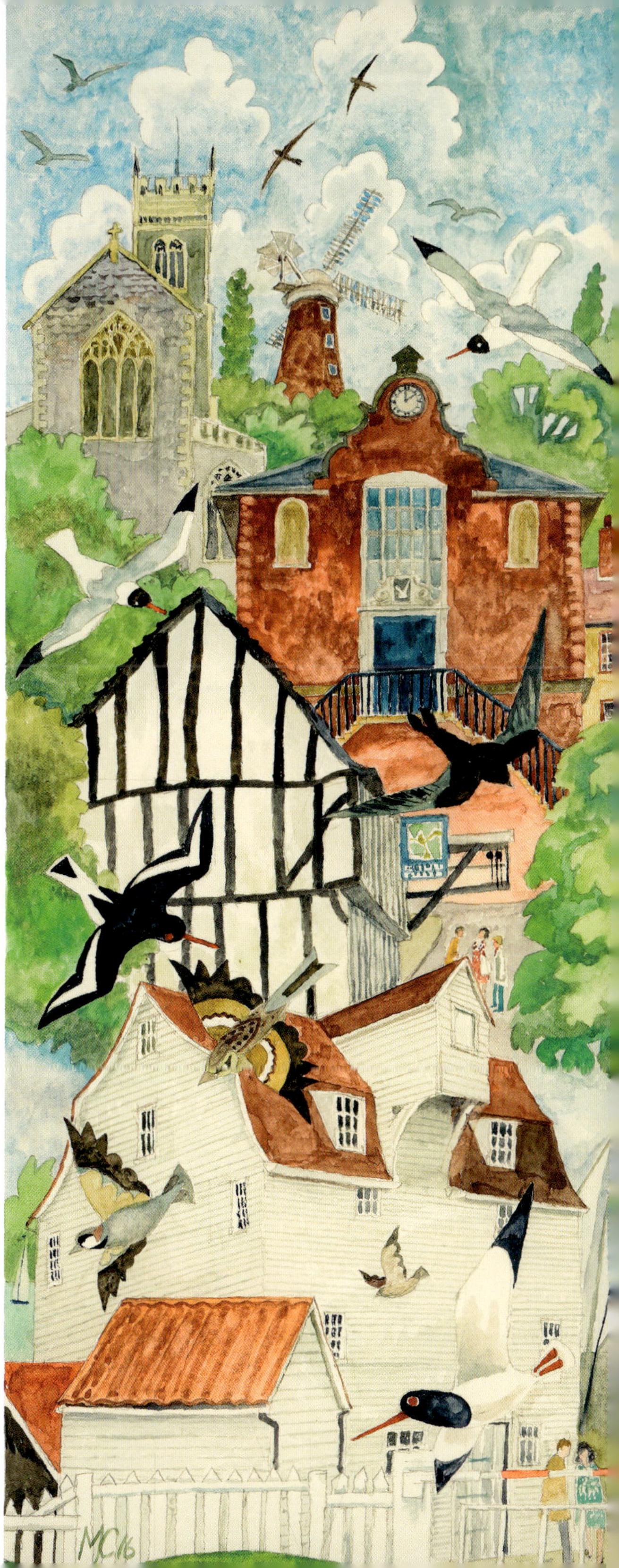

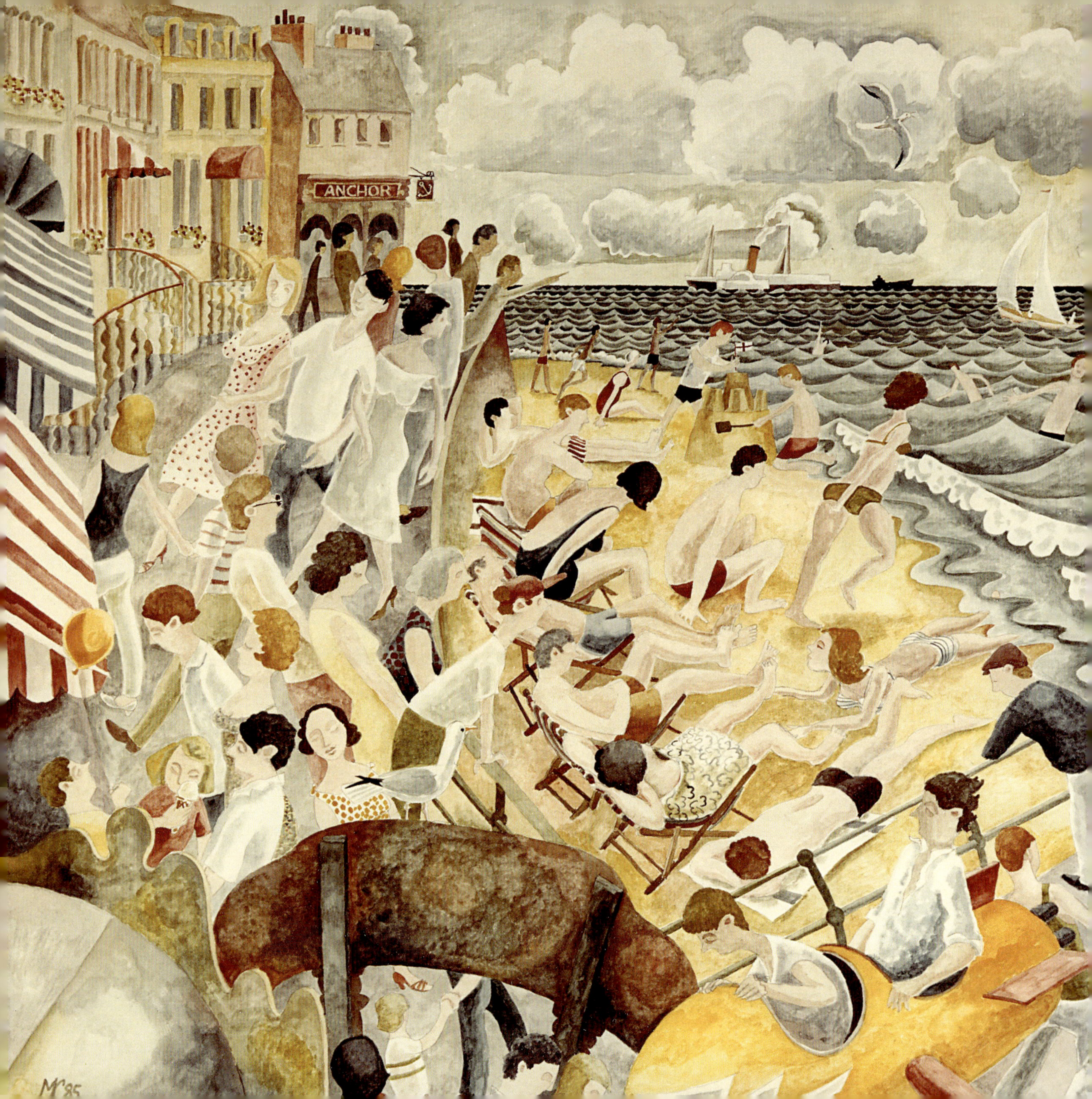

ANCHOR
MC'85

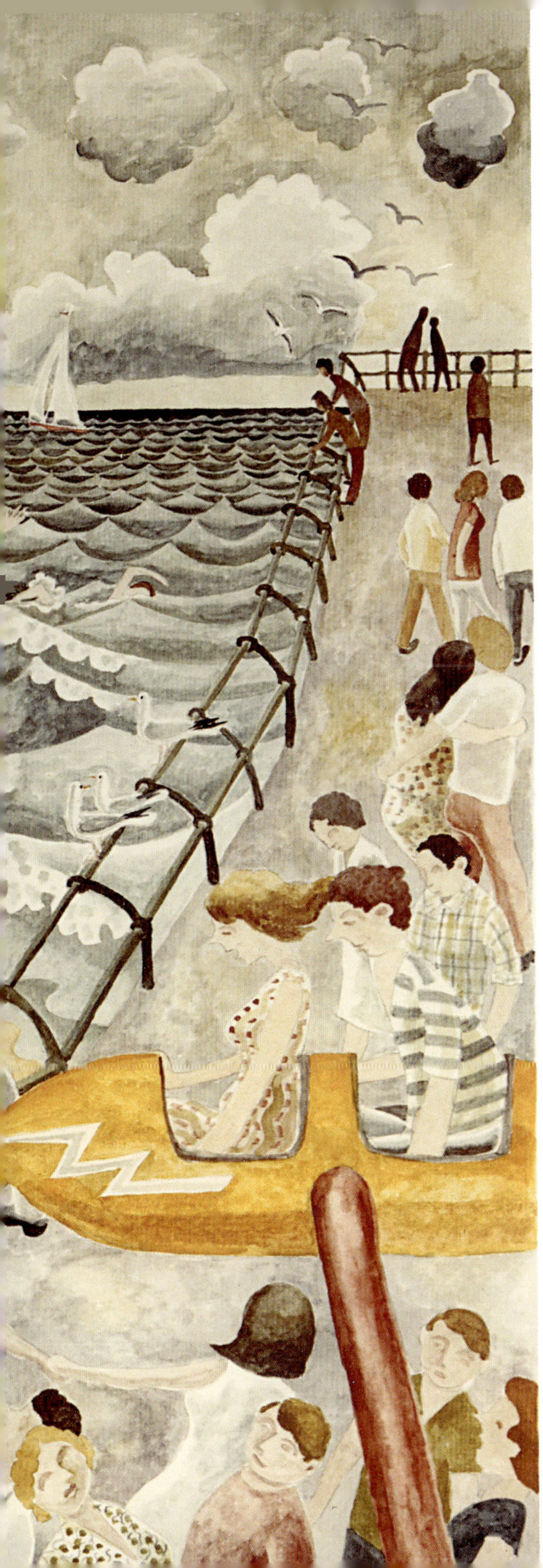

of promenades; and the replacement of traditional wooden beach huts.

Not only has there been the addition of new sea defences, but stretches of the coast have suffered constant and increasing erosion due to inadequate original measures. Occasionally it has been necessary to sacrifice traditional coastal landscape to the sea in order to create natural barriers such as saltmarsh habitats.

Some seaside towns have been transformed by the addition of marina complexes, commercial shipping facilities and major retail/residential expansion. Others have contracted, with shopping centres revealing more gaps than neglected teeth, boarded-up boarding houses and rundown amusement arcades spilling fading light onto cracked pavements.

There are gems, glittering throughout recession and packing in the crowds no matter what the economic and natural environment throw at them. Visitors to the likes of Aldeburgh and Southwold will see little obvious change from their Victorian forebears, other than higher prices, more fashionable shops and a chronic absence of parking spaces.

Michael Coulter's coast is a mixture of towns and unspoilt beaches; of hidden creeks and bustling ports; of fishing boats and waders probing the mud with elongated beaks. His interpretation of locations has changed, not only as a result of the places themselves, but because he seeks out new points of interest or a different perspective. The somewhat 'Burraesque' groups of people that typified early paintings are nowadays a rarity, but the flowers, foliage and fauna of wild and populated places bring with them a new vibrancy.

Art education in Hereford, Stafford and Leeds would hardly have filled Michael's head with ideas of painting the sea and shore. In fact, early work owed far more to farmers than to fishermen. It took several years based at Woolverstone to open his eyes to the potential of the local landscape. Far from the drama of the Pennines, the gentle undulation of Suffolk left him initially unmoved. Head filled with the rather dark characters of Edward Burra, Michael enlivened his scenes with often amusing individuals and farm animals that betrayed his equal enthusiasm for the styles of Edward Bawden and Eric Ravilious.

A remarkable series of paintings from a tour of two rivers represents perhaps a breakthrough in terms of the artist's relationship with his adopted county and its waterside locations. His 1989 journey along the Orwell and Stour to the coast

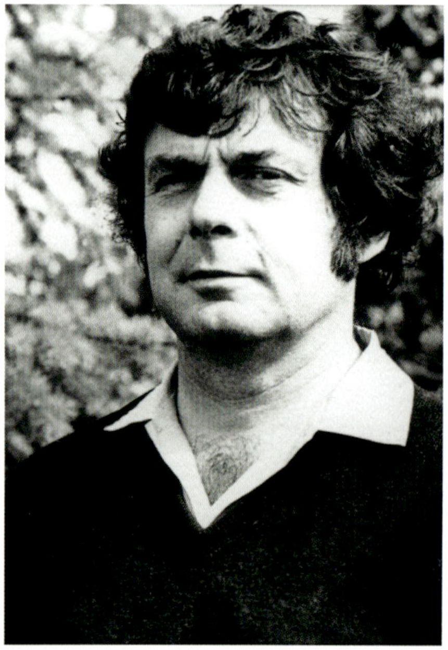

may have provided only glimpses of the sea, but certainly resulted in a life-long fascination with boats that has spawned many pictures.

During the first of the 'Two Rivers' expeditions, Michael headed from Ipswich along the Orwell past Woolverstone to the Shotley Peninsula, leading him across the county border into Essex. People tend to forget that Ipswich itself is a port, providing its own maritime connections and subject matter. The artistic journey also took in Felixstowe and Harwich, with these locations remaining popular with the artist for decades.

Michael taught art and rugby at Woolverstone for two decades, fitting his own artistic endeavours around the demands of his day job. Given the opportunity to take early retirement in 1987, he beat the closure of the school by three years and threw himself into the type of joyful work that has since become very familiar through his exhibitions, charity work and greetings cards. Suffolk, Essex and Norfolk locations were easy to teach, while the artist overcame his early resistance to the lowlands of East Anglia and developed a close allegiance with the coast – which certainly provided some of the drama he had been missing.

Woolverstone was to make another appearance in 1989, by way of the painting reproduced on page 34. It forms a busy shipping highway on the River Orwell. The ship seen in the picture is a collier going to supply Cliff Quay Power Station in

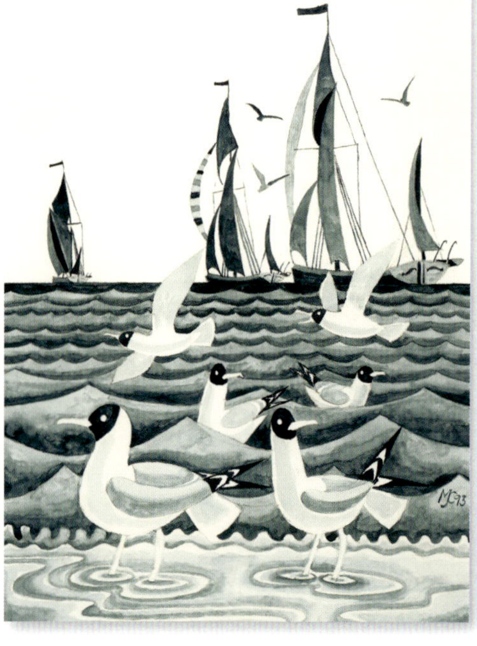

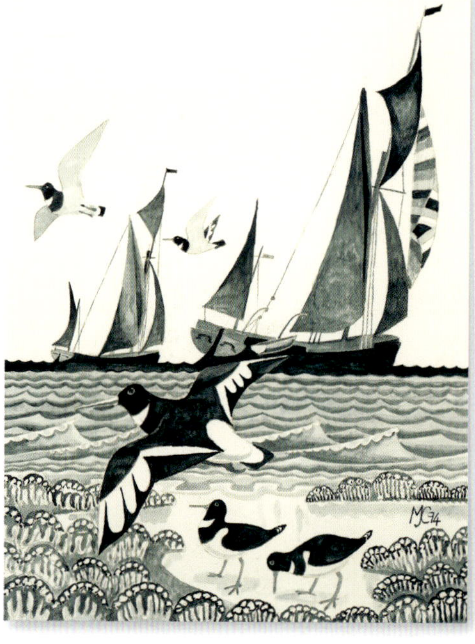

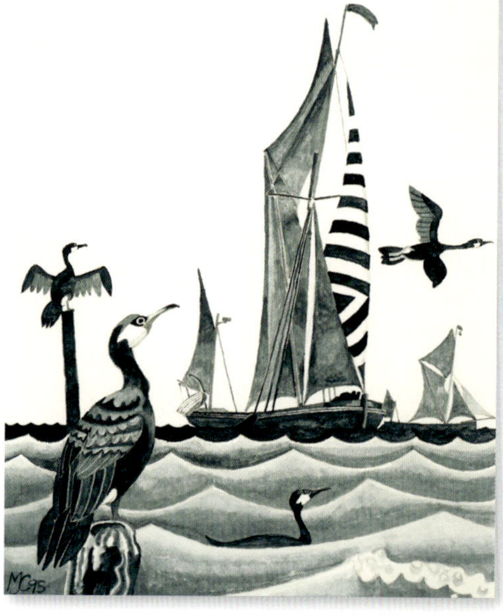

Ipswich with coal (the chimneys can be seen in the background). Like many of Michael's paintings, it provides a glimpse of a vanished past, as the plant was demolished in 1994. The artist was to paint Woolverstone Hall itself in 2012 on behalf of its most recent occupant, Ipswich High School for Girls.

The slow seduction of Suffolk continued once Michael had become a professional artist; he has since explored virtually every inch of its coastline and inland beauty spots, enjoying the open skies, gentle hills and flowing rivers. He has seldom been tempted to stray, but a period in the early 1990s saw two exhibitions of Dorset paintings that kept him planted temporarily in south-western soil. This book reproduces for the first time a large portfolio of the Dorset work that brings together such unlikely elements as the onshore Wytch Farm oilfield, Abbotsbury swans, peacocks on Brownsea Island, naval helicopters over Chesil Beach and the atmospheric Cobb at Lyme Regis.

Wildlife and nature has arguably become a larger element of Michael's art, even though the interest was there from the start. His stylised birds capture very effectively the essence of each species, without following slavishly the 'feather maps' and ornithological precision of some dedicated wildlife artists. Birds outnumber people in many contemporary paintings and the focus may be more on the blooms than on the boats in some coastal scenes. This has helped attract a new audience to the artist's work and resulted in his ongoing involvement with Suffolk Wildlife Trust, for which he produces an annual painting.

This book doesn't pretend to be a gazetteer of Britain's coastal locations, but is a comprehensive collection of the artist's seaside-inspired creations. Readers can travel from King's Lynn and Wells-next-the-Sea in Norfolk, past the Suffolk treasures of Southwold, Aldeburgh and Orford to the mighty container ports at Felixstowe and Harwich. Flitting through Hastings, Dungeness and Romney Marshes, they can take in Dorset's dramatic coastline before making stops in Falmouth, Tresco and glimpsing the Irish Sea. This three-decade journey from Woolverstone School has seen the artist establish a highly recognisable style of painting that has kept pace with the changing coastal landscape before him.

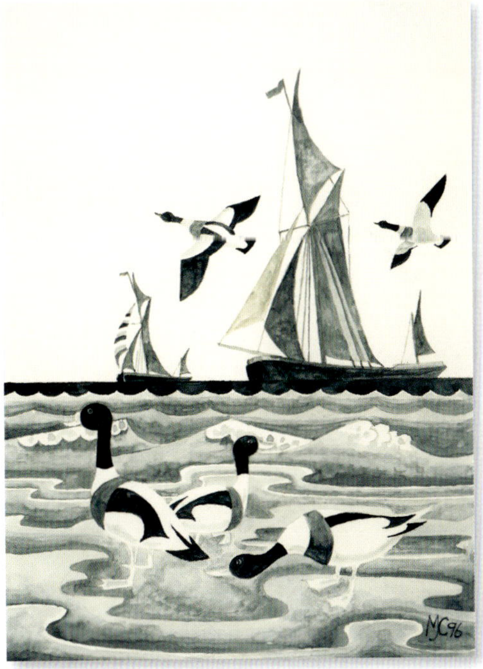

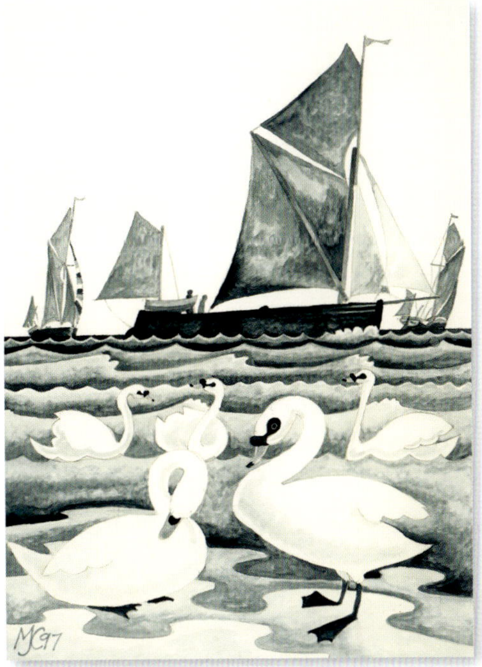

Page 8: 'Promenade' (1985).
Facing page, top left: the artist as a younger man (in his rugby playing days!)
From left to right: Cover designs for the annual Barge Match programme, dating from 1993 to 1997. Barge Match scenes can also be found on pages 44 and 48.

SUFFOLK

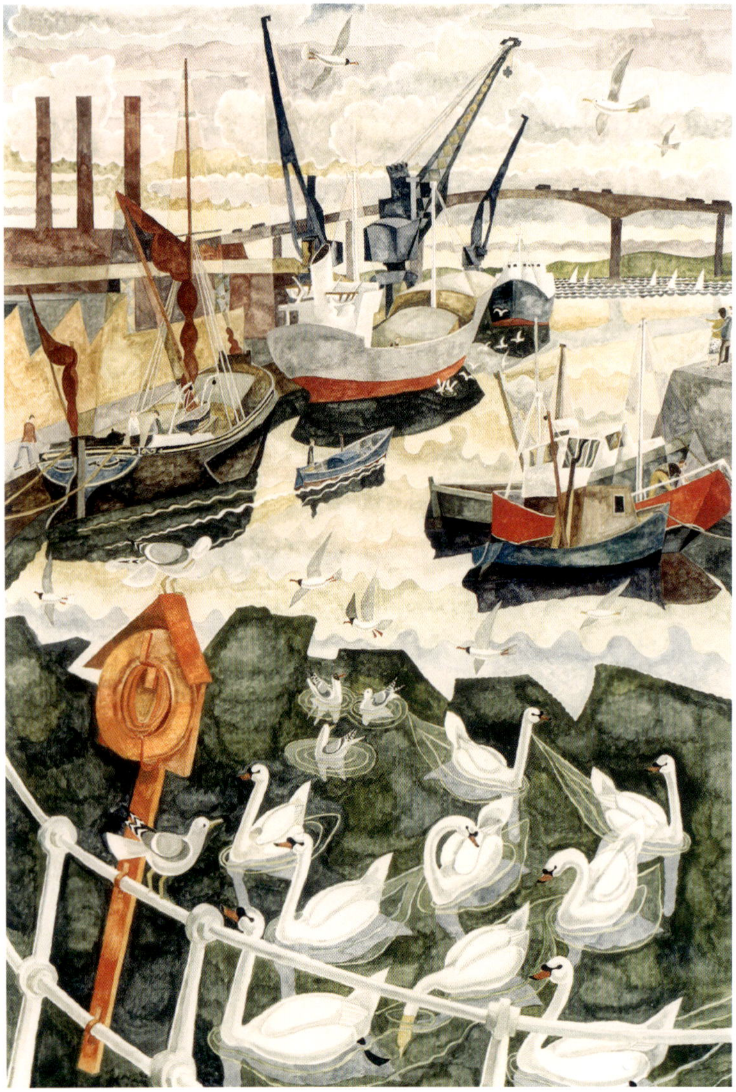

Michael's adopted county of Suffolk has around 80km of coastline extending south from the former fishing port of Lowestoft to the container port of Felixstowe. Popular tourist towns nestle between expanses of important natural environment, RSPB reserves, Anglo-Saxon burial sites and the odd nuclear power station. The coastal strip contains an area of heathland known as the Sandlings, which runs most of the length of the county's eastern edge. Some 20 per cent of Suffolk's population is based in Ipswich where the docks, pictured left, have changed greatly during the artist's time as a professional painter. Other more remote locations, such as Shingle Street on page 14, change little but for the meanderings of the beach itself as the sea resculpts it constantly. The Orwell Bridge seen in the background on the left and again on page 36 has been a striking addition to the Suffolk landscape even if, frustratingly, it offers barely a glimpse of the watery panorama below it.

Left: 'Memories of Ipswich Docks' (1991). This image helps cement the connection between the county's inland capital and the sea 19km down river. Michael's limited colour palette in these formative years provided a more sepia-like hue, replaced gradually by a broader watercolour range.
Facing page, clockwise from top left: 'Sizewell' (2011); 'Evening Sunset' (2014); 'Trimley Marshes with Shoveller Ducks and Lapwings' (2017); 'Beach Scene' (1997). The power station at Sizewell is surrounded by natural beauty such as the RSPB Minsmere reserve, while the murmuration of Starlings has a striking background of Blythburgh Church.

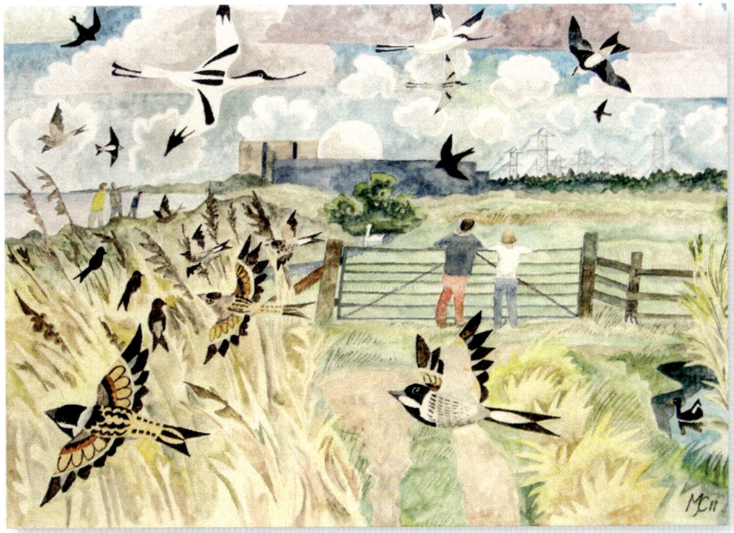
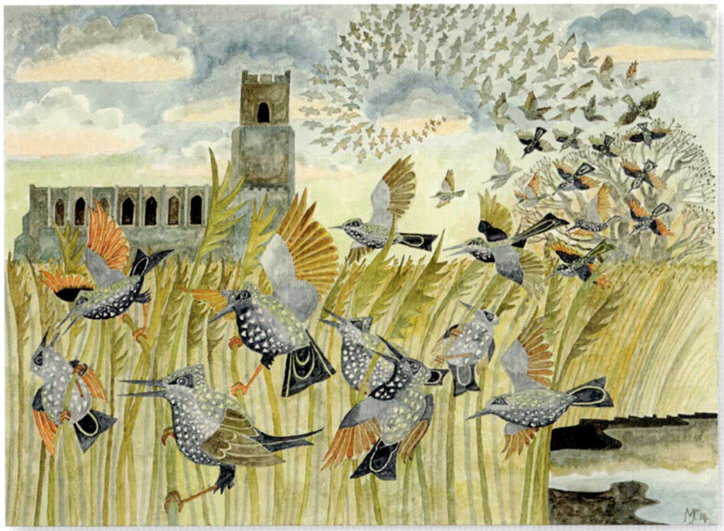
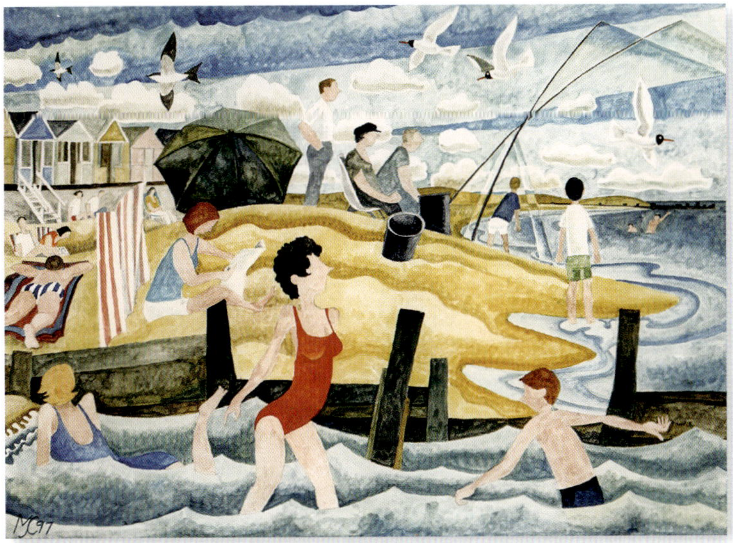
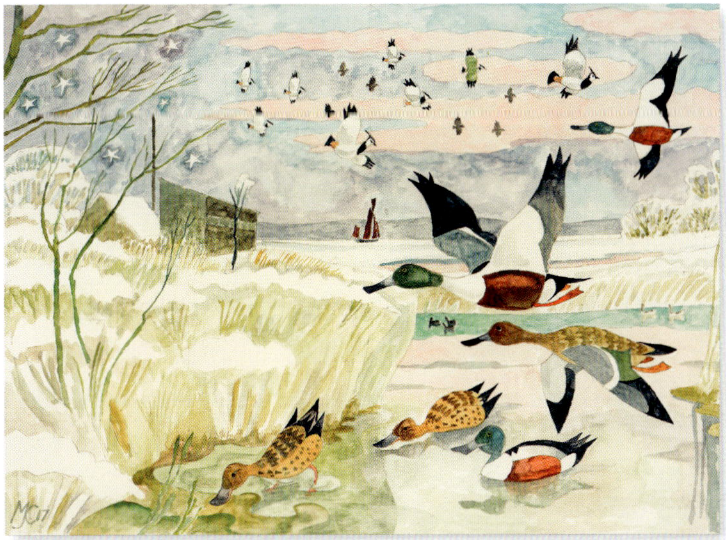

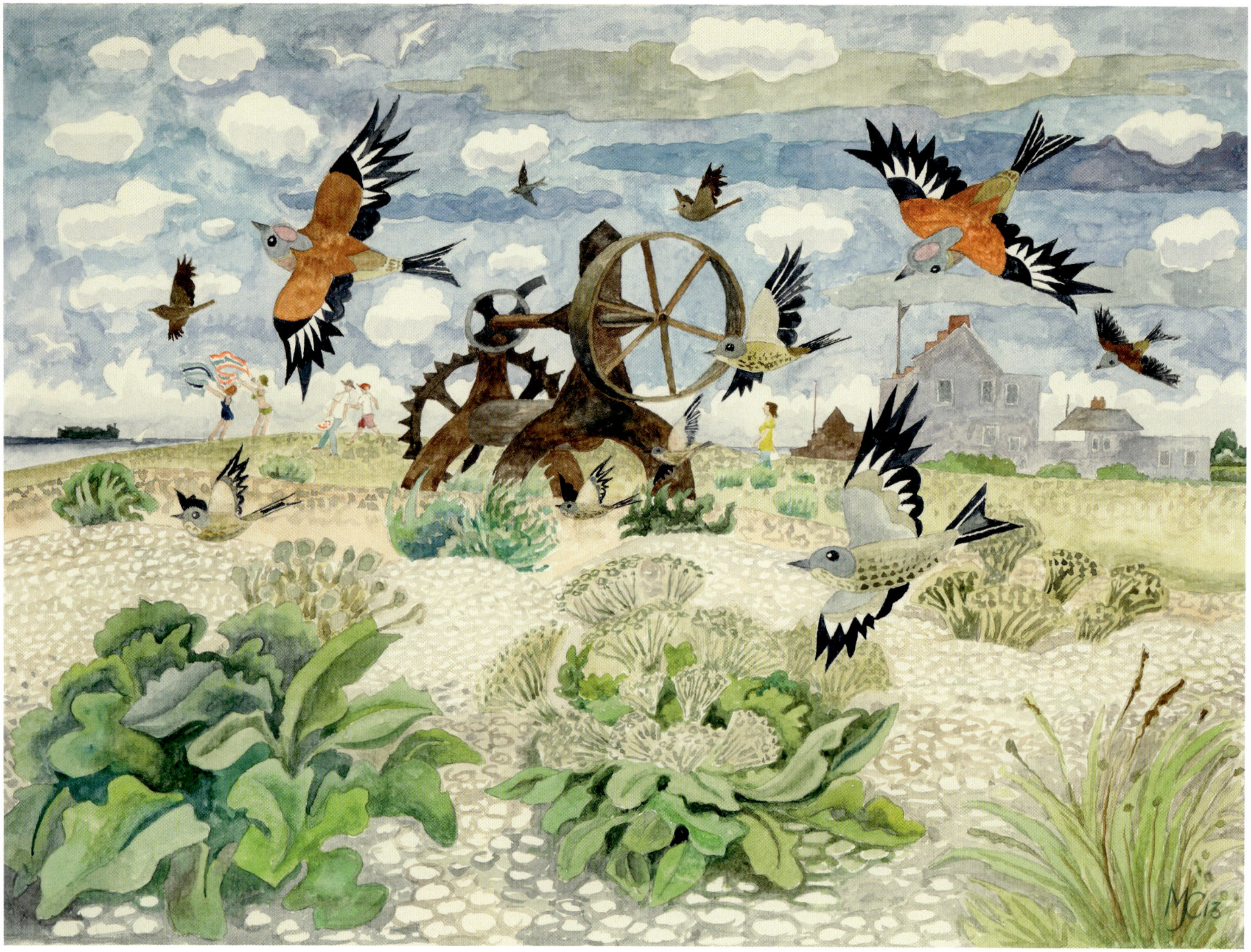

'Shingle Street' (2013) "The remoteness of Shingle Street is like going back several decades in time. Simple pleasures, doing nothing in particular. Staring out to sea; walking among the Sea Kale and Valerian on the stony beach; taking a picnic or renting a coastguard cottage. As soon as you drive across the bridge and take a deep breath, you are back to the 1950s and can relax – wonderful."

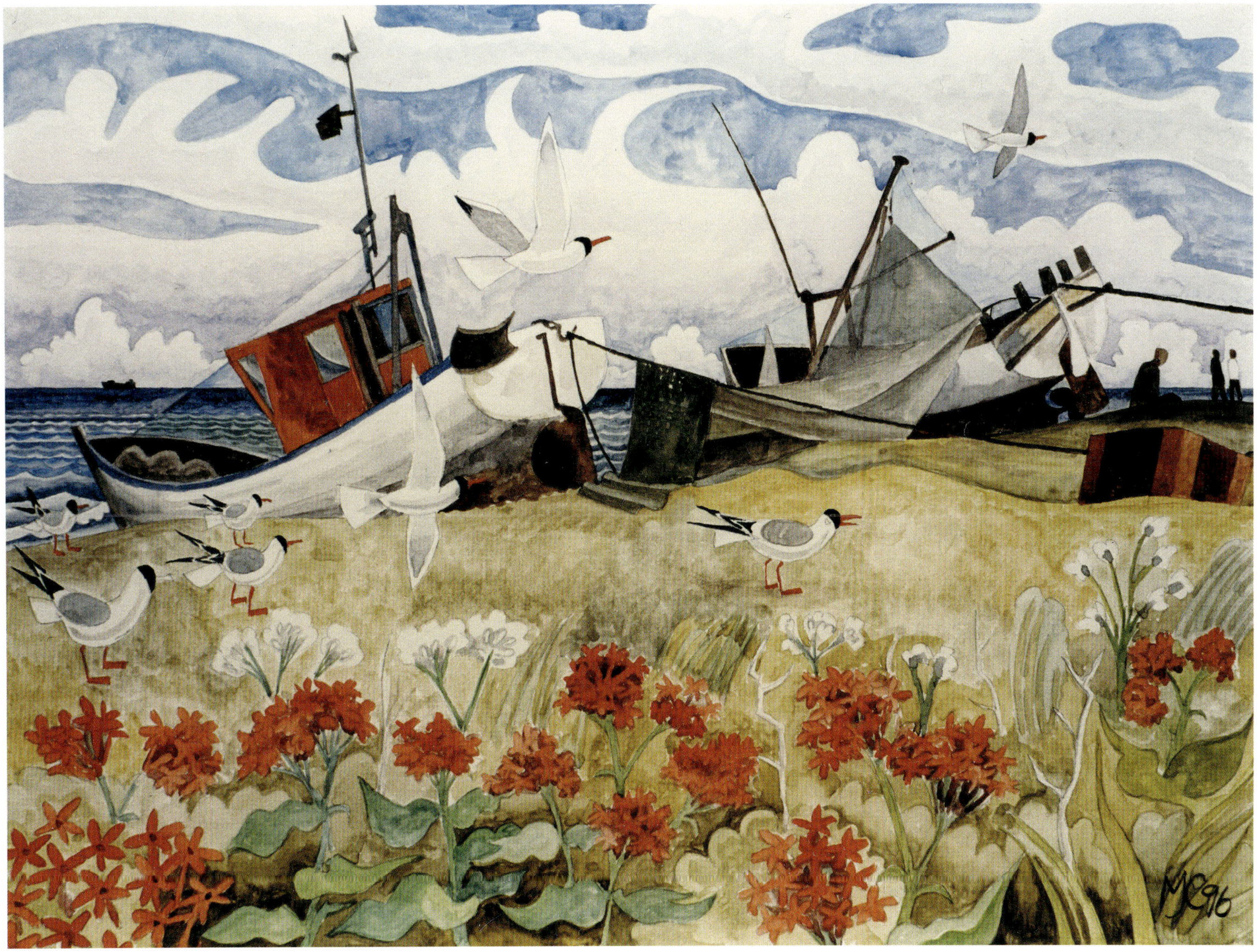

'On Aldeburgh Beach' (1996) "The fascination of boats arranged higgledy-piggledy on a shingle beach has been a feature of almost every artist's subject matter for hundreds of years. The working and retired boats at Aldeburgh are not stage-managed into a tidy composition; they create their own natural form that is different every time you visit. Rustic, part of the landscape, beautiful."

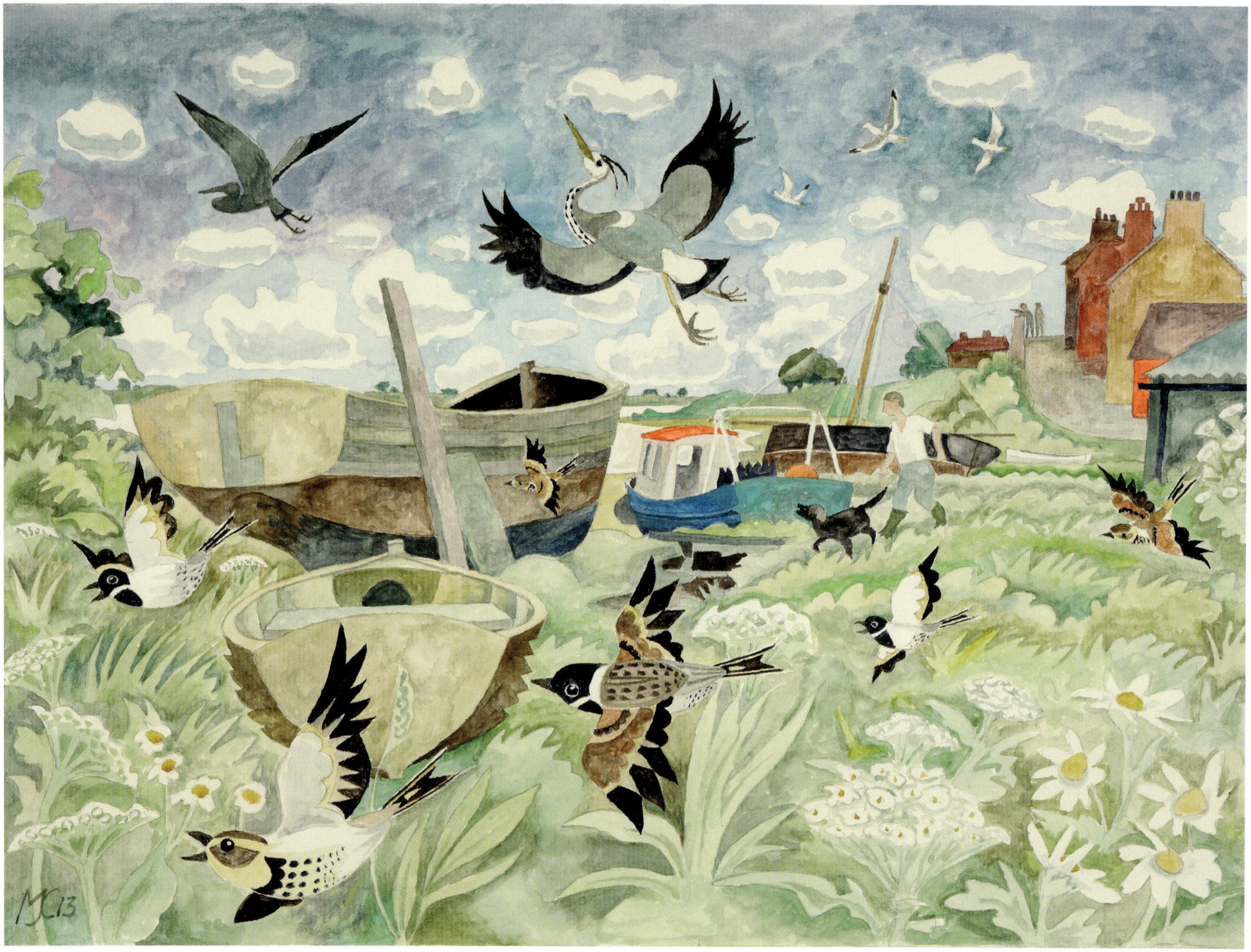

'Flight from the Saltings' (2013) "It is always pleasurable walking beside the sea or along the marshes. Birds are there to observe at leisure. There is something familiar and something new to see every day. Time stands still."

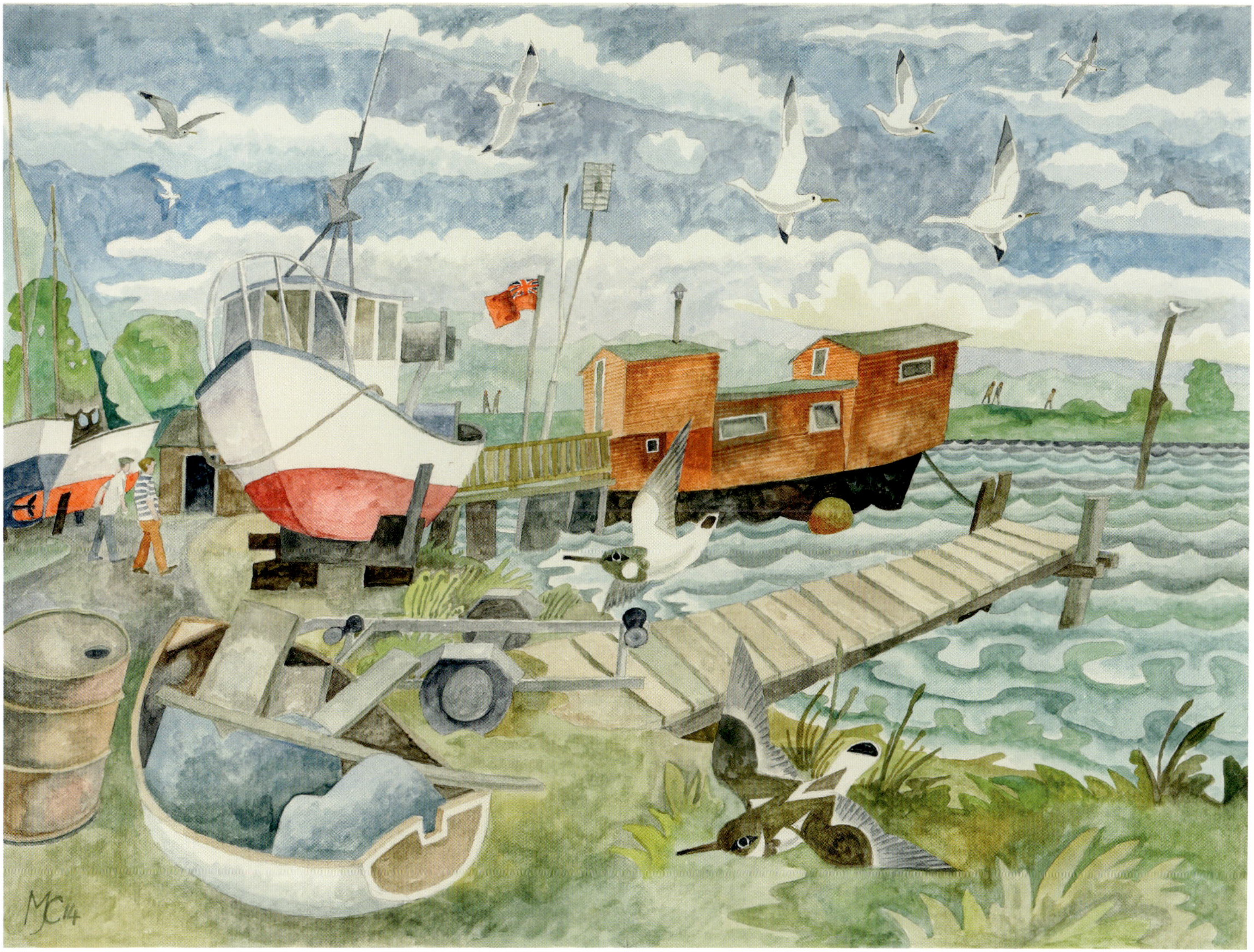

'Boatyard at High Tide' (2014) Michael's painting is based on images from Felixstowe Ferry, a destination popular with the artist and tourists. "Living on a boat may seem romantic, and perhaps it is. It certainly looks interesting!"

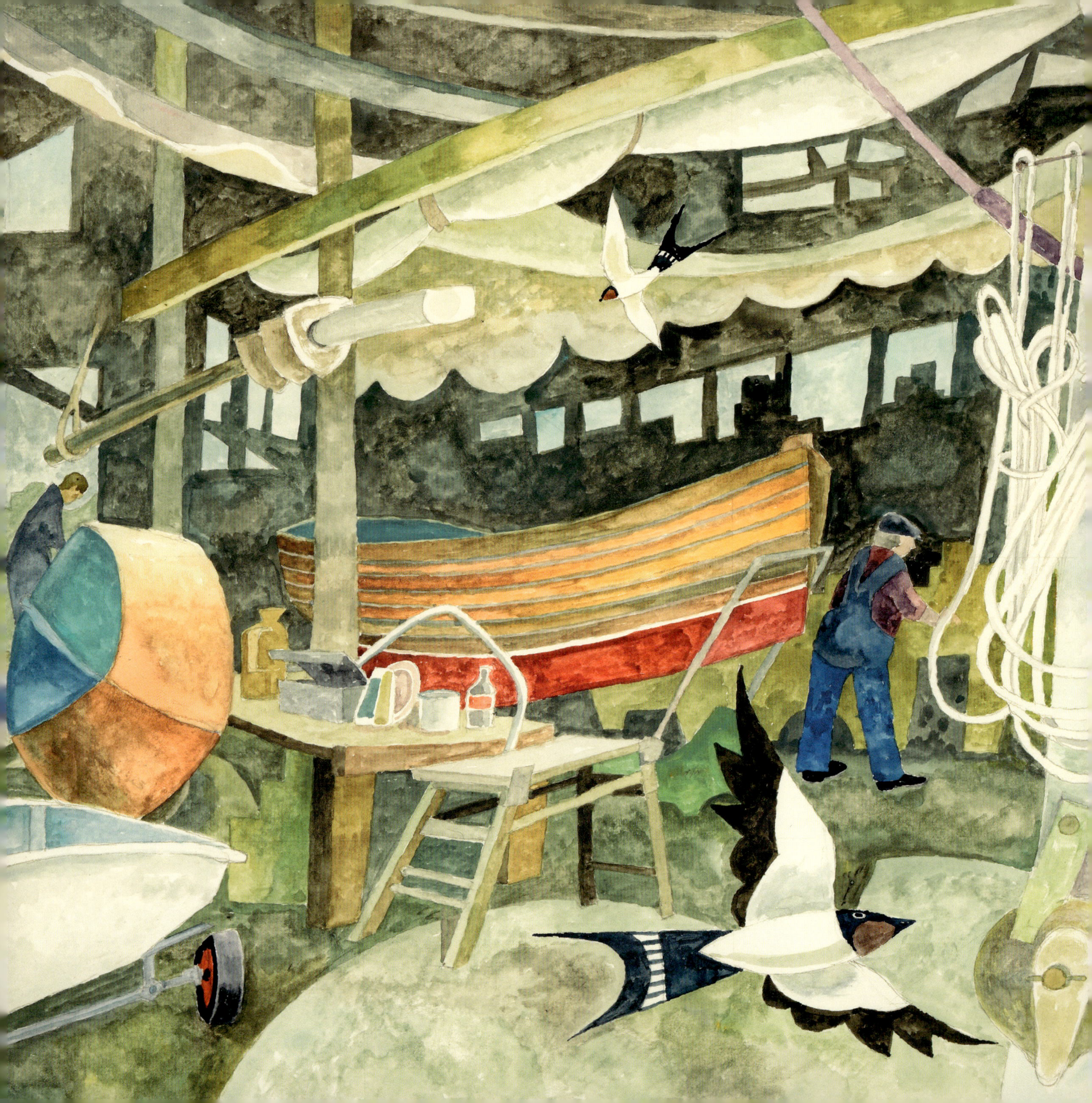

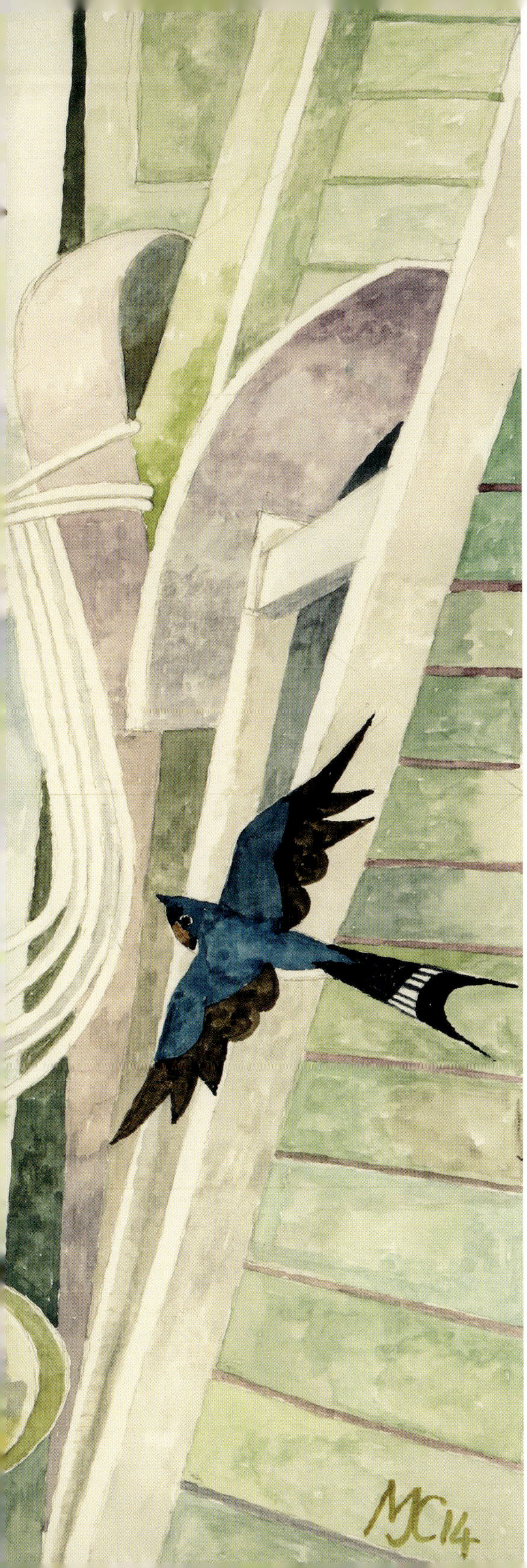

'The Boat Shed' (2014) The scene as observed while walking past an old boat shed. "Traditional skills are still practised in these tucked-away places. Visiting Swallows like to nest in these ageing buildings."

'August Creek' (1997)

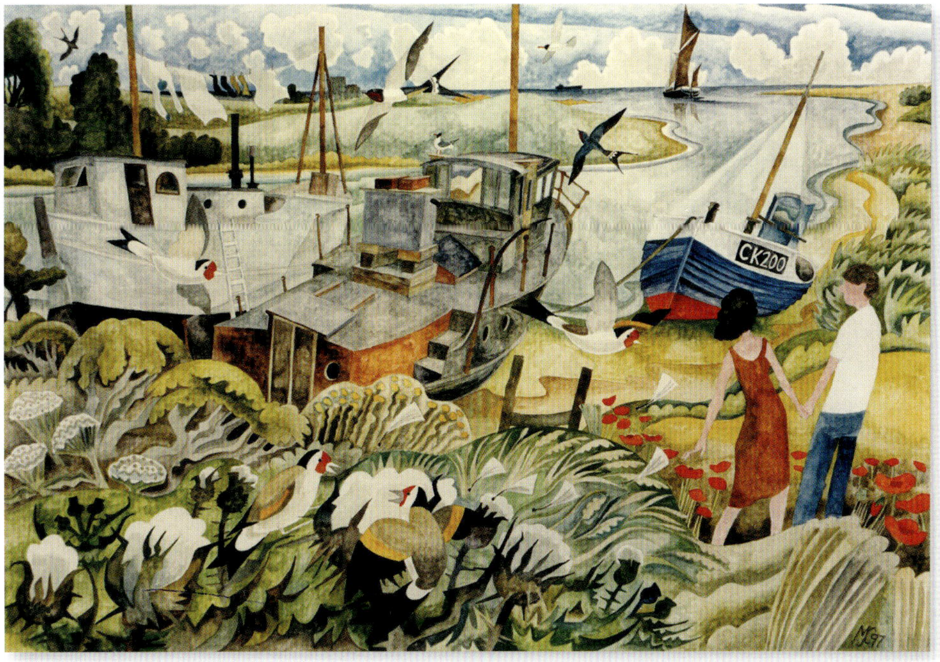

'Summer and Finches, Blythburgh' (2015) The village of Blythburgh stands within an Area of Outstanding Natural Beauty just 6km inland from Southwold. The dominant feature is Holy Trinity Church, standing on high ground and overlooking the marshland of the Blyth Valley. Here, Michael's dog walkers have surprised a charm of Goldfinches feasting on the seedheads.

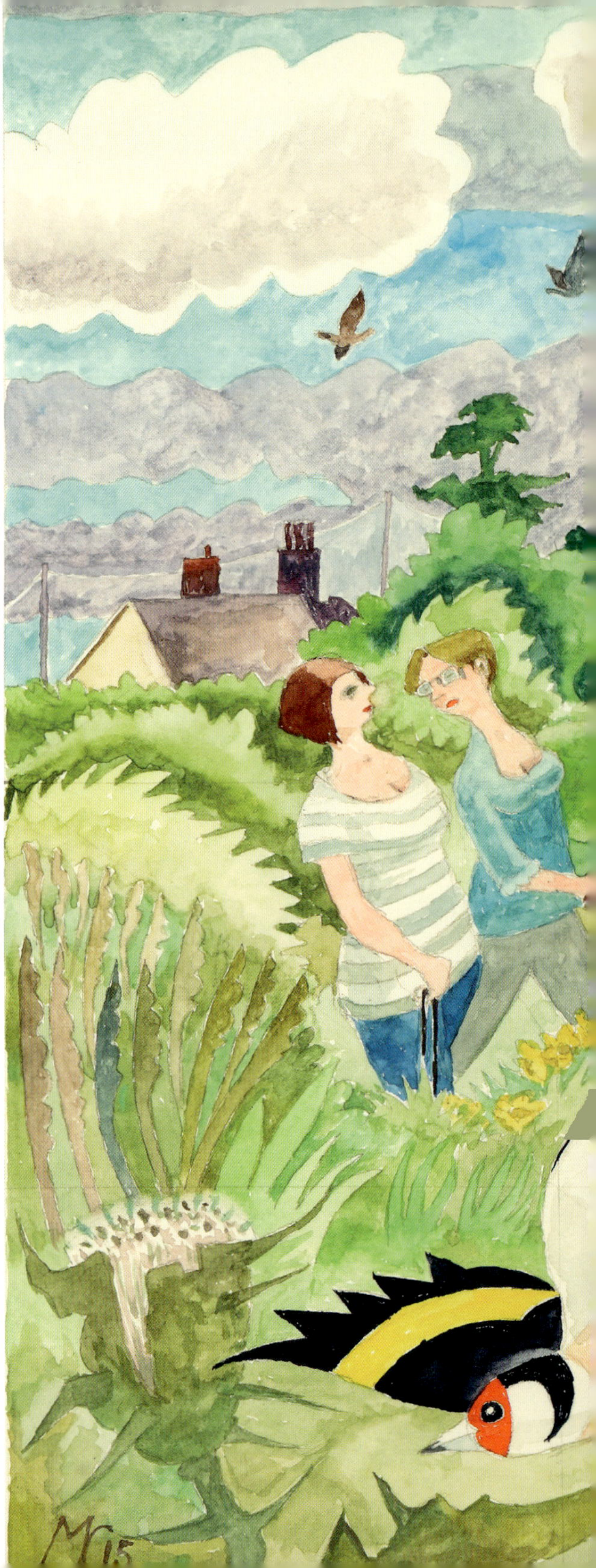

'Winter at Iken Cliff' (1993)

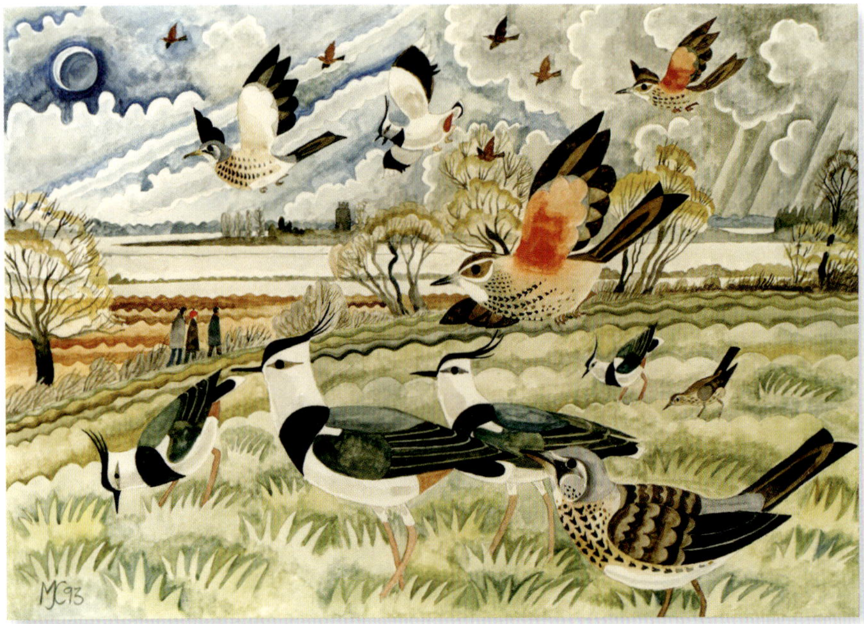

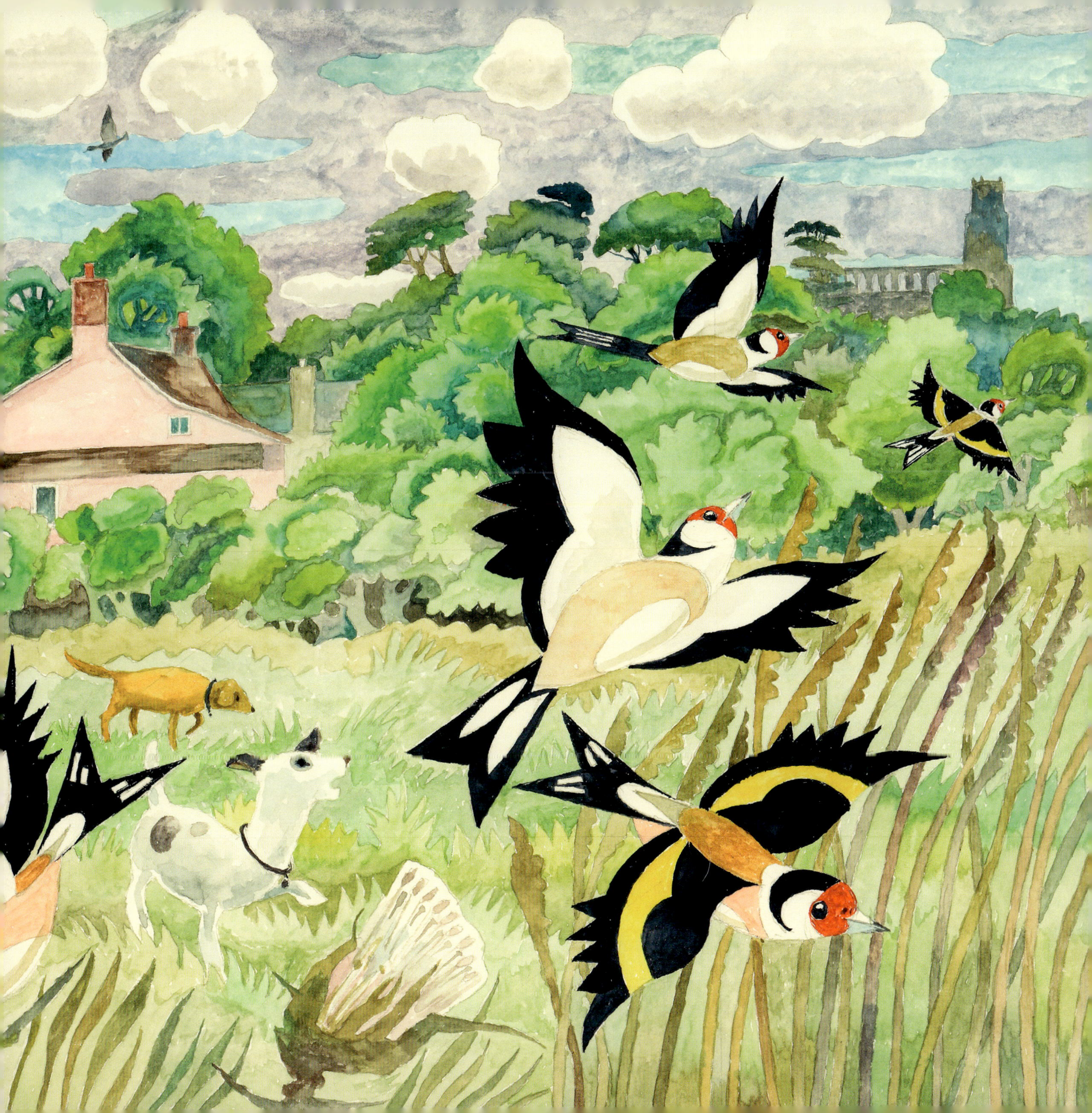

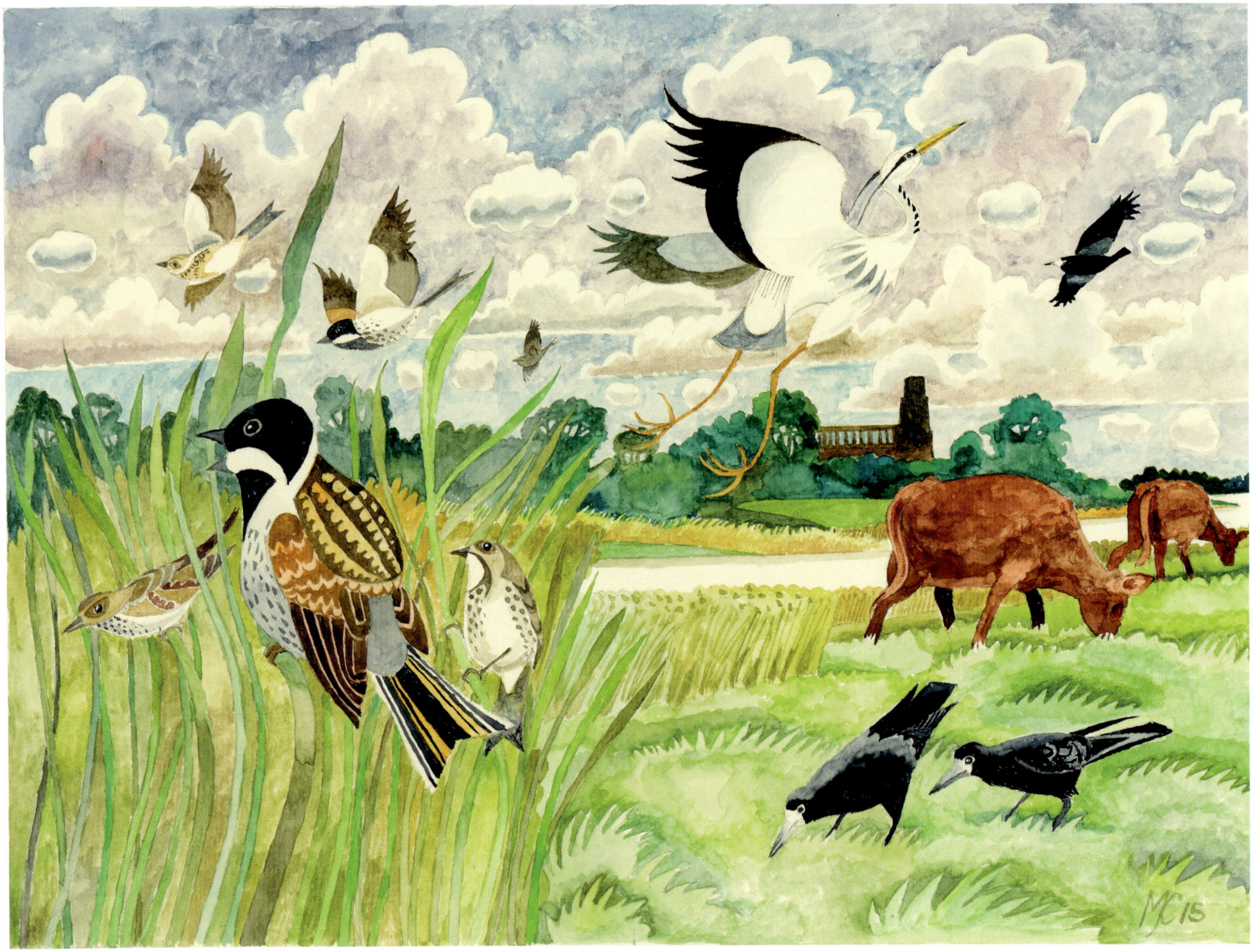

'Blythburgh Marshes' (2015) The River Blyth gives the village its name, and runs from its source near Laxfield to a tidal estuary between Southwold and Walberswick just 6km away. Holy Trinity Church is in the background, but the foreground is dominated by Michael's birds including a startled Grey Heron and a singing Reed Bunting. Rooks graze alongside the cows on the river bank.

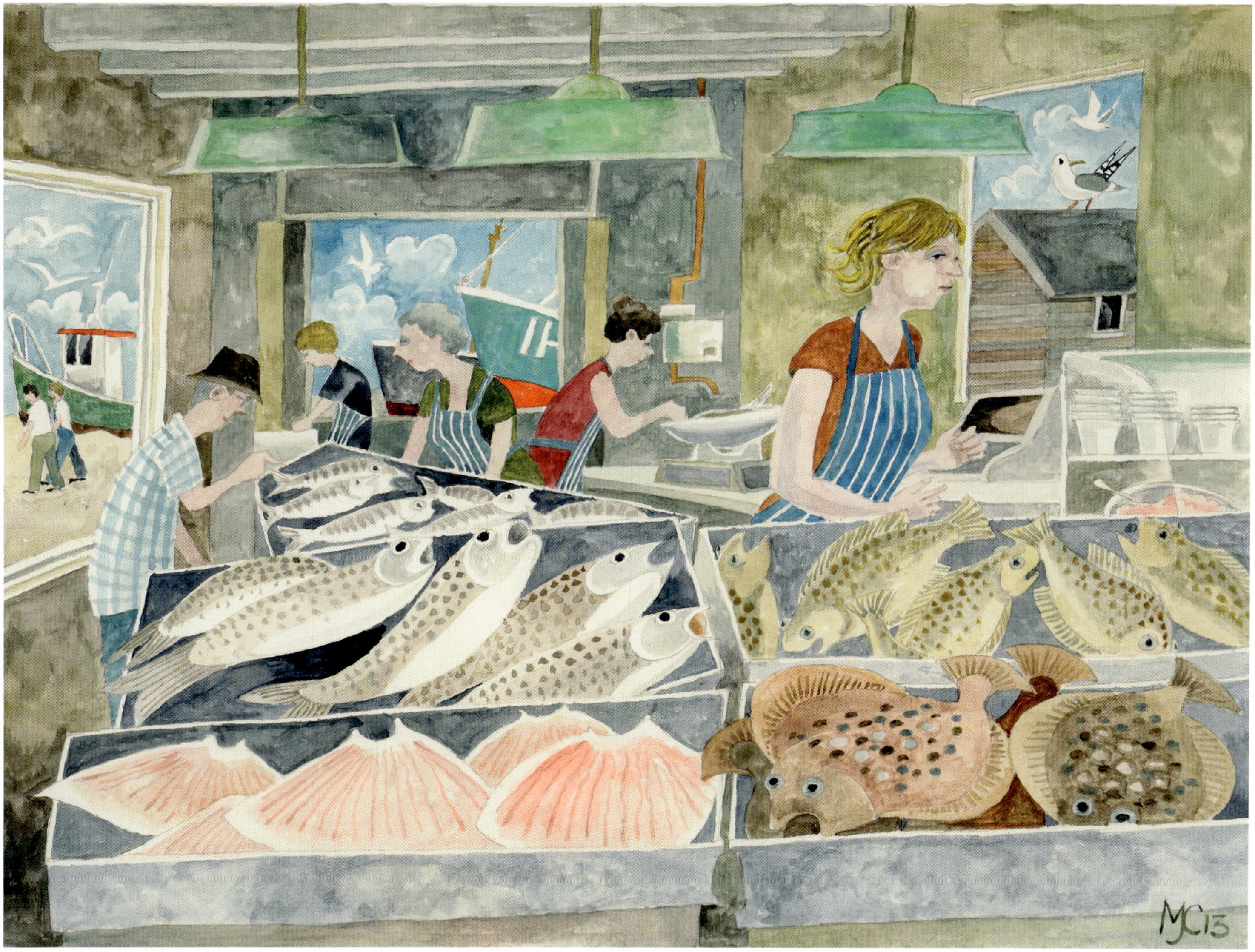

'Fresh from the Sea' (2013) Felixstowe Ferry makes one of several appearances in this collection. Located just a stone's throw from the huge container port, it represents a step back to the time of small-boat fishing. "Felixstowe Ferry has for many years sported a hut on the beach selling fresh fish, straight from the boat. Our favourite is a bag of picked shrimps or prawns to be taken away and eaten with bread and butter."

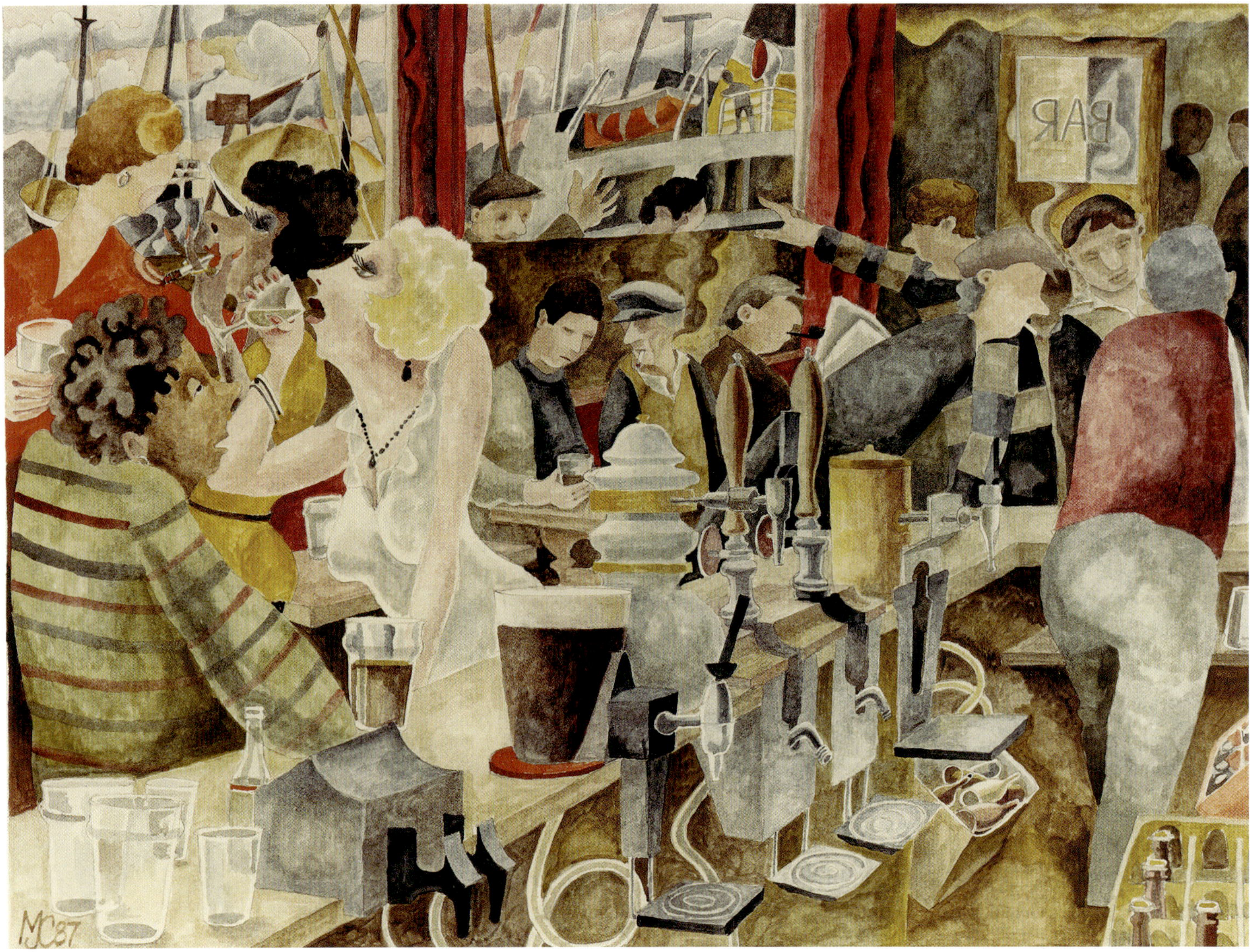

'Dockside Pub' (1987) Michael took up the offer of early retirement from his teaching career in 1987, leaving Woolverstone School and becoming a professional artist. This early painting therefore reflects a formative style influenced by the figurative work of Edward Burra and the subtle colour palette of Eric Ravilious. The dockside pub at Ipswich is captured in great detail, with some fascinating characters monopolising the bar.

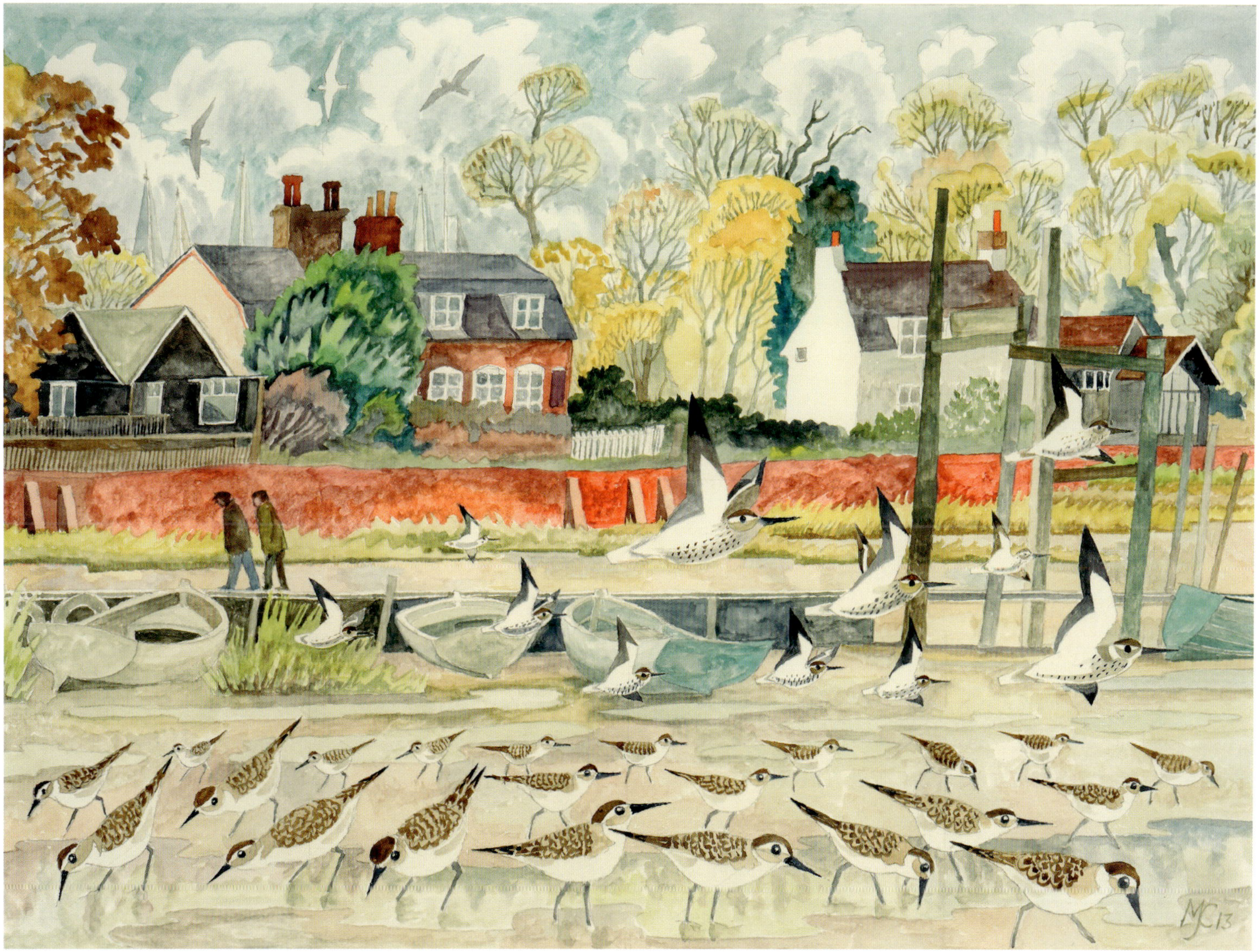

'Coast Guard Cottages at Pin Mill' (2013) Pin Mill was once a busy cargo landing point, a centre for the repair of Thames sailing barges and home to many small industries such as sail-making and a maltings. "To get the view I waited for low tide and then strode down the hard and looked back. Years ago, many a barge would be moored up high and dry on this hard that stretches out into the river. The black building to the left is the Pin Mill sailing club. Plenty of good times have been had in there."

'Buntings and a Barge' (2013) "A fanciful view of the River Orwell in summer. A walk from Pin Mill to Woolverstone along the river, over fields and through the woods, is one I never tire of. It never fails to please time and time again."

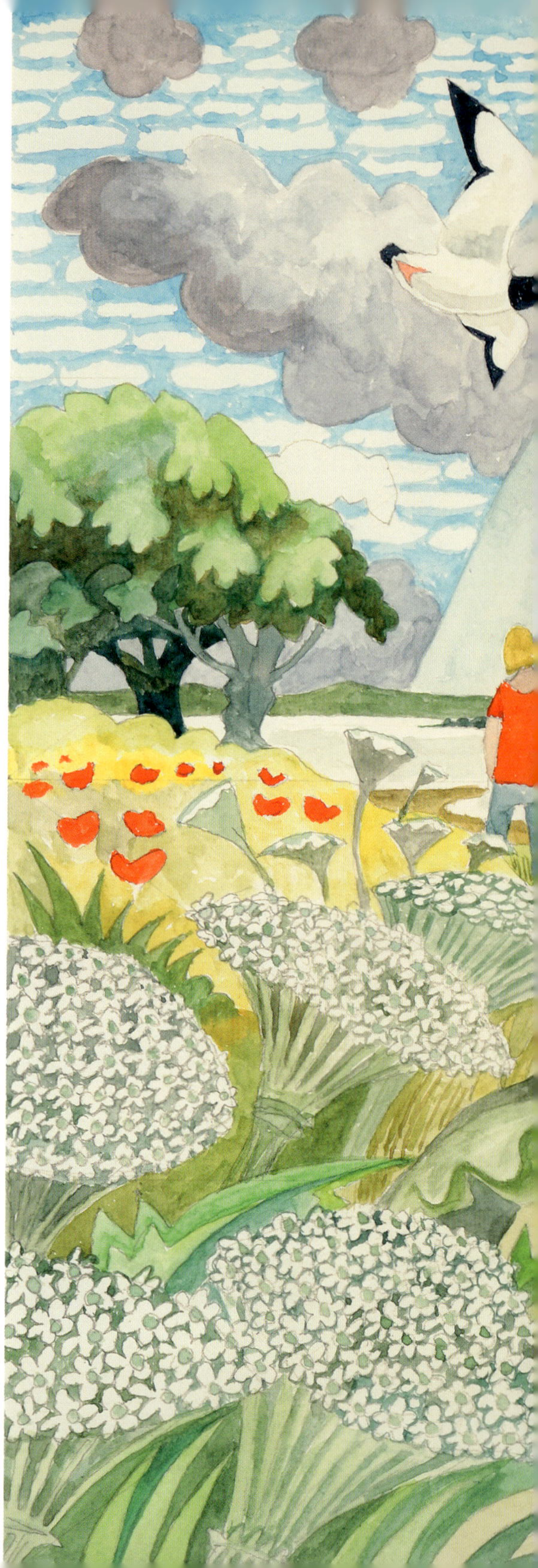

'Freston Tower, Christmas' (2001)

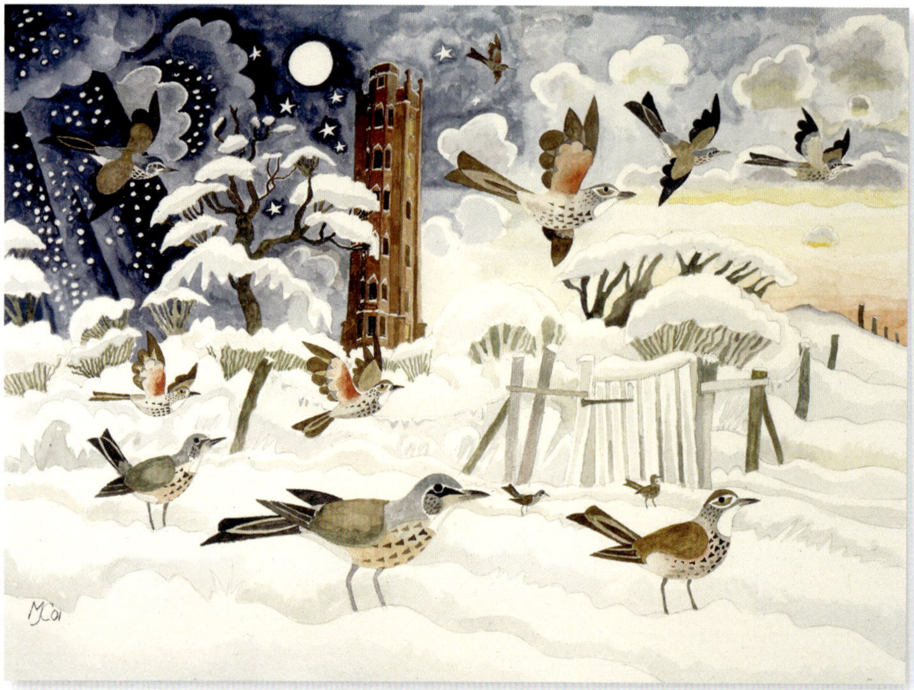

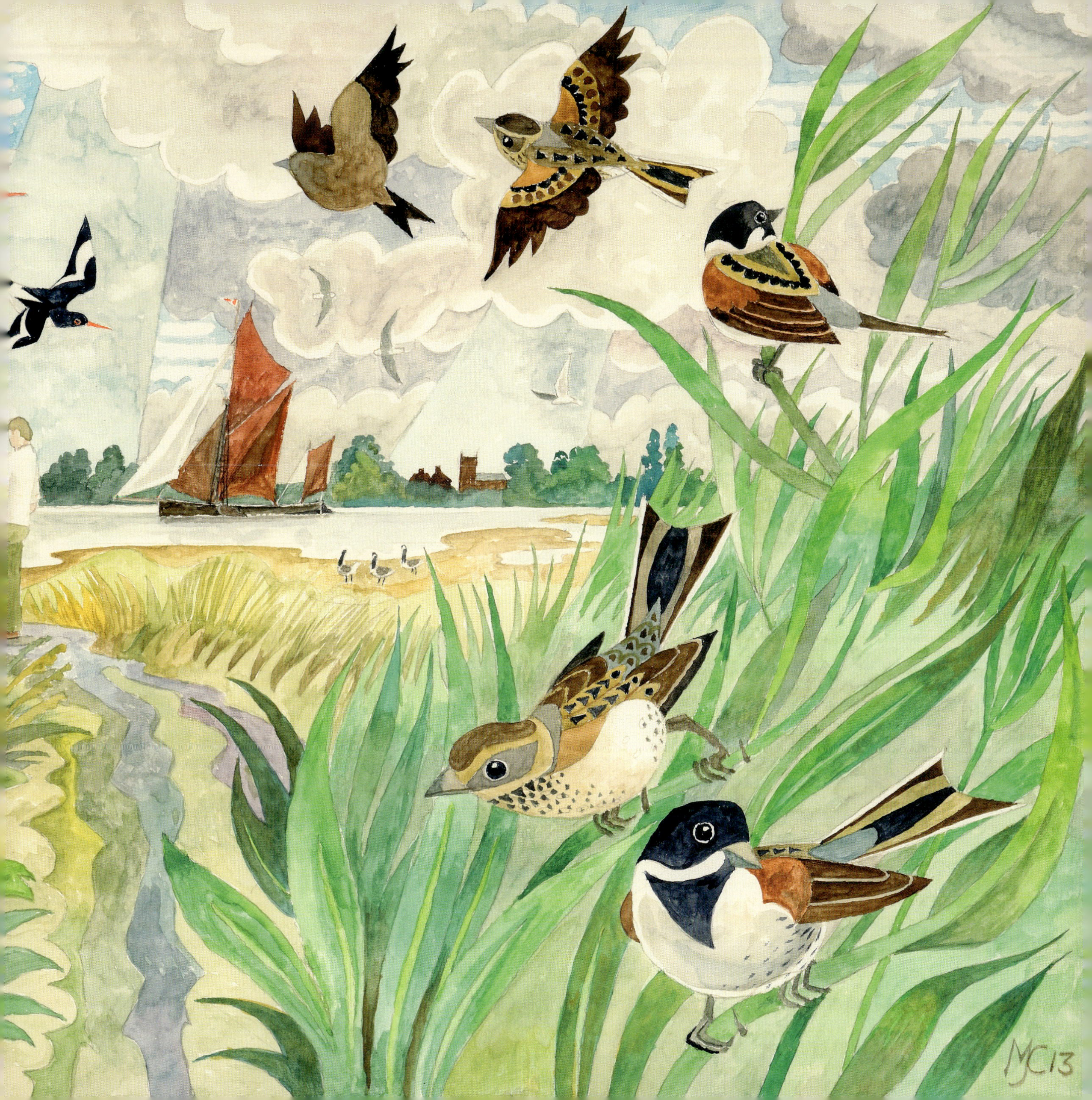
MJC13

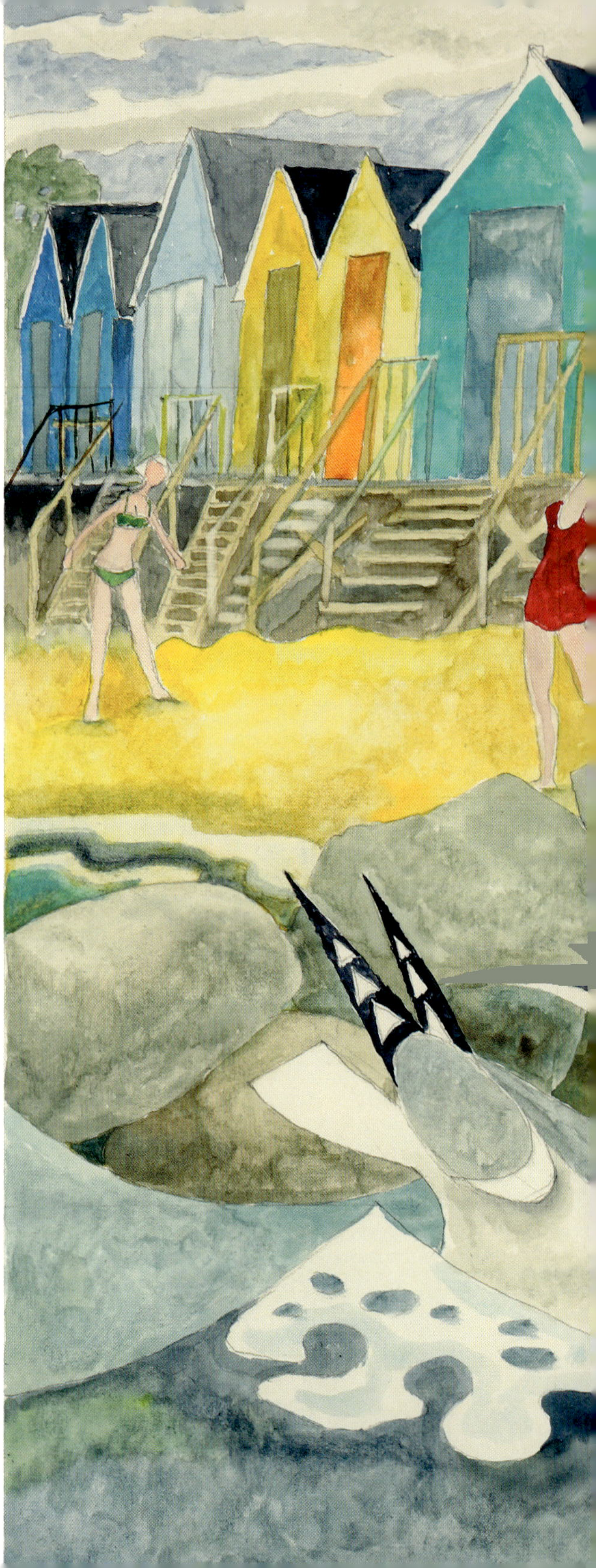

'Gulls and Local Huts' (2010) "Based on old Felixstowe beach huts. The sand has been washed away by the sea, so steps to the huts have been installed. The promenade is a pleasure to stroll along. Improvements have been made, rocks now prevent the erosion by the sea and offer protection against the wind."

'The Beach, Southwold' (1990)

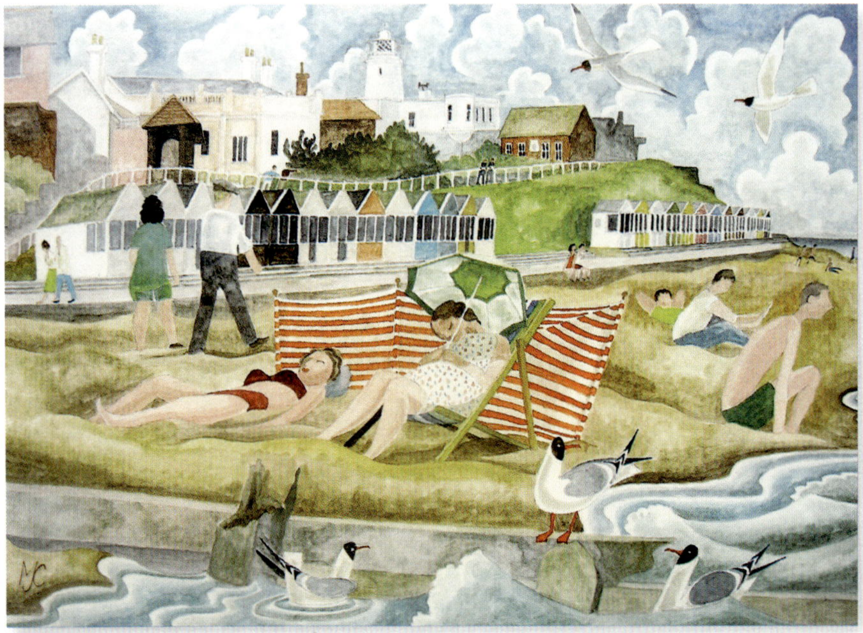

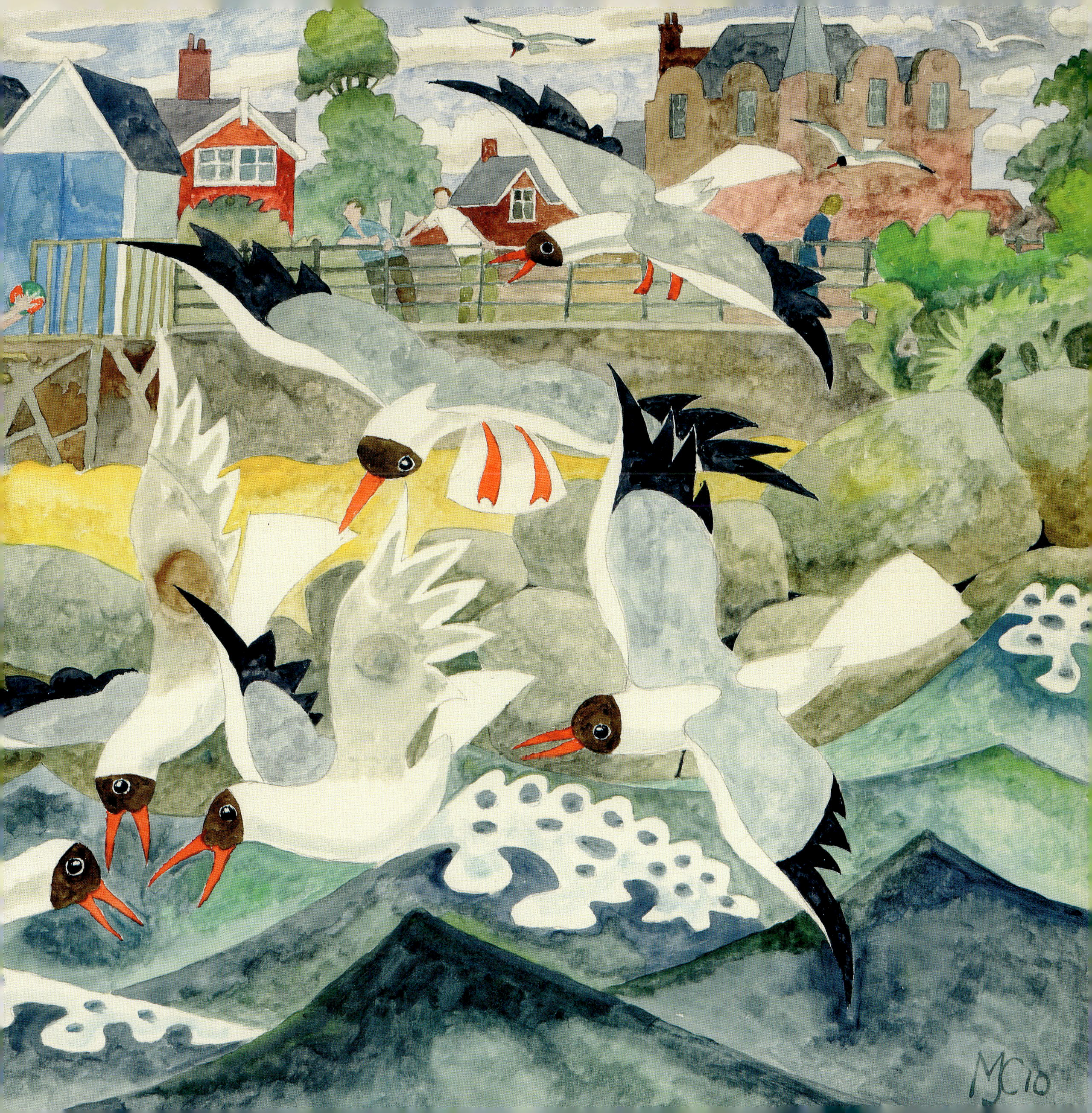
MC10

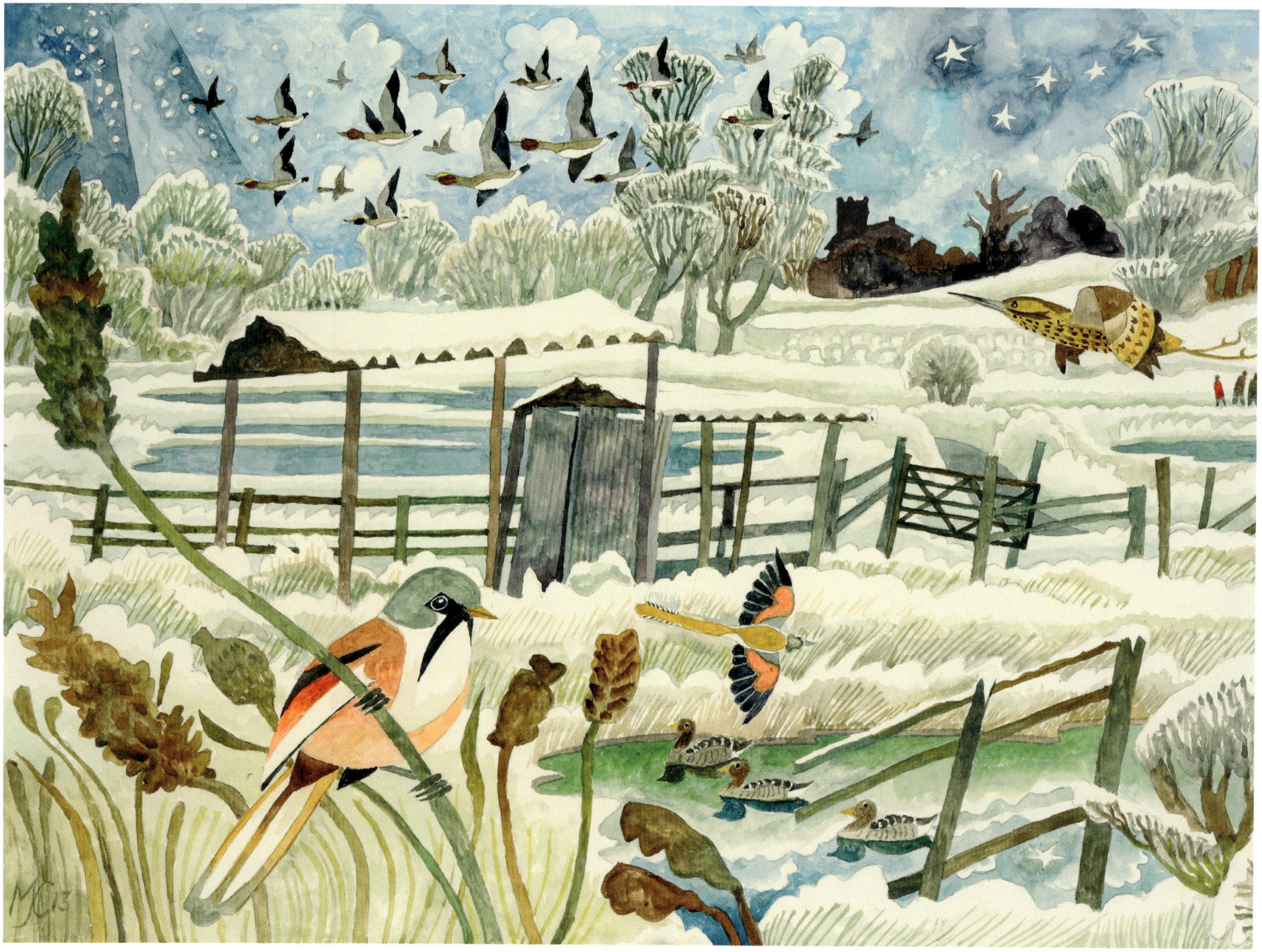

'Oulton Marshes' (2013) "For many years now I have donated a picture every Christmas to the Suffolk Wildlife Trust to use for the charity's annual Christmas card. The Oulton Marshes reserve offers a great deal of interest, represents an ideal habitat for birds, and holds memories of long walks in the snow."

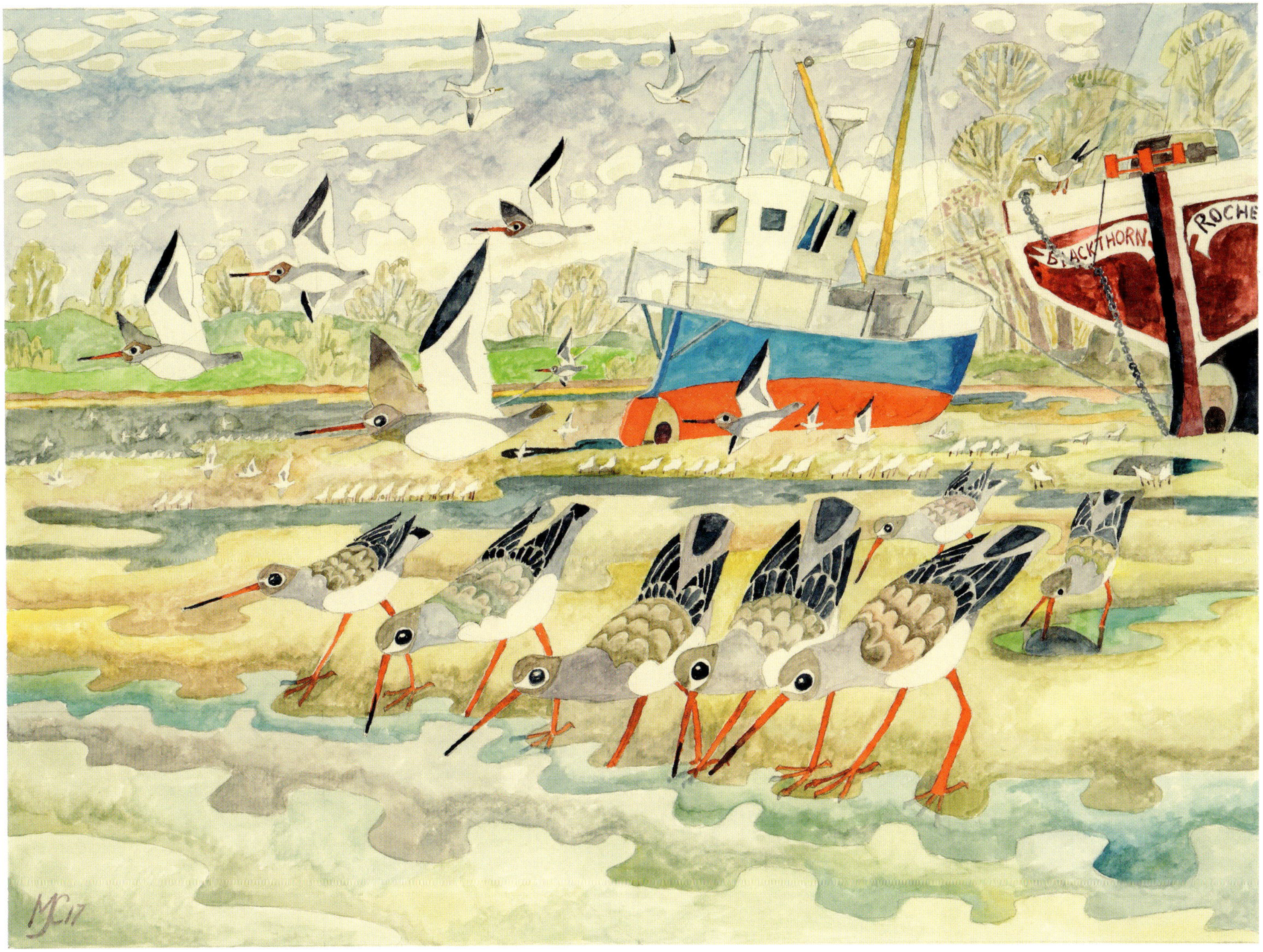

'Waders' (2017) In the background to Michael's depiction of feeding waders probing the sand at low tide can be seen the Thames sailing barge Blackthorn (built 1887, Rochester), a regular competitor in local barge racing and a familiar sight in coastal Suffolk, particularly Iken and Snape on the River Alde.

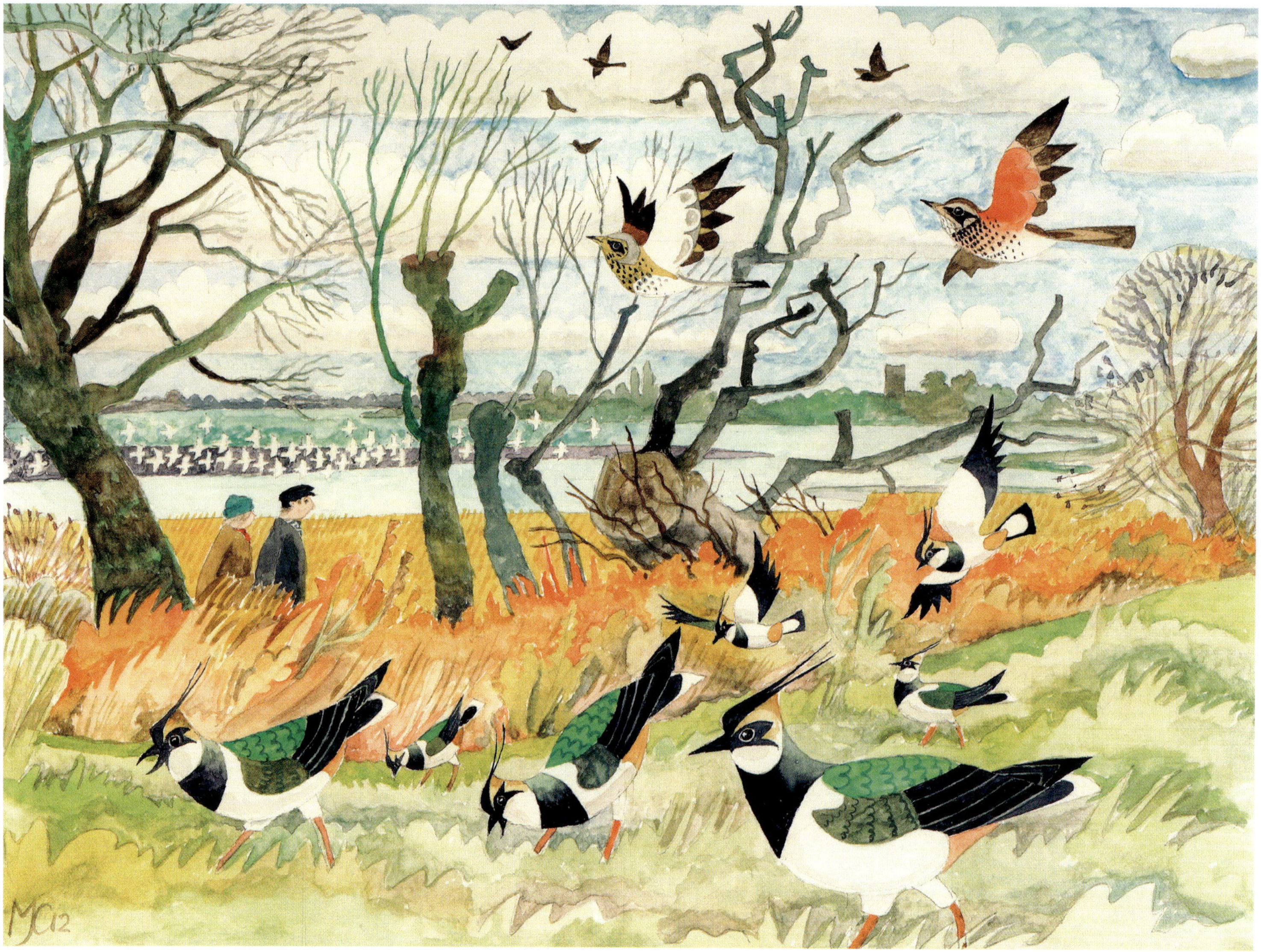

'February, Iken Cliff' (2012) "I don't often cause offence, but I'd painted a felled tree with the raw saw marks of this ancient beauty in full view. It had been commissioned by some friends, dedicated nature lovers, and the sight of this slaughter cut them to the quick. So I painted a few twigs in front of the offending tree stump – still no good. I then painted their garden instead, which went down very well. The Iken Cliff picture happily sold elsewhere."

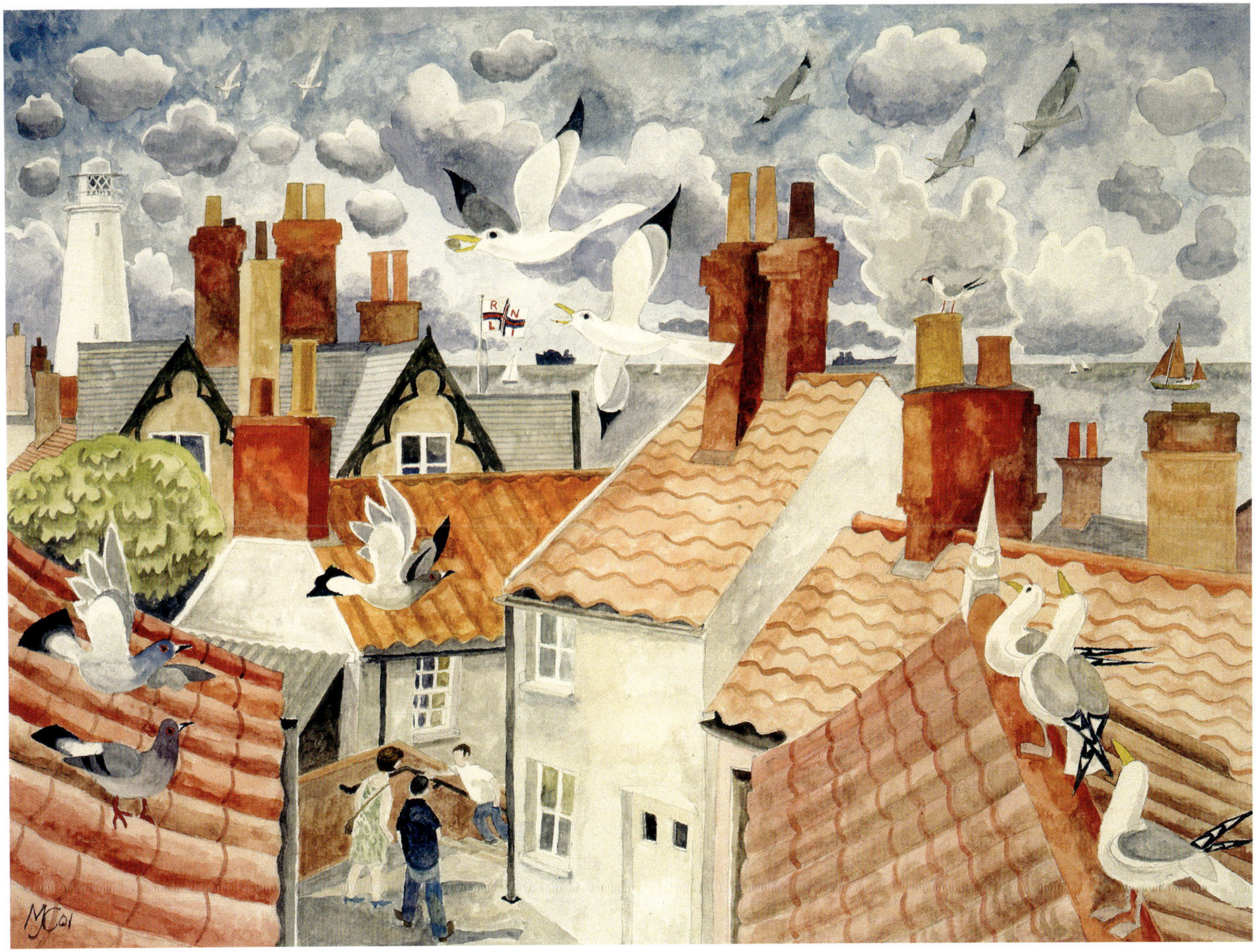

'Seaside Rooftops' (2001) Fans of Aldeburgh may think this is based on the view from the top of the Town Steps leading off the High Street. There is a spectacular outlook to the sea over the multi-coloured tiled roofs of shops and cottages. In fact, this painting is of no specific location. "Sometimes I use artistic licence and paint what I like. This is a made-up picture that could be based in Aldeburgh or Southwold. A typical scene of the area, but nowhere in particular."

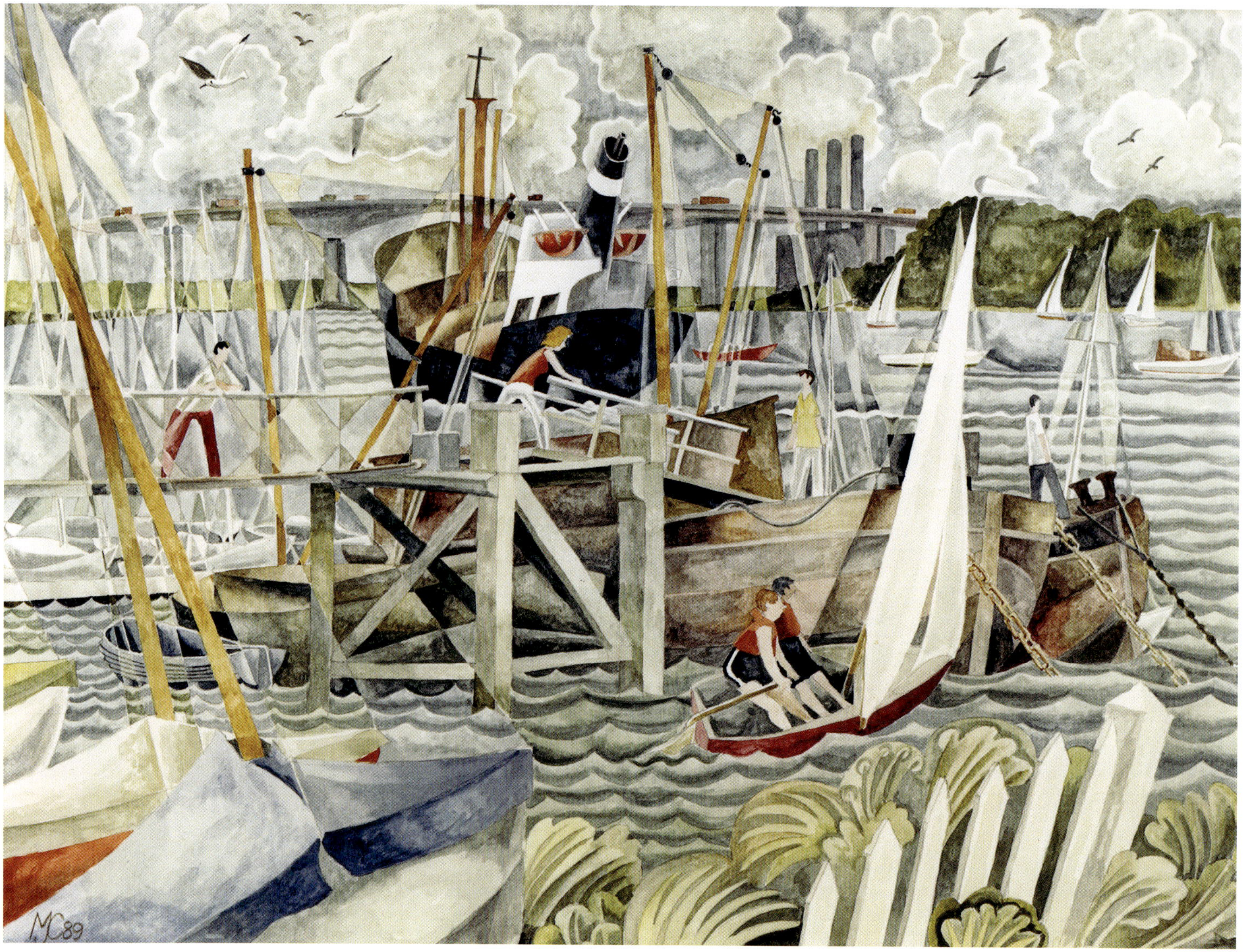

'Woolverstone Pier' (1989) "Watching people bobbing about in little boats is always amusing. Sailing with the breeze and tacking against it. Always busy, changing sides, pulling in the sheets and tying fast. Good times. Woolverstone is a busy shipping highway on the River Orwell. I remember several years ago a Russian cargo ship came out of Ipswich Docks and bumped and crashed its enormous bulk, in slow motion, threading carelessly through the moorings on either side of the river, sinking boats at every turn and damaging the rest. Horrifying for some. It doesn't happen often. The ship here is a collier going to supply Ipswich Cliff Quay power station (since demolished) with coal – the chimneys can be seen in the background."

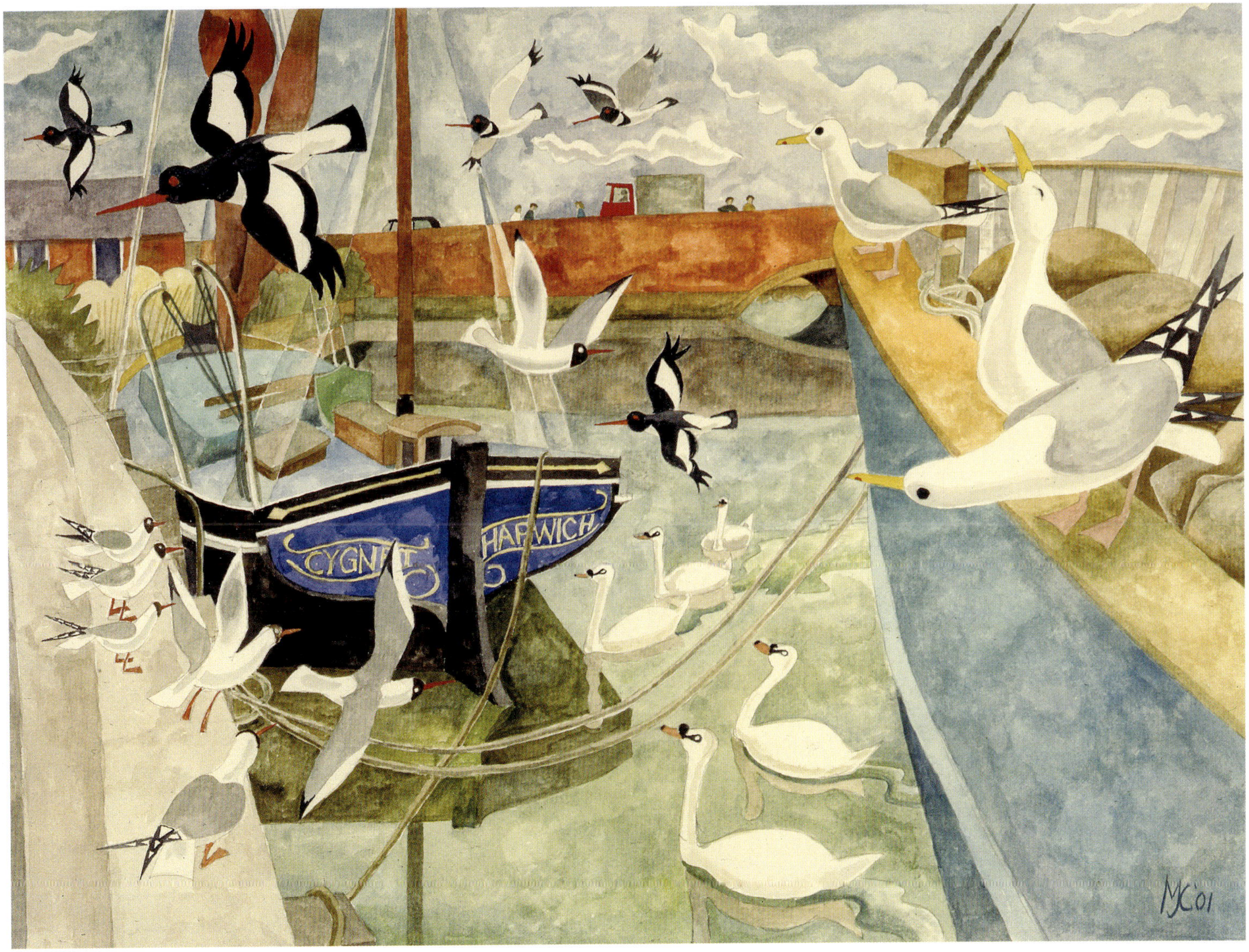

'Cygnet at Snape' (2001) Snape has a wonderful location on the River Alde, which runs through marshland to the village of Iken and eventually meets the sea at Shingle Street. The old sailing barge Cygnet is typical of those that used to serve the maltings, before they were transformed into a concert hall and shopping complex. "Snape is at the end of a meandering muddy estuary, the site of the Aldeburgh Festival and other cultural pursuits, a hot spot for visitors. Father Christmas arrives here in December by sailing up the river in a barge, the red sails slowly appearing above the tall reed beds, before landing on the quay to huge welcoming crowds, Morris Dancers and hot dogs."

'Meadow beside the Orwell Bridge' (1989) Referred to in the book's introduction, the series of paintings with the theme 'Two Rivers' saw Michael follow the Orwell and Stour and paint places at various points. This picture is from that collection, created in 1989, not long after the artist left Woolverstone School. "A very early painting, hence the strange colours that have deteriorated over time thanks to the shortcomings of photography before the digital era. Cows grazing on the marshes by the River Orwell. The Orwell Bridge is quite a feature in the landscape. It was a huge feat of engineering. A few days before it was open to traffic it was pedestrianised for a day. The public were invited to walk across and admire the spectacular views and stand about in the middle of the road. They turned out in their hordes. It opened to traffic in 1982."

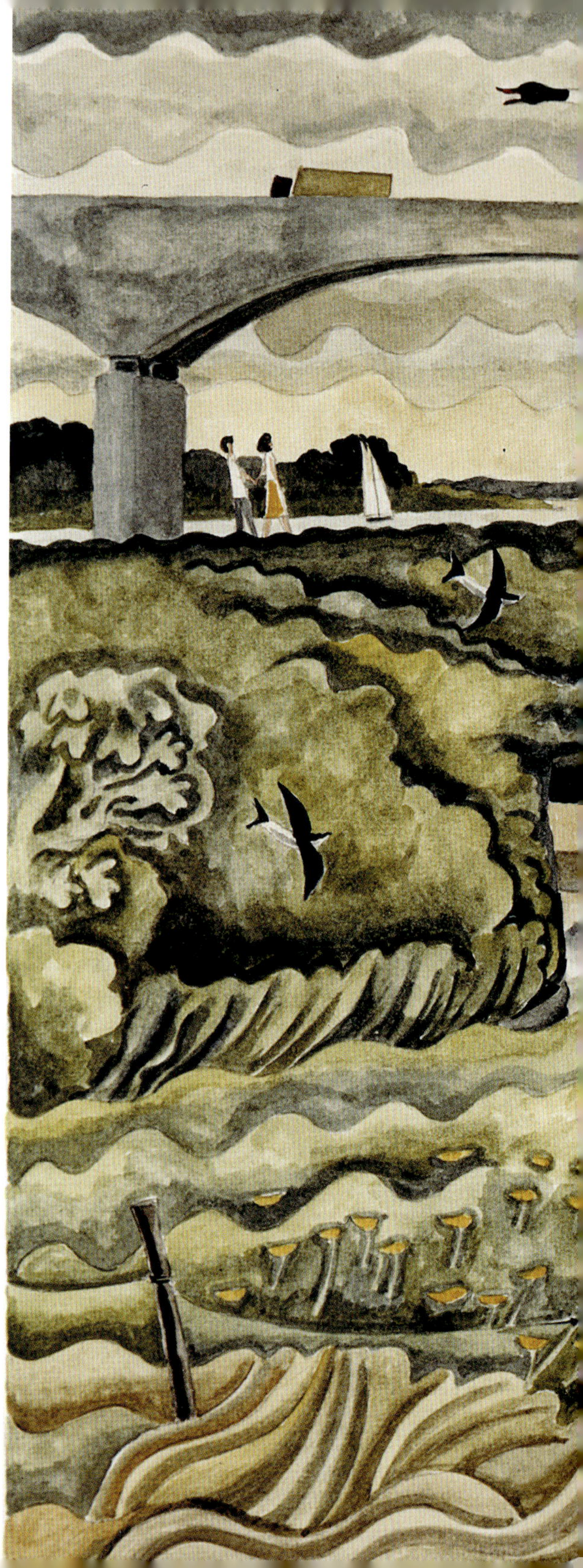

'At the Docks' (1985)

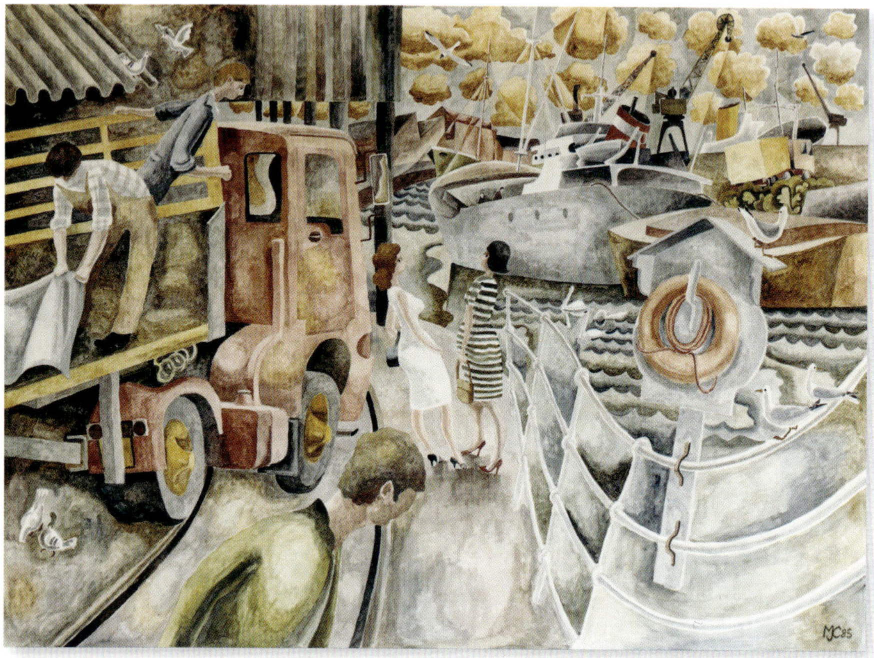

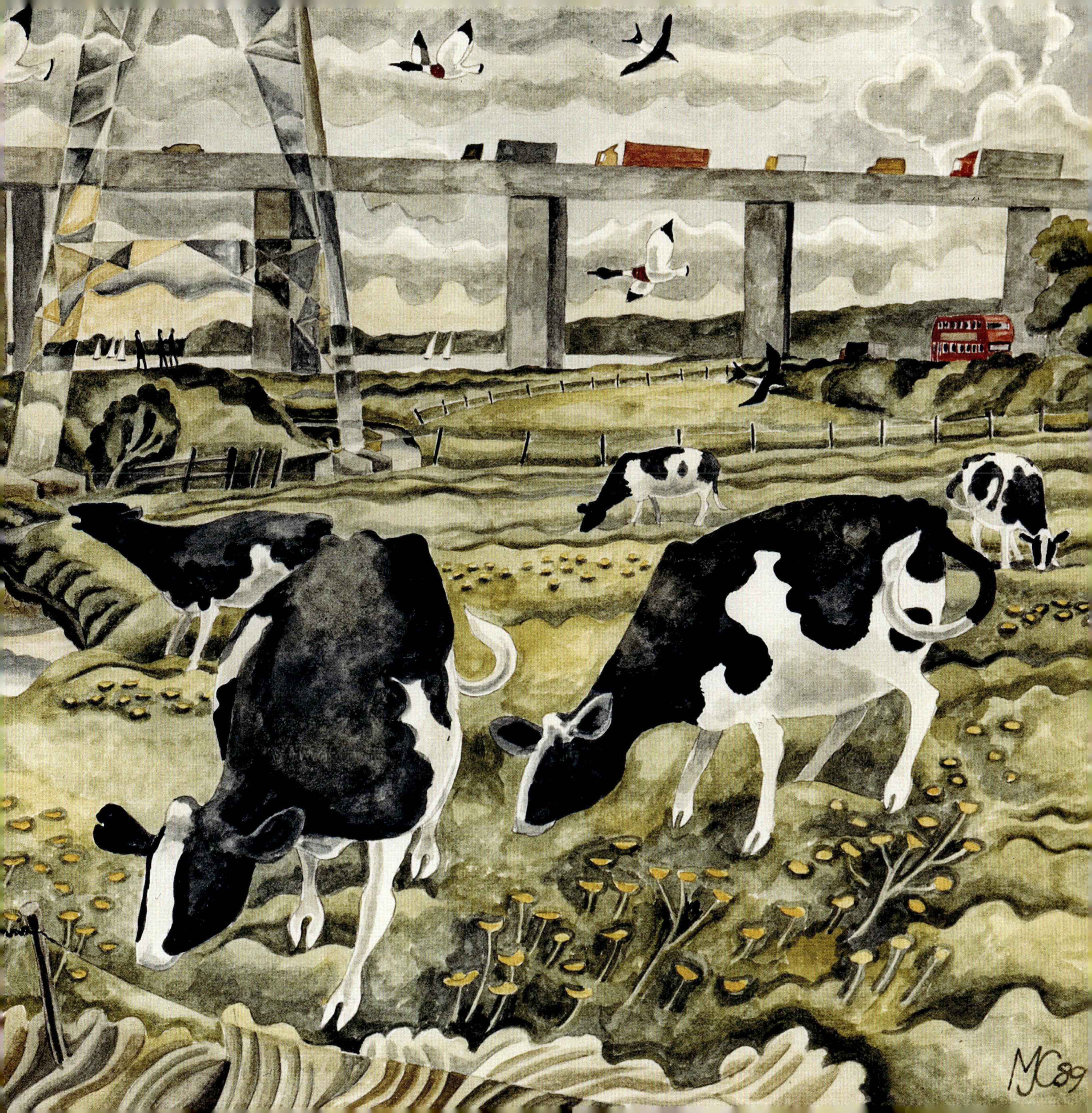

'A Red Bus at the Bristol, Shotley' (1989) Another image produced in 1989 as part of the 'Two Rivers' sequence of paintings, we encounter traffic on the Shotley Peninsula, with an Ipswich-bound red bus passing The Bristol Arms. The peninsula is trapped between the Orwell and the Stour, with the pub at Shotley Gate providing a welcoming sight for walkers tackling the waterside tour. There has been a Bristol Arms overlooking the Stour since the 1800s, named after the Marquis of Bristol who owned the land and foreshore of Shotley Gate.

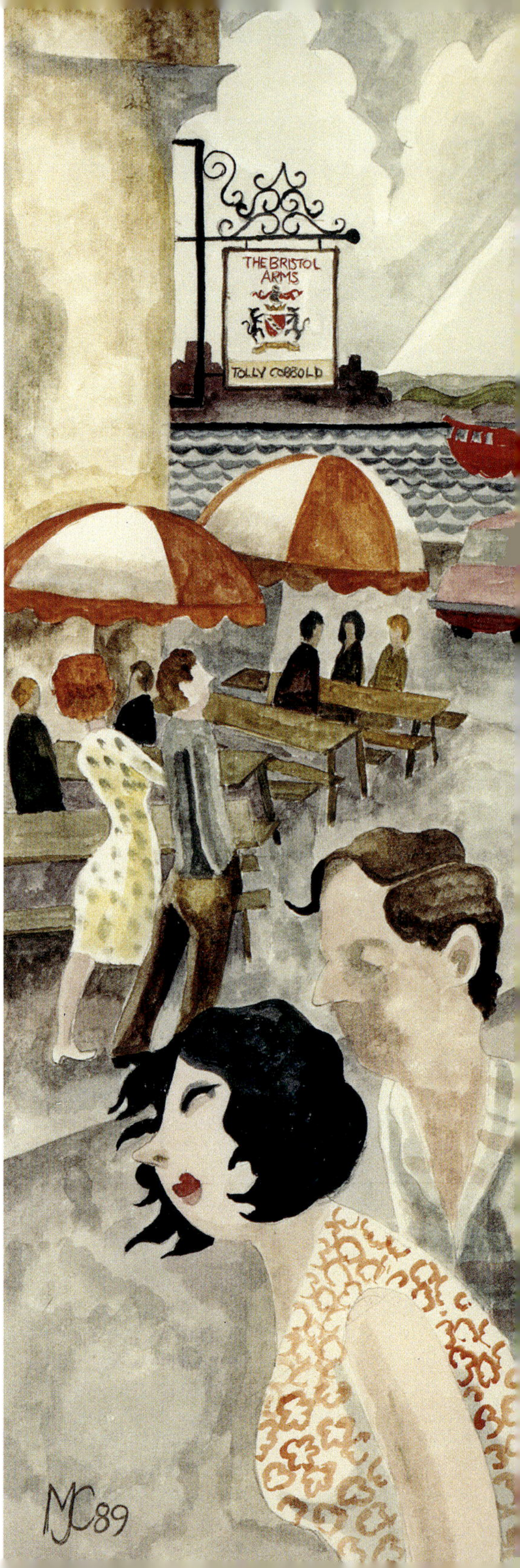

'Sea Scouts and Ragwort' (1985)

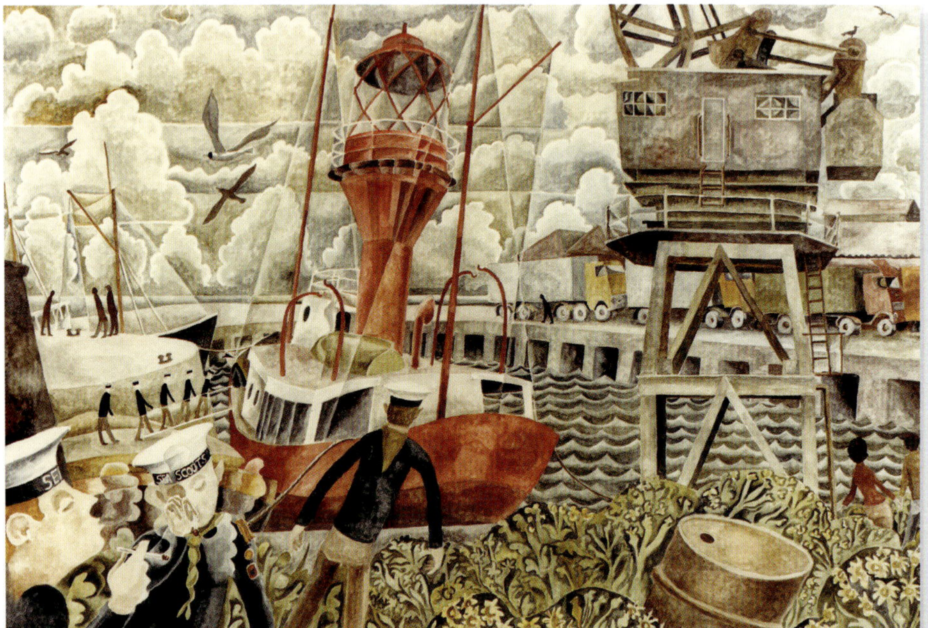

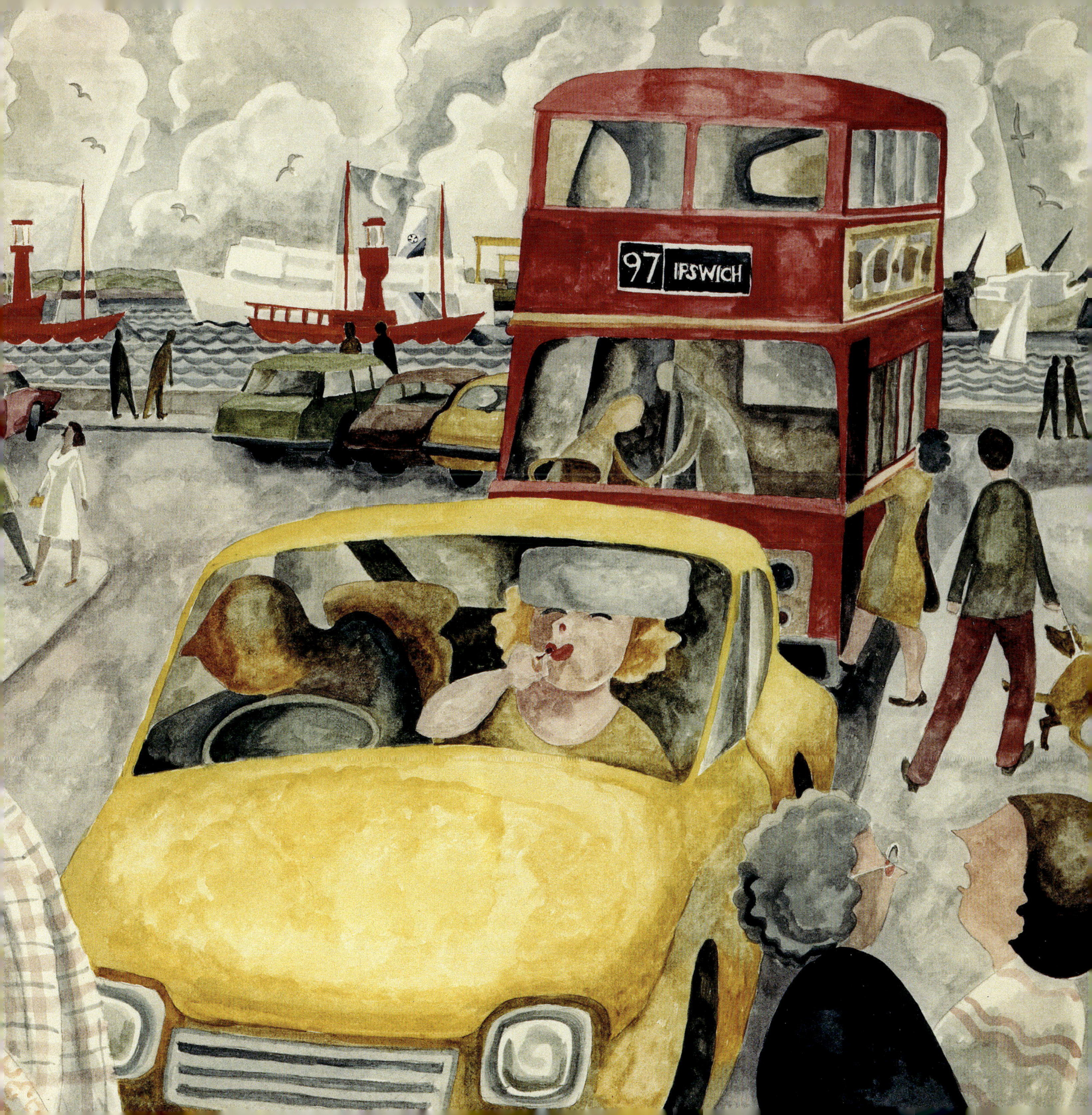
97 IPSWICH

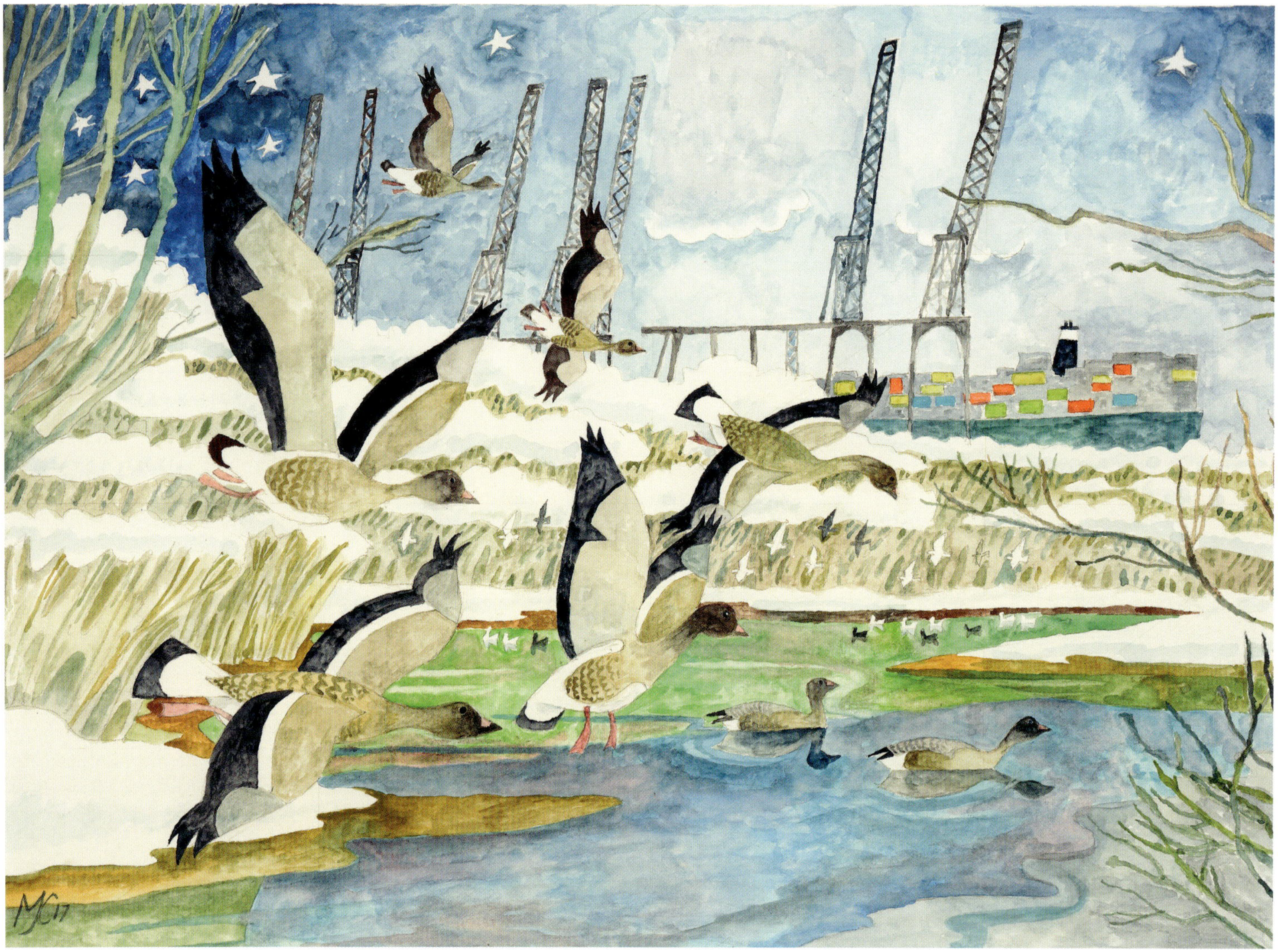

'Pink-footed Geese, Trimley Marsh' (2017) "The tranquil marshes and wildlife seem unperturbed by the heavy industry located just across the river wall at Felixstowe Docks, only a few hundred metres away. Winter-visiting Pink-footed Geese arrive in large numbers to create a great spectacle."

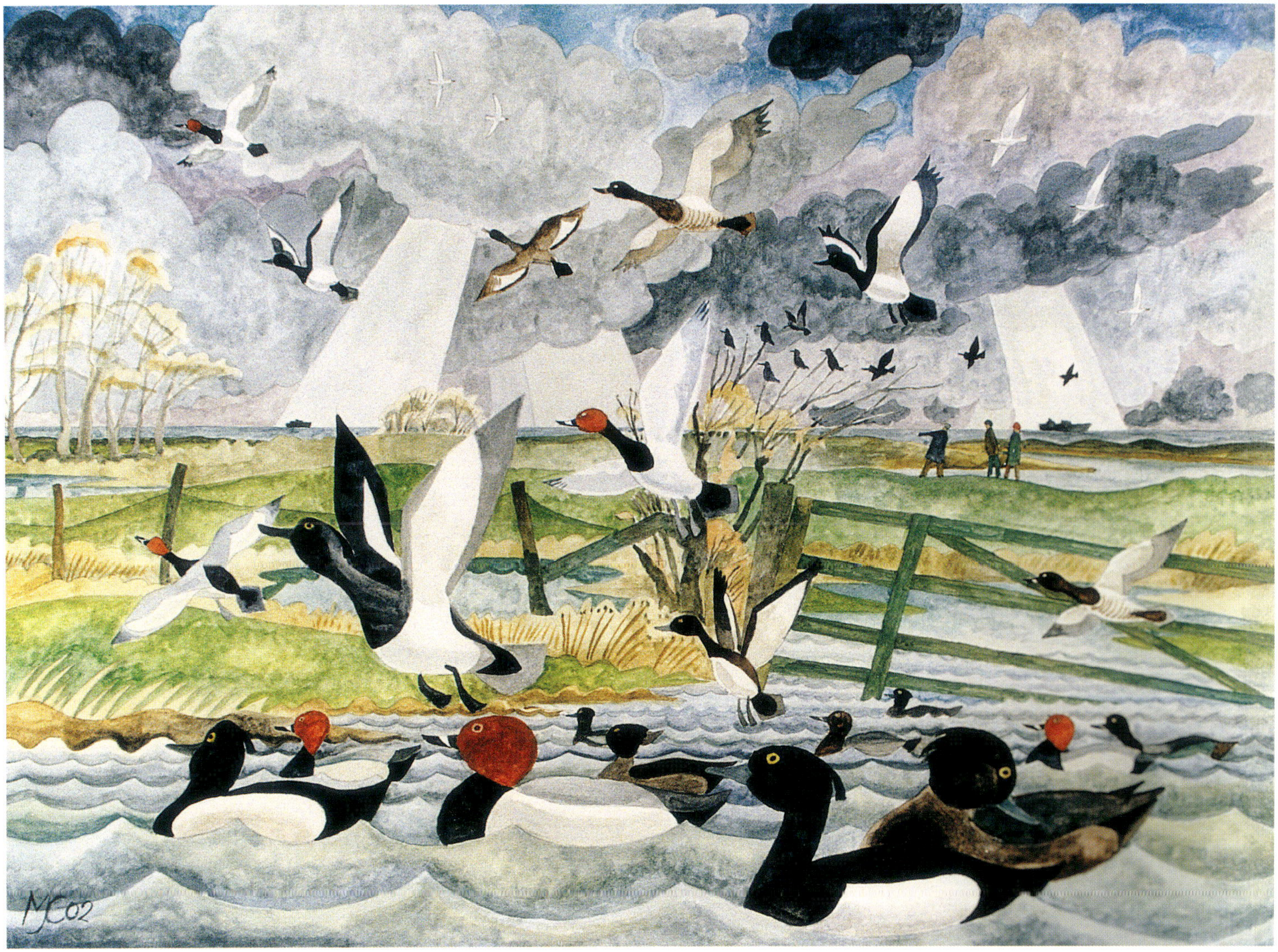

'Winter Ducks' (2002) "Pochard and Tufted Duck near Butley Creek". The location is a tributary of the Rive Ore and can be crossed using the Butley Ferry during summer months. Various wildfowl species can be found at the site, making it popular with walkers and twitchers.

'Thursday by the Sea' (2013) Jackdaws and Collared Doves flit in the foreground between Felixstowe beach huts – with the lower ones now accessed by steps thanks to beach erosion. The ever-present container ships head for the neighbouring port.

'Winter Seaside' (1998)

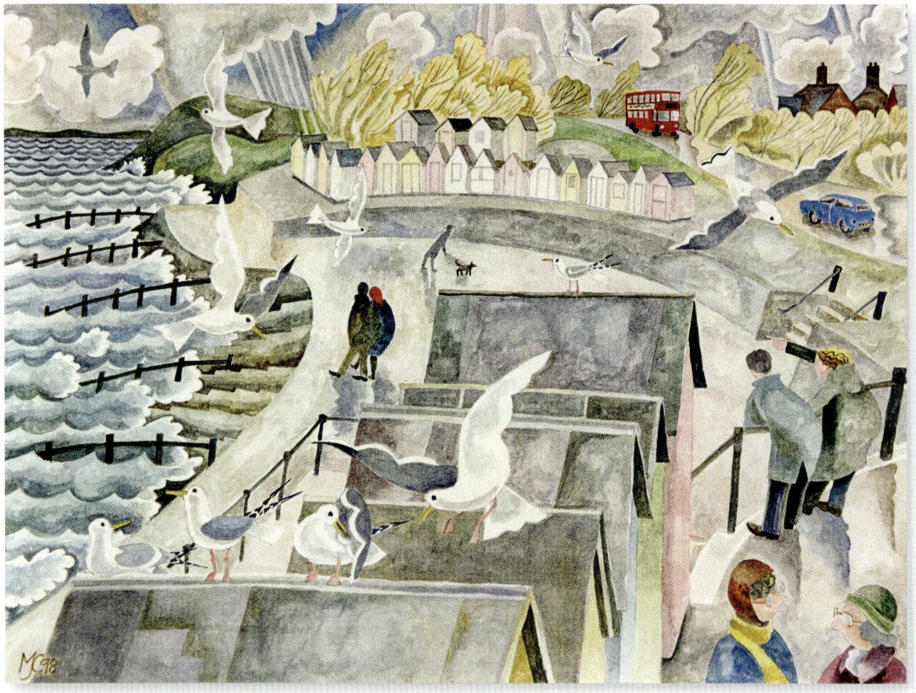

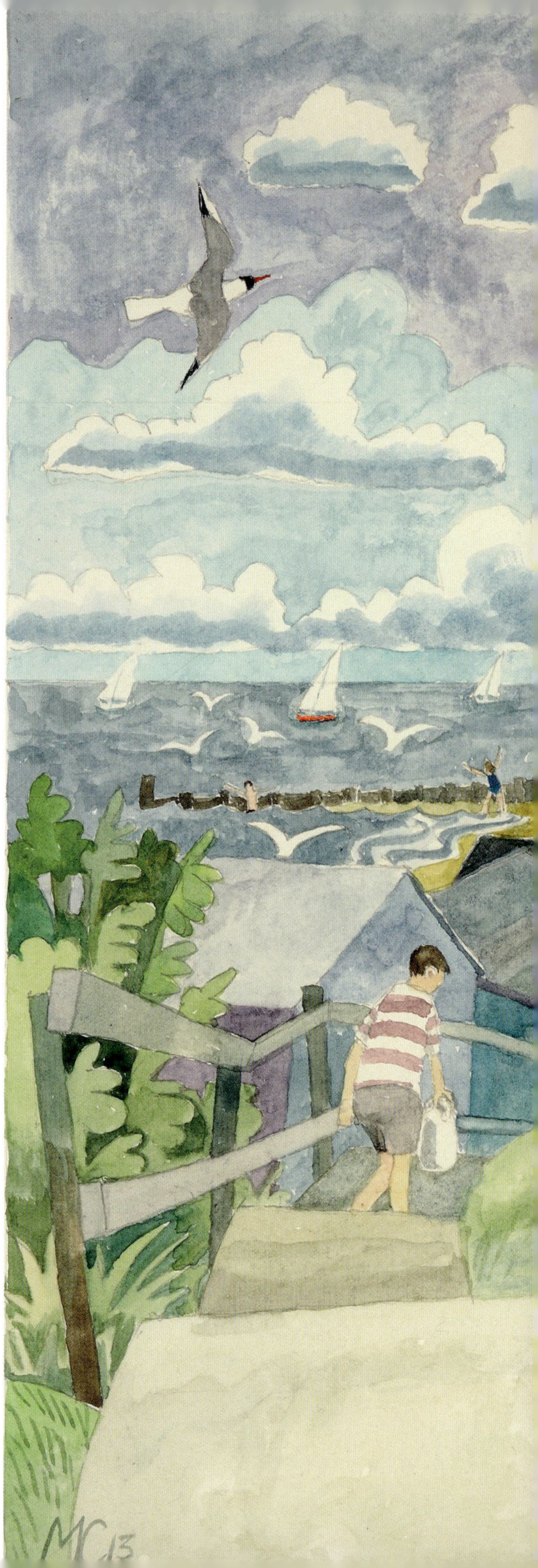

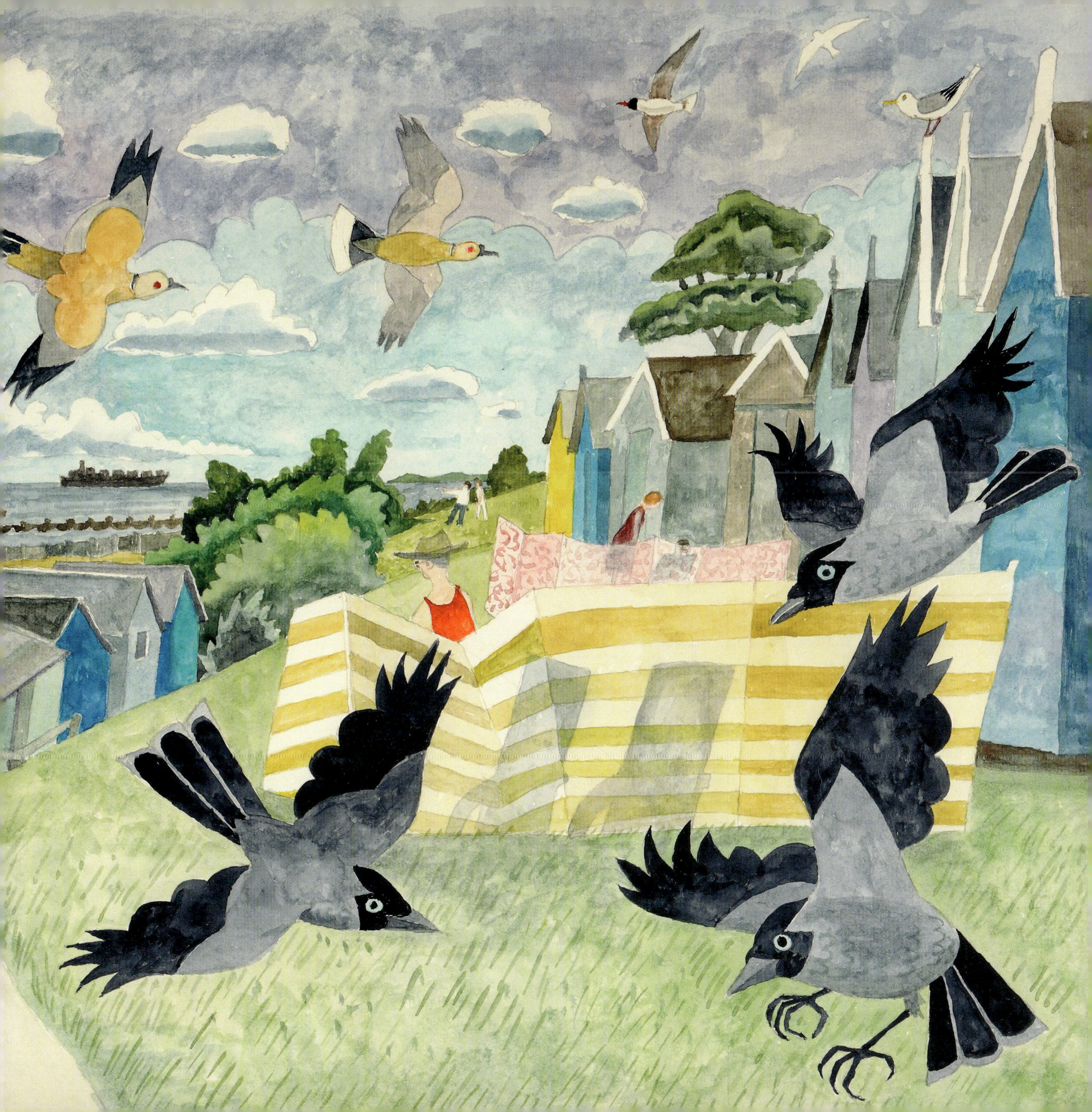

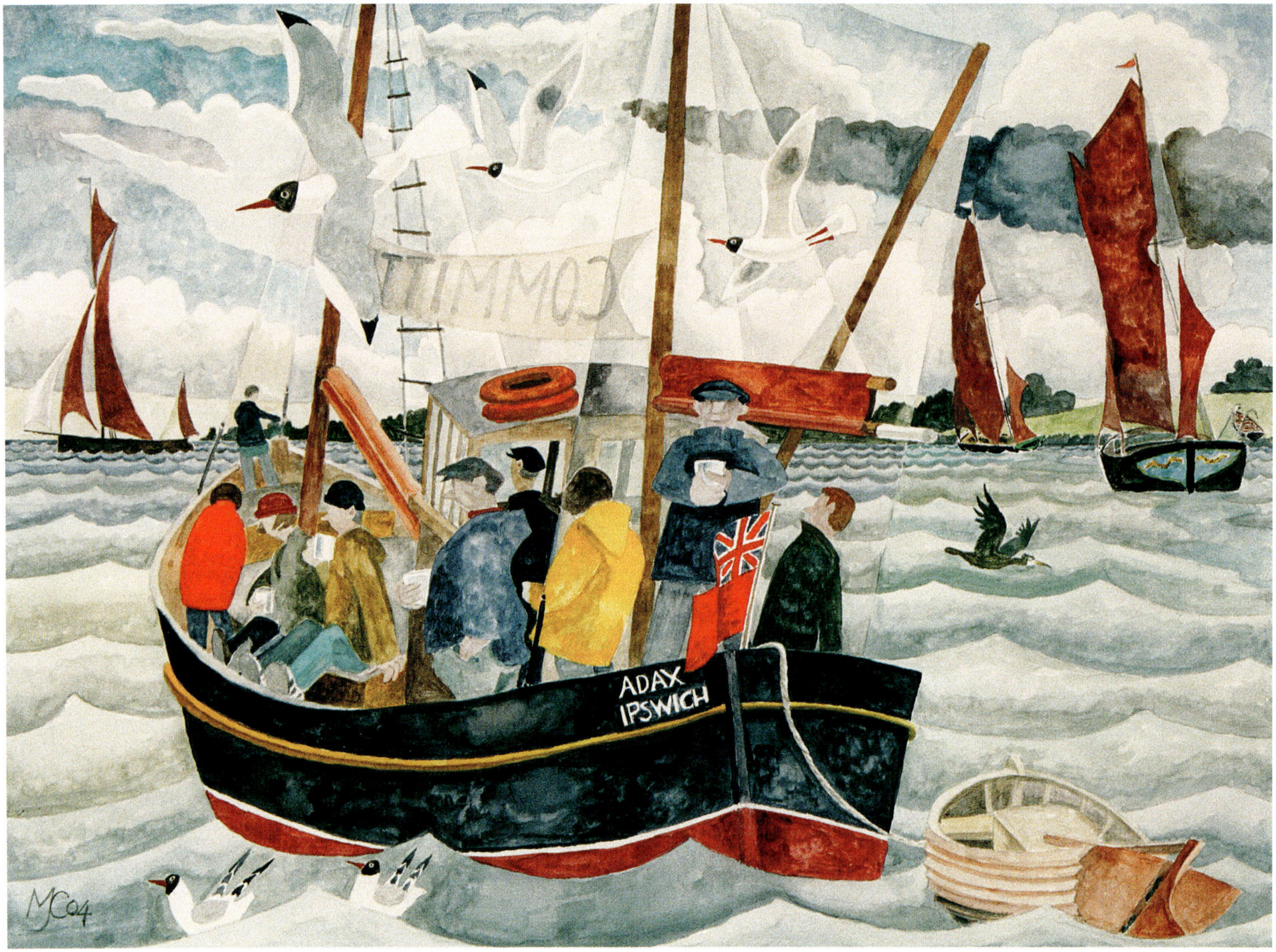

'The Barge Match Committee Boat' (2004) "Adax followed the barge match every year out to sea. I was one of the scrutineers of the race; our job was to make sure the barges kept to the course and rounded the buoys correctly. If one did not have sea legs, bobbing up and down or idling by a buoy could make the stomach churn and there is nothing worse than sea sickness. I passed the test, just!"

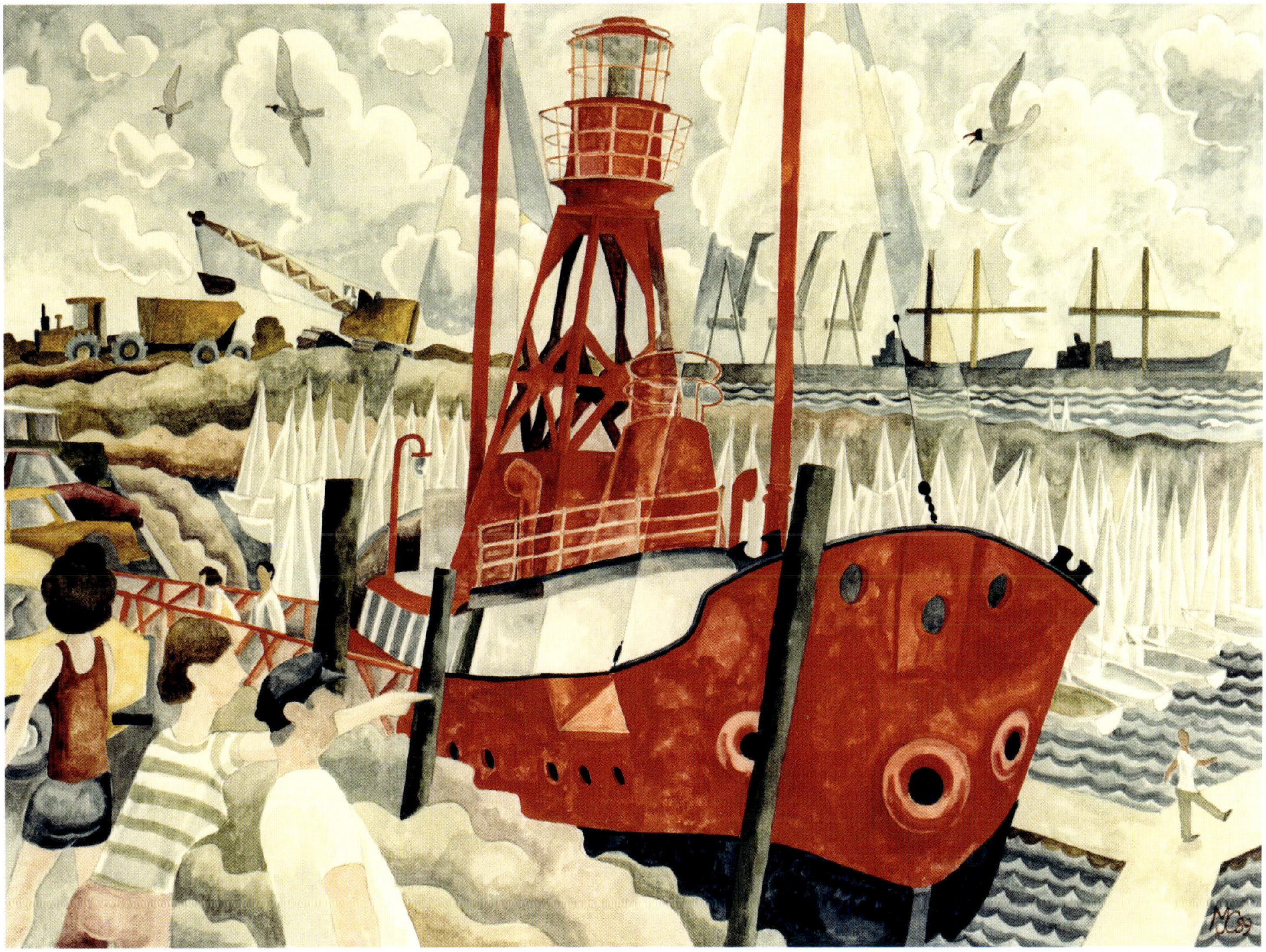

'Levington Marina' (1989) "Lightships were often brought into places on the Rivers Orwell and Stour for maintenance or retirement. The redundant Mid Barrow Light Vessel no 87 was moved to the Haven Ports Yacht Club. The marina was still in its infancy in 1989 and has grown considerably since this painting was completed. In the distance the docks are being extended with large working machinery."

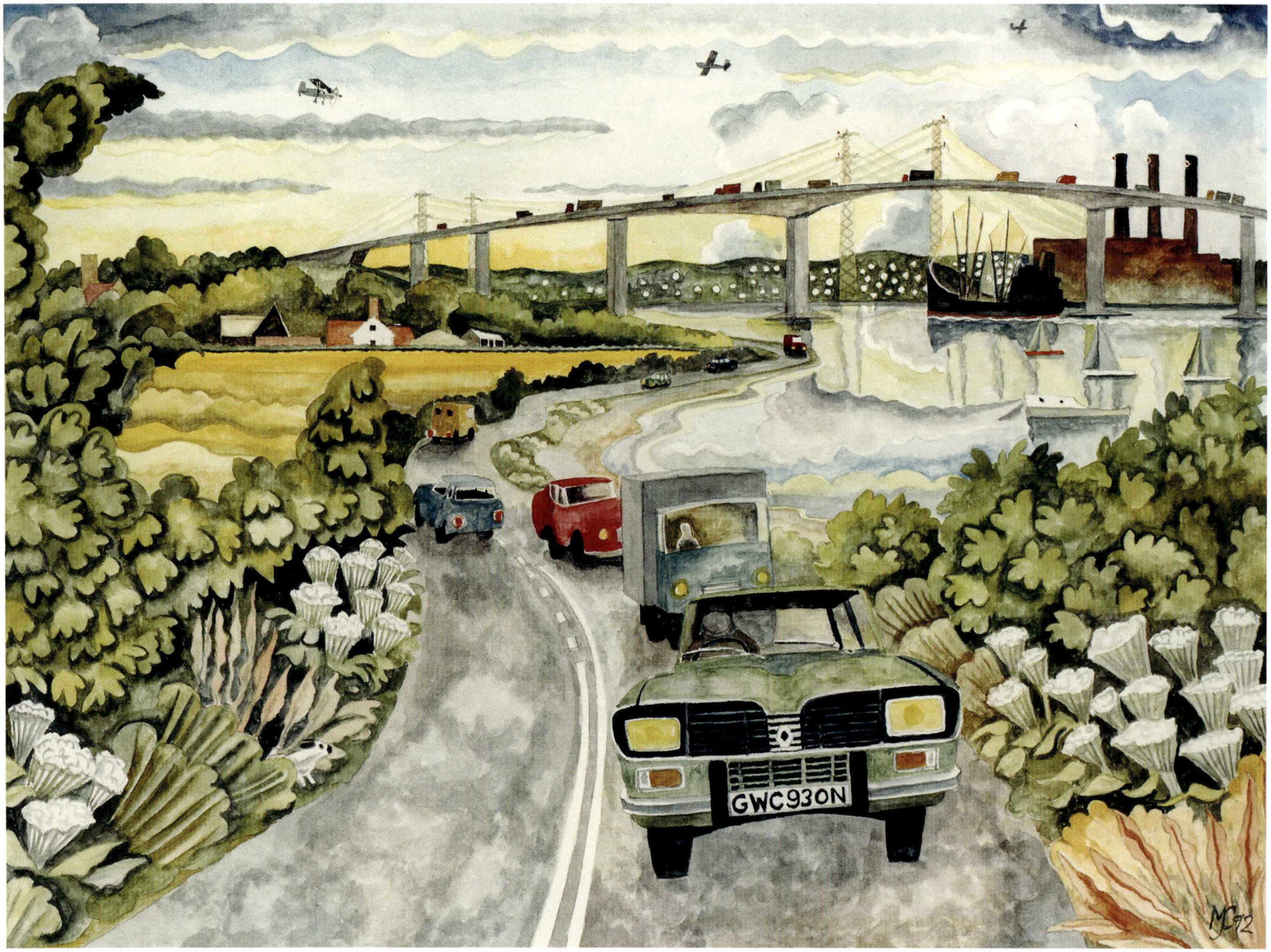

'The Strand from Freston Hill' (1992) "The car in the foreground is an old family favourite of the people who commissioned this painting. The Strand is an attractive riverside road where people stop and stare at the water and observe the wildlife feeding on the muddy flats. I have painted this stretch many times and from different directions. The Strand is busy with people and birds at all times of the day. The chimneys of the former Cliff Quay power station can be seen in the distance. They and the rest of the plant were demolished in 1994. Crowds gathered on the bridge and along the roads nearby to watch this old landmark disappear forever; in a few great blasts it tumbled down into rubble. Sad in a way – others may disagree."

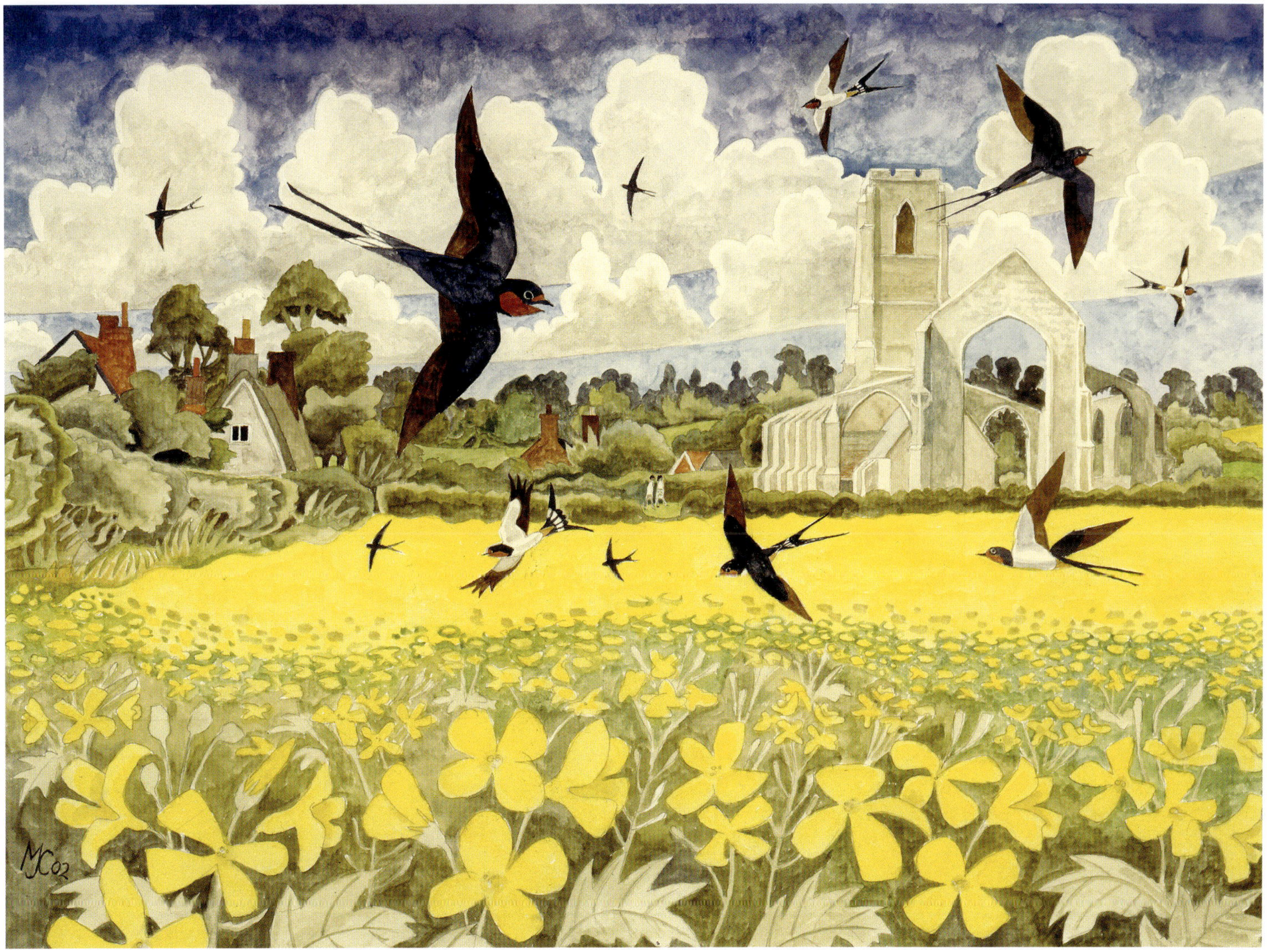

'Swallows and Mustard, Covehithe' (2001) Thanks to coastal erosion, not much is left of the village of Covehithe (6km north of Southwold) other than the remains of one church and a smaller one added later. Covehithe retreated more than 800 metres between the 1830s and 2001, according to Ordnance Survey maps. "I saw the Swallows swooping over the mustard and just had to capture that. What a glorious sight with a backdrop of the old ruined church. This little hamlet is slowly crumbling into the sea. The road comes to a sudden jagged stop and the rest is over the cliff. A beautiful beach offers nesting places in the cliffs for Sand Martins."

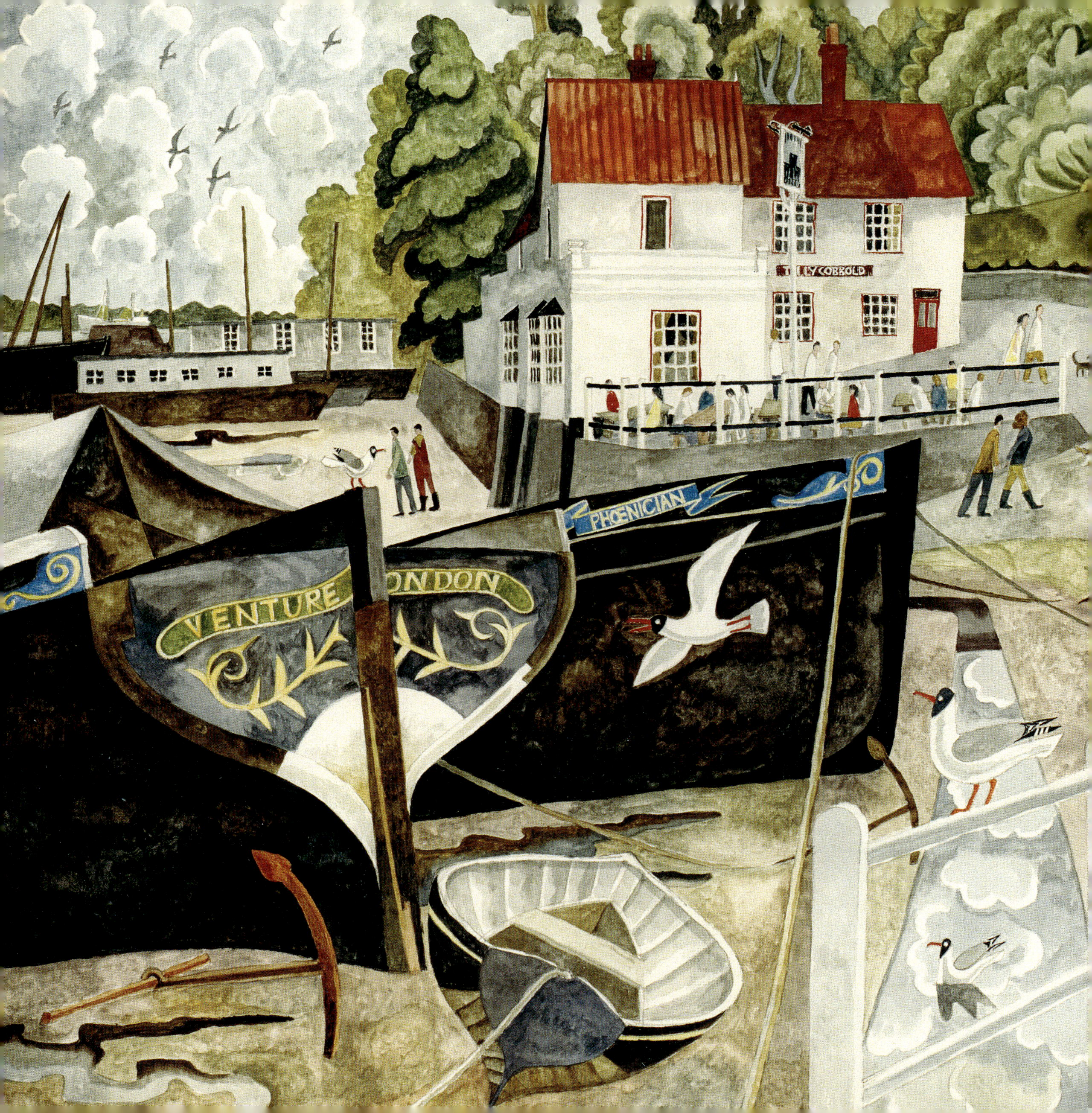
LY COBBOLD
PHŒNICIAN
VENTURE
ONDON

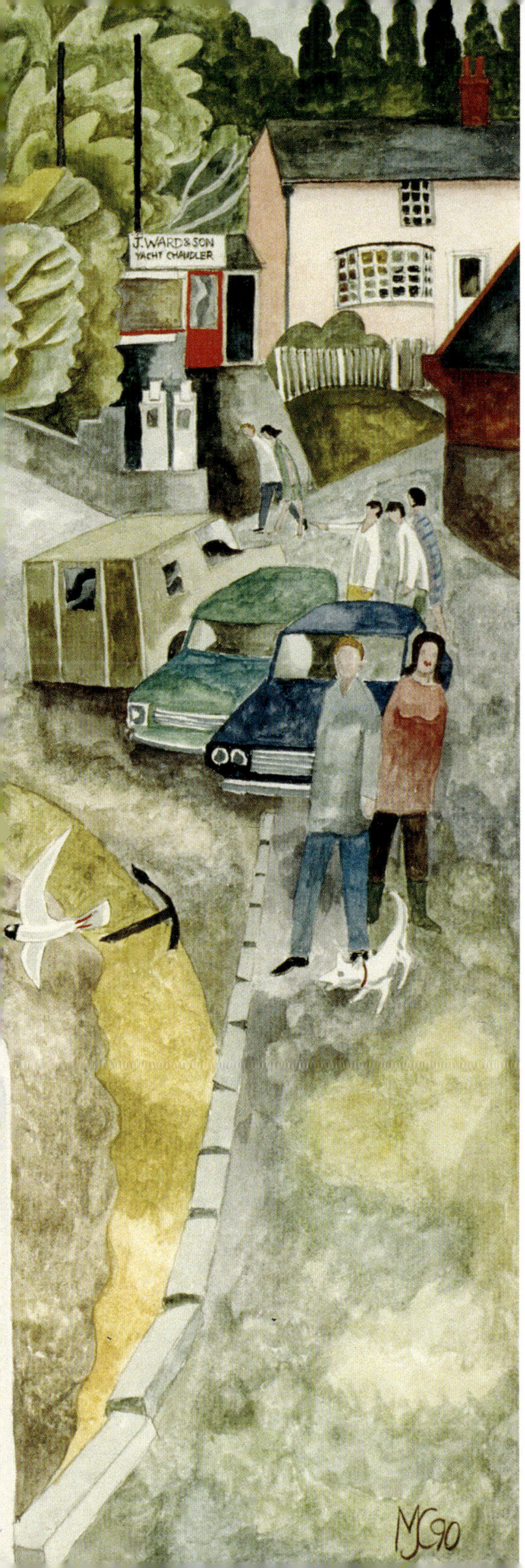

'Barges at the Butt and Oyster' (1990) "I have painted this scene many times from all vantage points. The pub, at Pin Mill, has changed colour from white to cream and now it is pink; this is one of the older paintings. The barges come and go. People paddle in the stream as they have done for generations. Cars get marooned on the wrong side of the spring tides if they are not mindful."

'At the Outer Ridge' (1991)

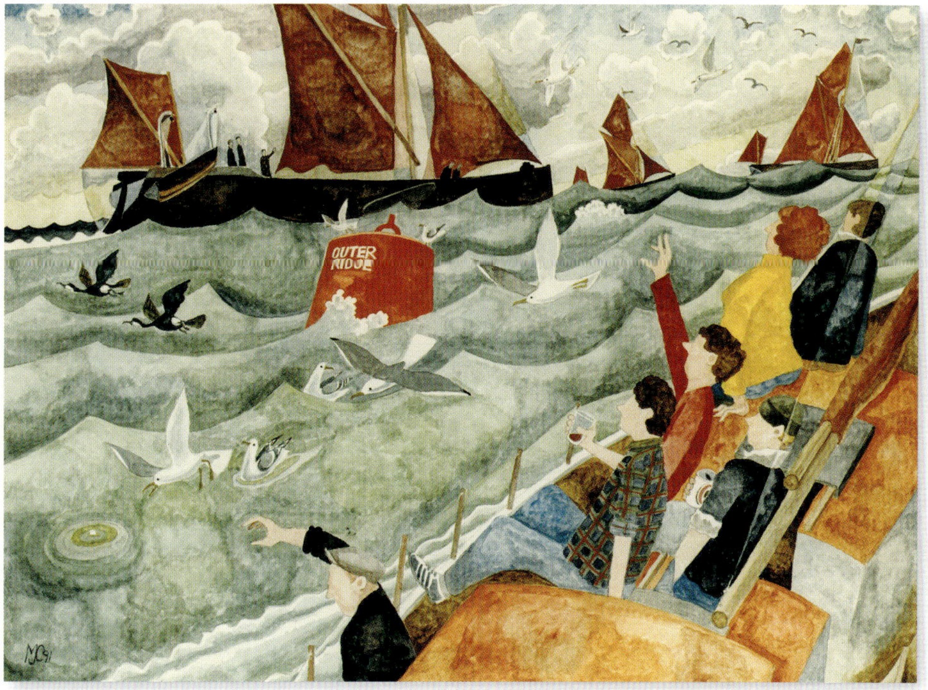

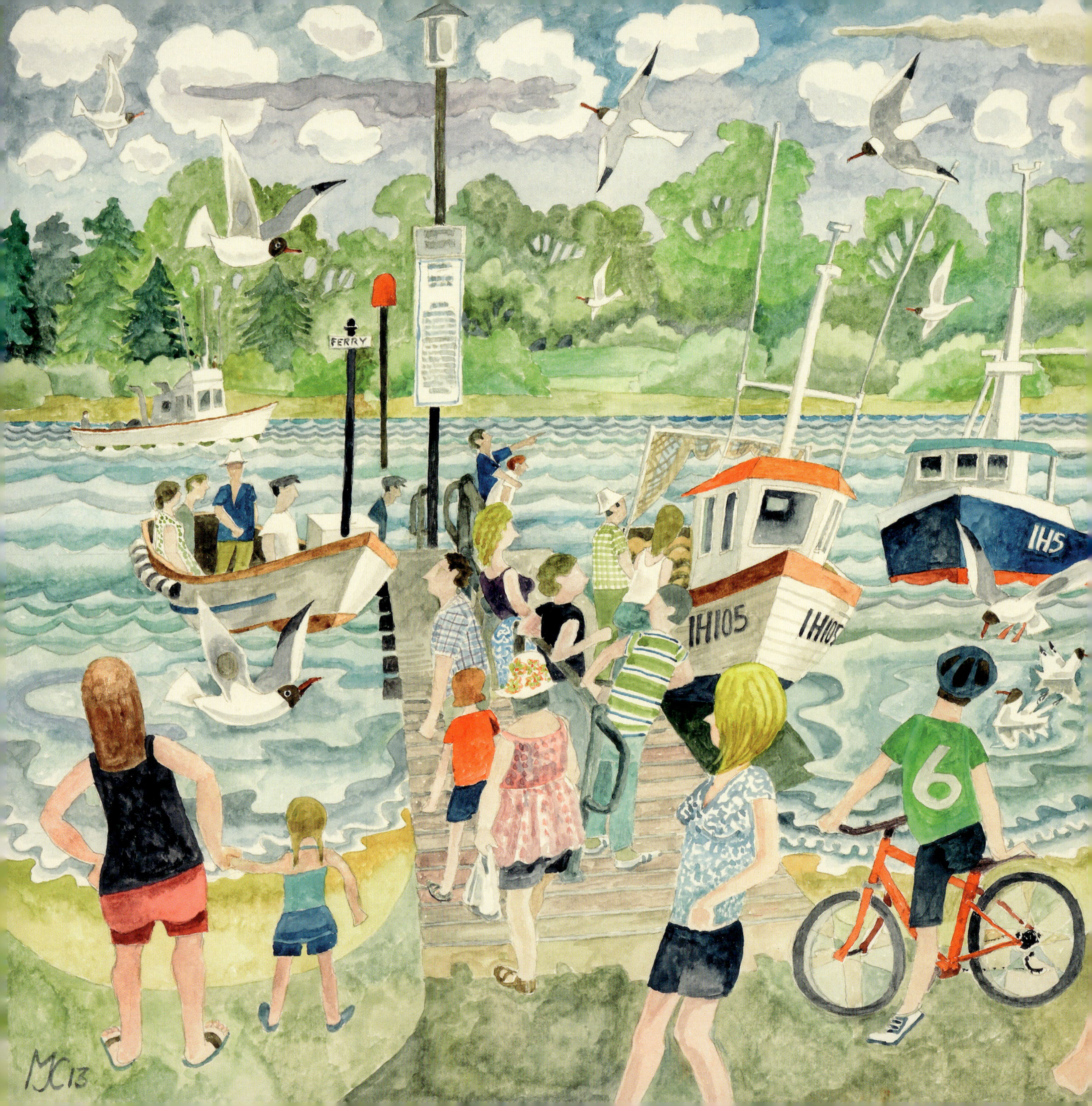
FERRY
IH105
IH5
6

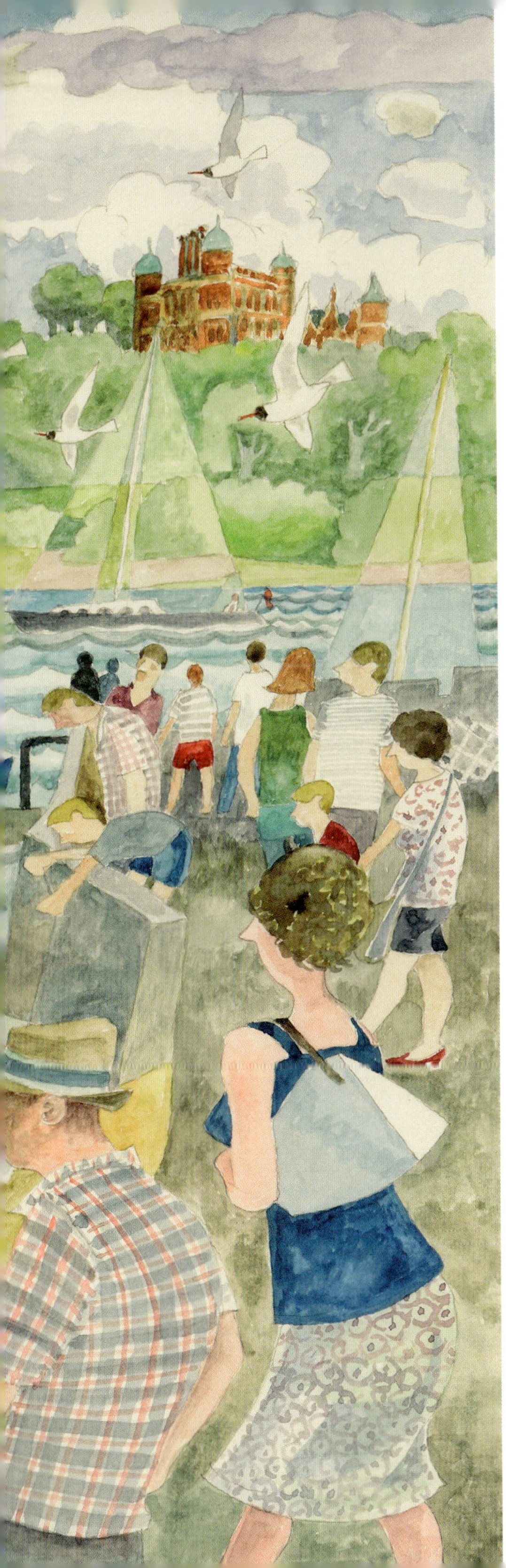

'Holiday at Felixstowe Ferry' (2013) "A hive of activity in the summer with holidaymakers enjoying the ferry over the dangerous, fast-running River Deben that rushes out to the North Sea. Children crabbing from the jetty and the wall. Locals cycle for miles and have fish and chips nearby. A strong sailing community dominates this part of Felixstowe. One can look across the river to Bawdsey beach and reminisce about the secret wartime activities that went on over there; the first radar station in the country was at Bawdsey Manor."

'Dinghy Sailors' (2005)

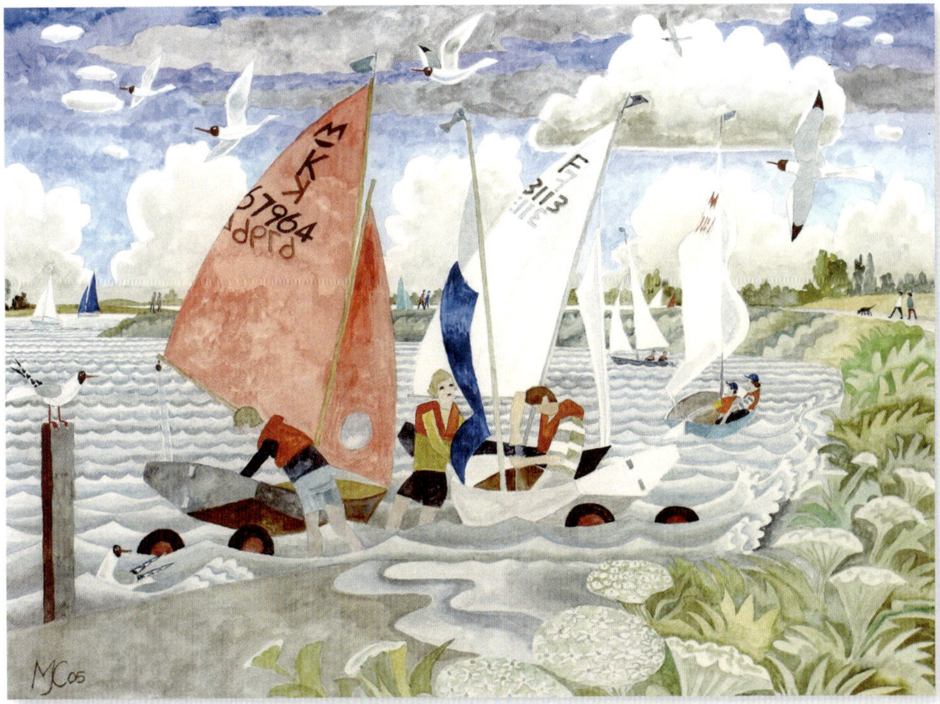

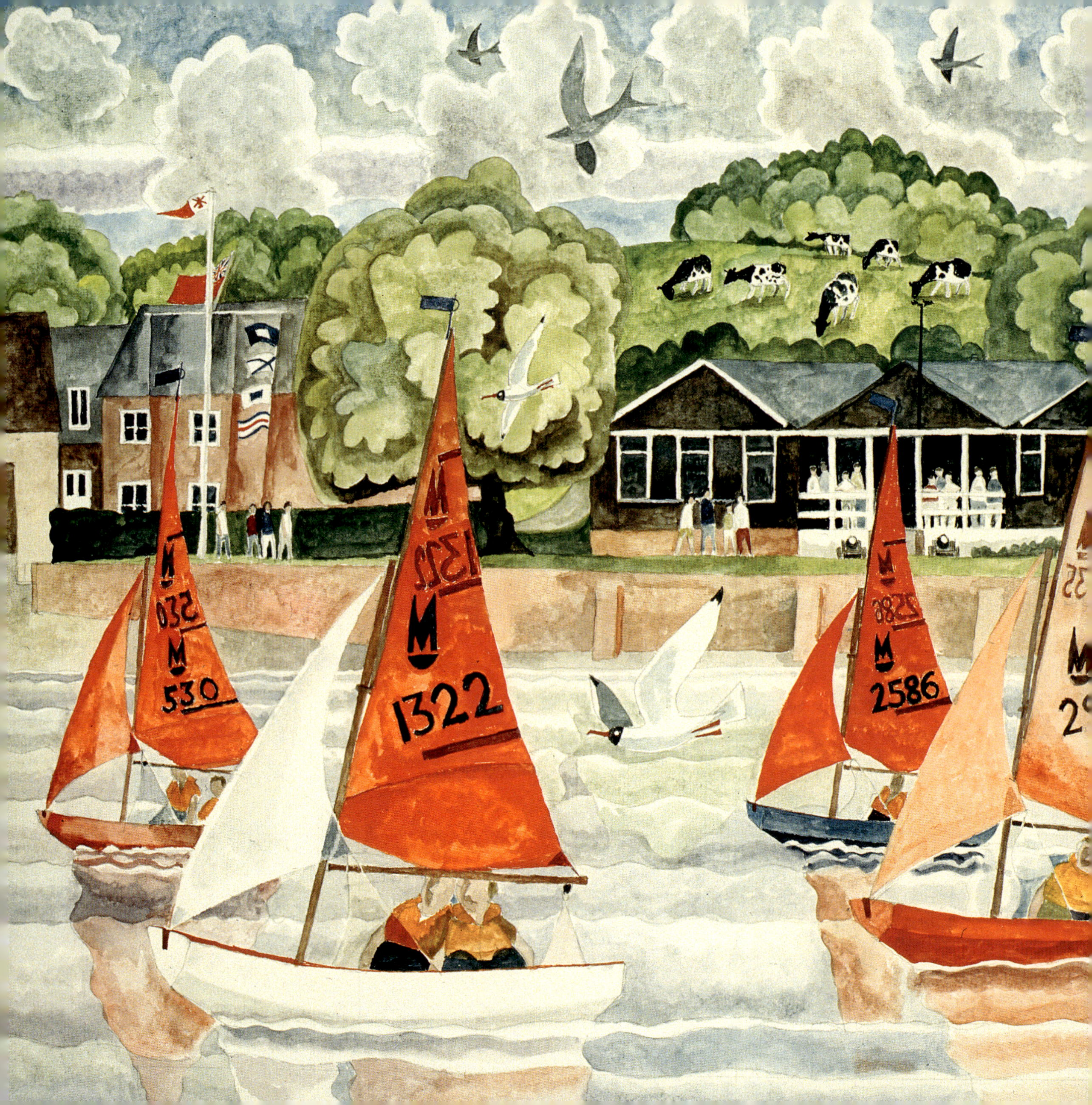
530
1322
2586

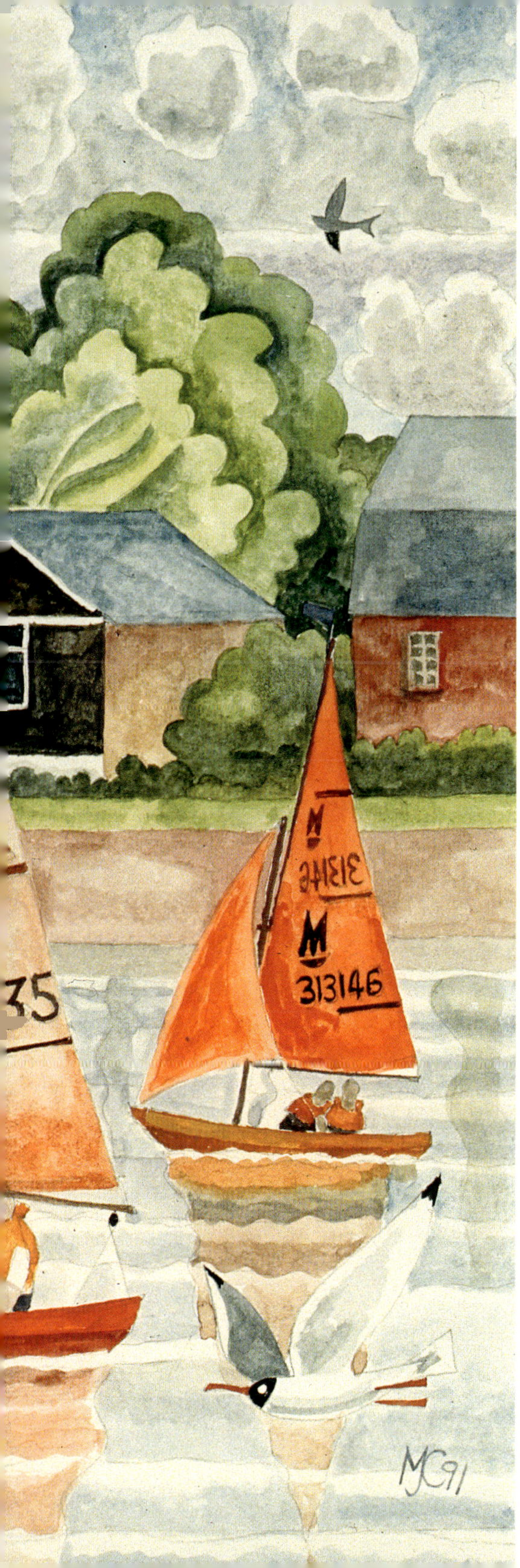

'Pin Mill Sailing Club, High Tide Summer' (1991) "I was commissioned to paint a parade of all the Mirrors [Mirror-class sailing dinghies] at the club. The red sails reflect nicely in the water."

'Sailing at Waldringfield' (1991)

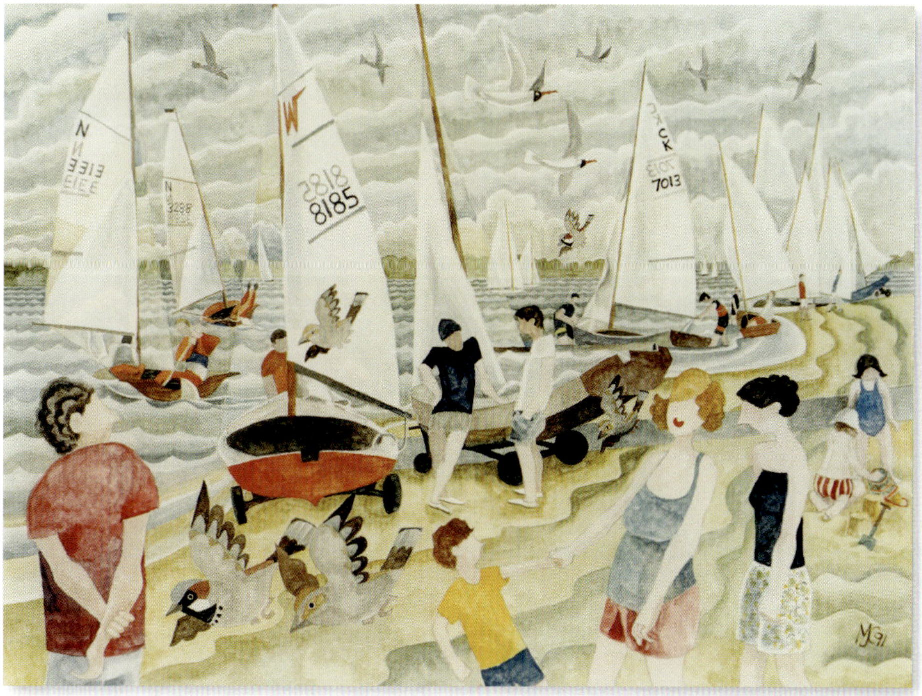

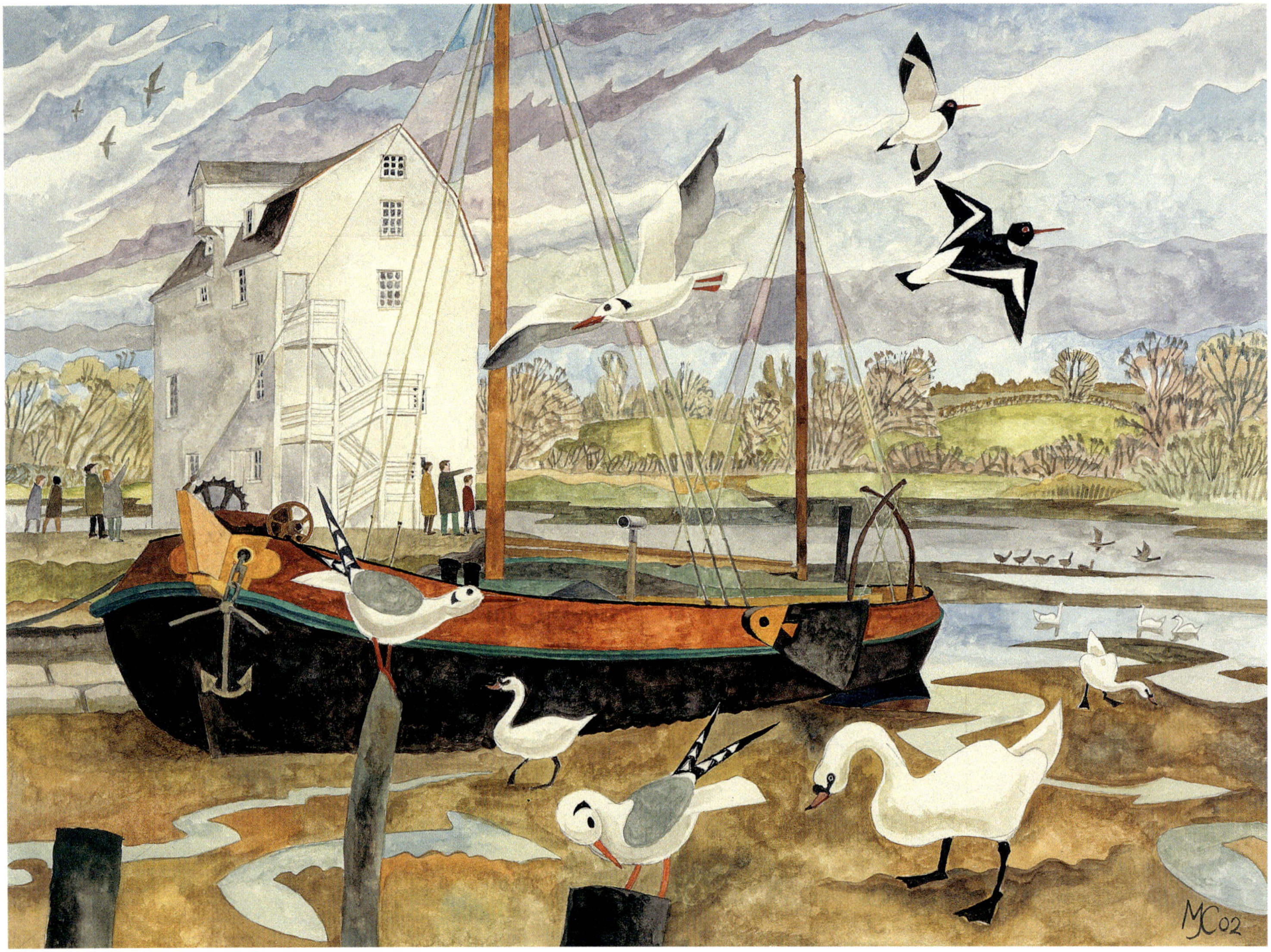

'Woodbridge Tide Mill' (2002) The earliest record of a tide mill at Woodbridge on the River Deben is for 1170. The present building dates from 1793, and by the 1950s was the last working example in Britain. It was salvaged in 1968 and opened to the public in 1973. Restoration work has since brought it back into working order.

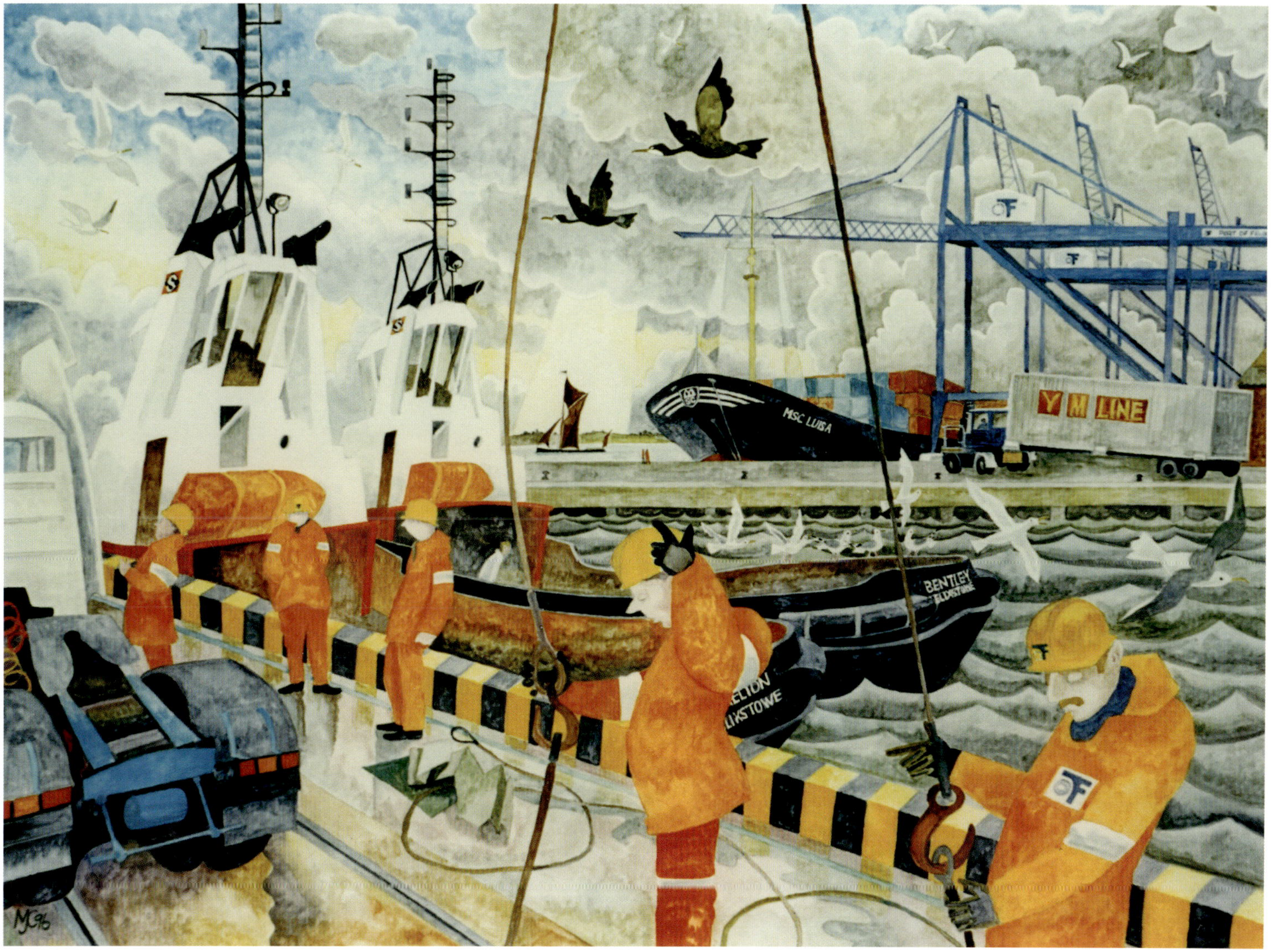

'The Port of Felixstowe' (1996) "I get many interesting projects and this was one of them. The brief was to paint the Port of Felixstowe in action. I was given a hard hat, I wasn't allowed to drive myself or walk freely about. I wasn't allowed to take photographs myself. I was escorted in a car by an official, for my safety and their security. I could ask to stop the car for a photo opportunity if it wasn't too busy an area. The noise was incredible. Trailers were driving about at speed with containers. Cranes were hauling up and down. They took the photographs I needed and these were sent onto me later. A bit cloak and dagger. This was commissioned by Managing Director Peter Bennett to hang in his office. A very enjoyable day. I felt quite privileged to be able to peer into this intriguing place the public can only glance at through the wire fence."

'Long Shore Fish Sale, Lowestoft' (1990) "To gain access to the market I had to get permission from the Port Authority. I was told to arrive for the sale sharp at 7.00am. I arrived at 6.45am one cold February morning. Not a soul in sight. After waiting for what seemed like an eternity and shuffling about, a few fishermen arrived with their boxes of fish from small boats. The sale actually started at 8.30am. Never mind; I got my picture."

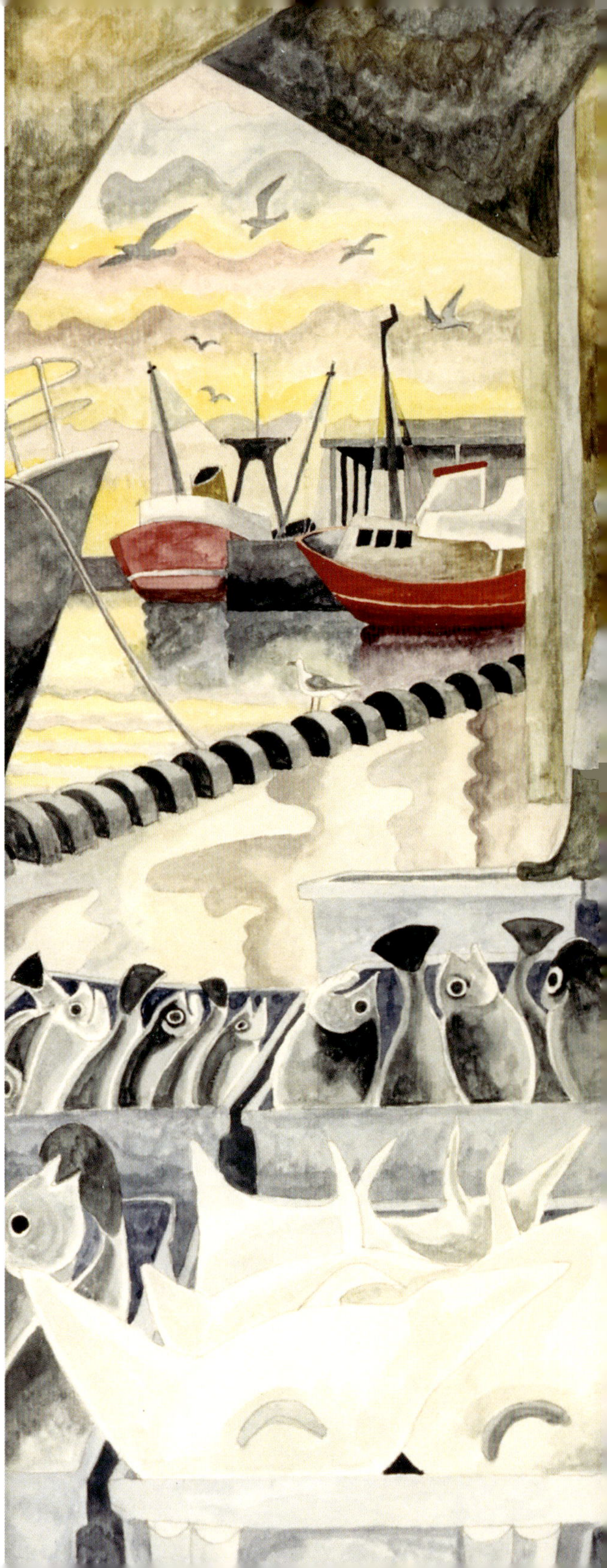

'Dunwich' (1990)

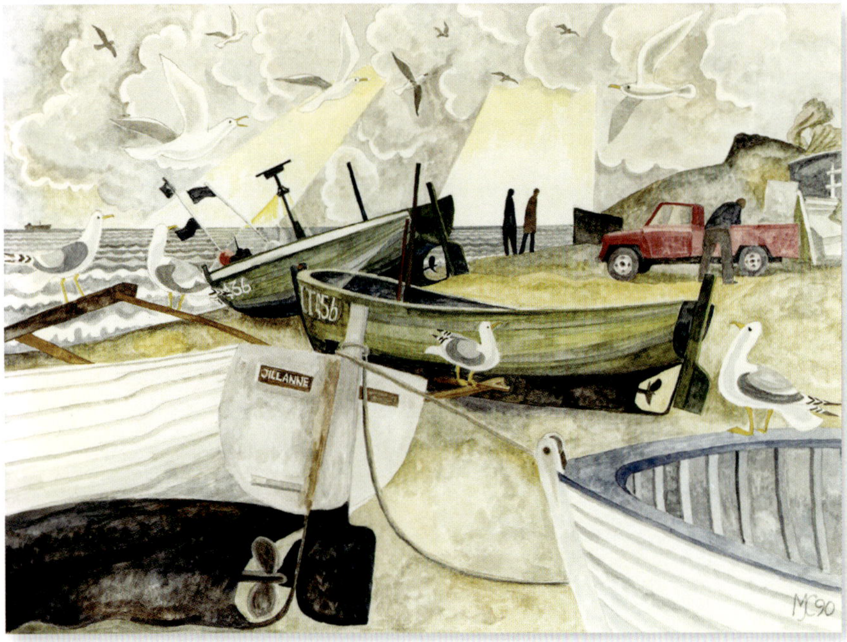

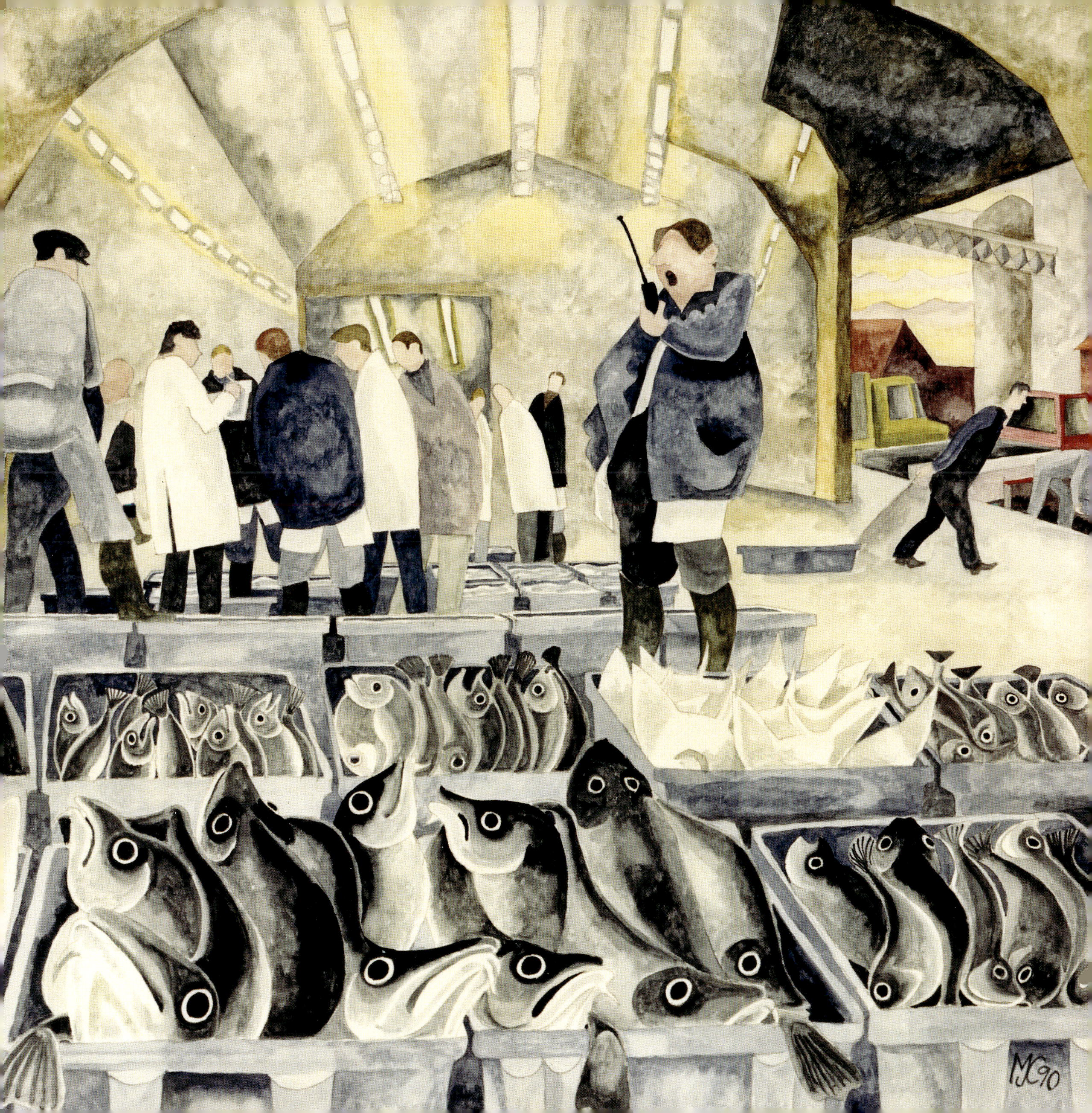
MJC90

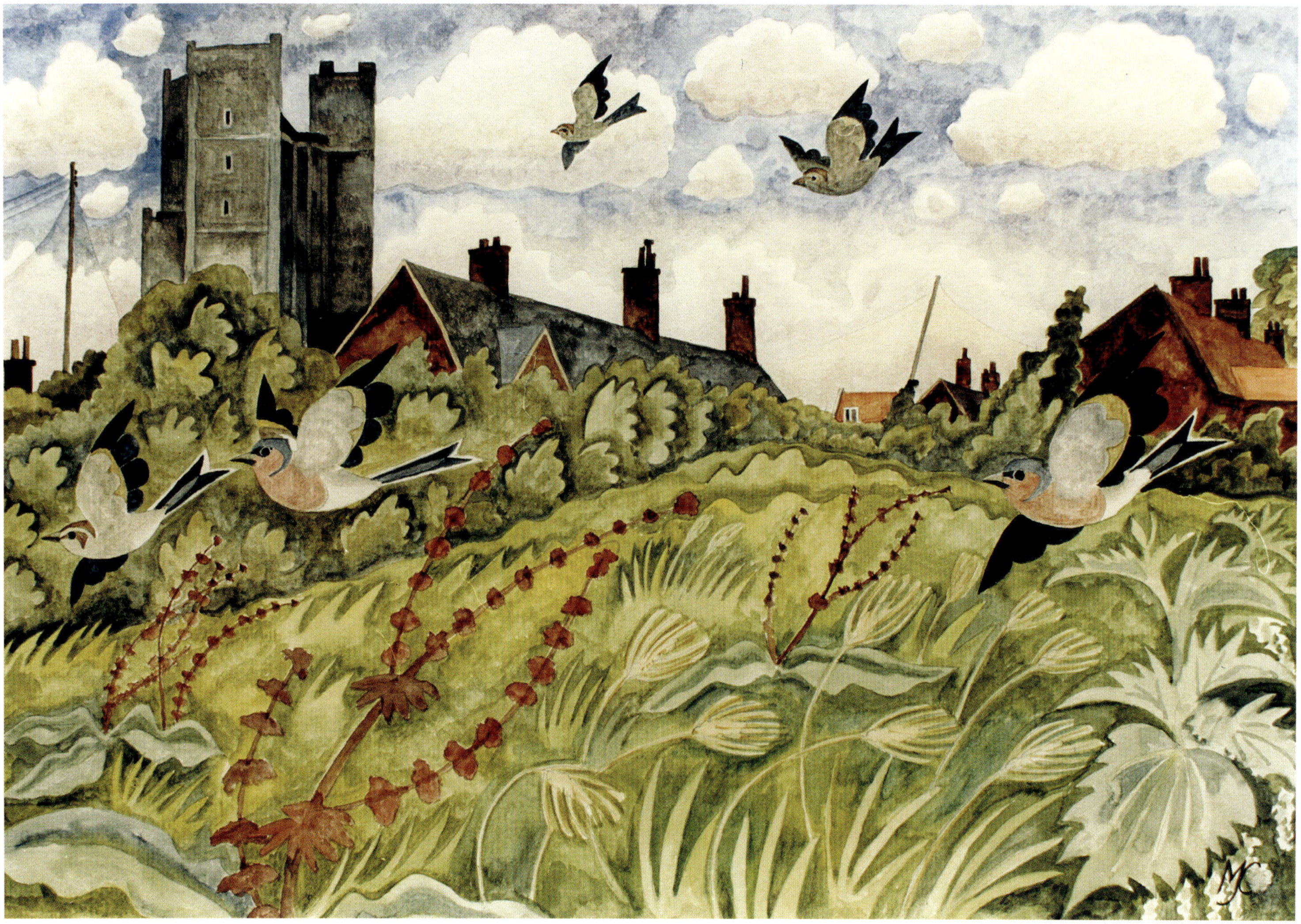

'Orford Castle' (1994) Dating from around 1170 and built on the order of King Henry II, the surviving keep at Orford Castle is one of Suffolk's architectural treasures. "The wild field of flowers and brambles no longer exists and has been developed for housing."

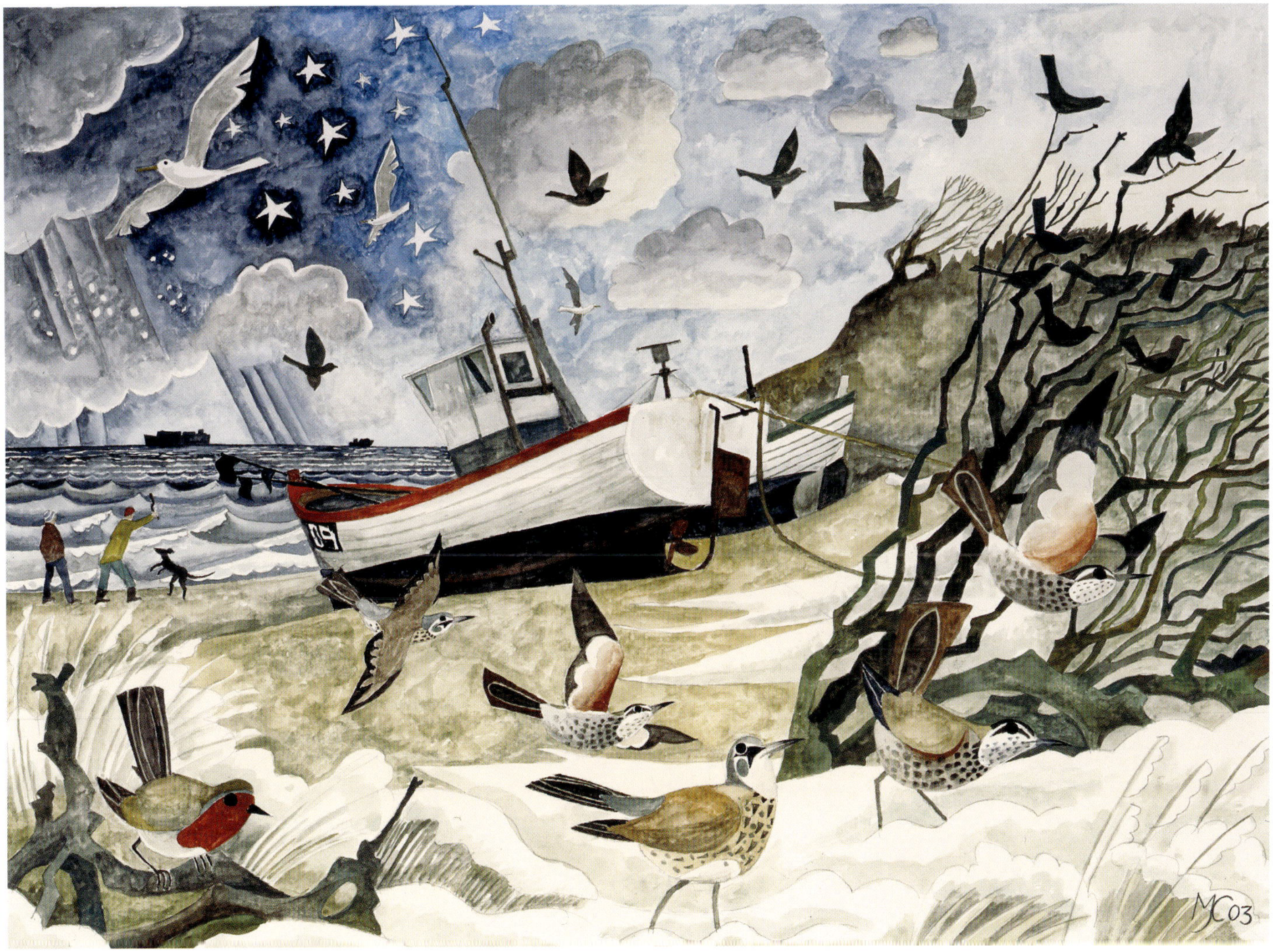

'The Coast at Christmas Time, Dunwich' (2003) "Based loosely on Dunwich, the ancient East Anglian port that fell into the sea. The church bells from under the water are supposed to be heard on stormy nights."

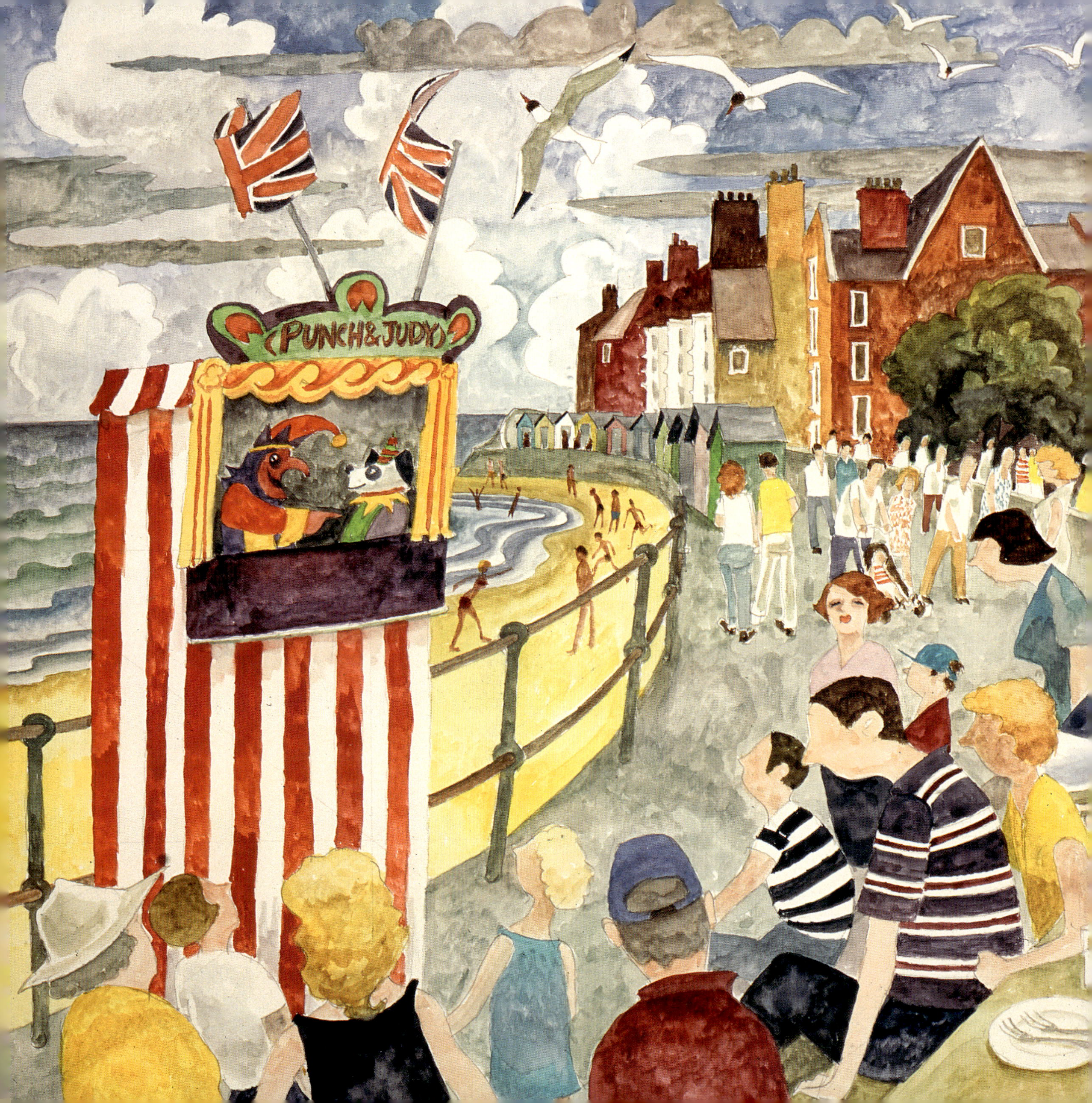
PUNCH&JUDY

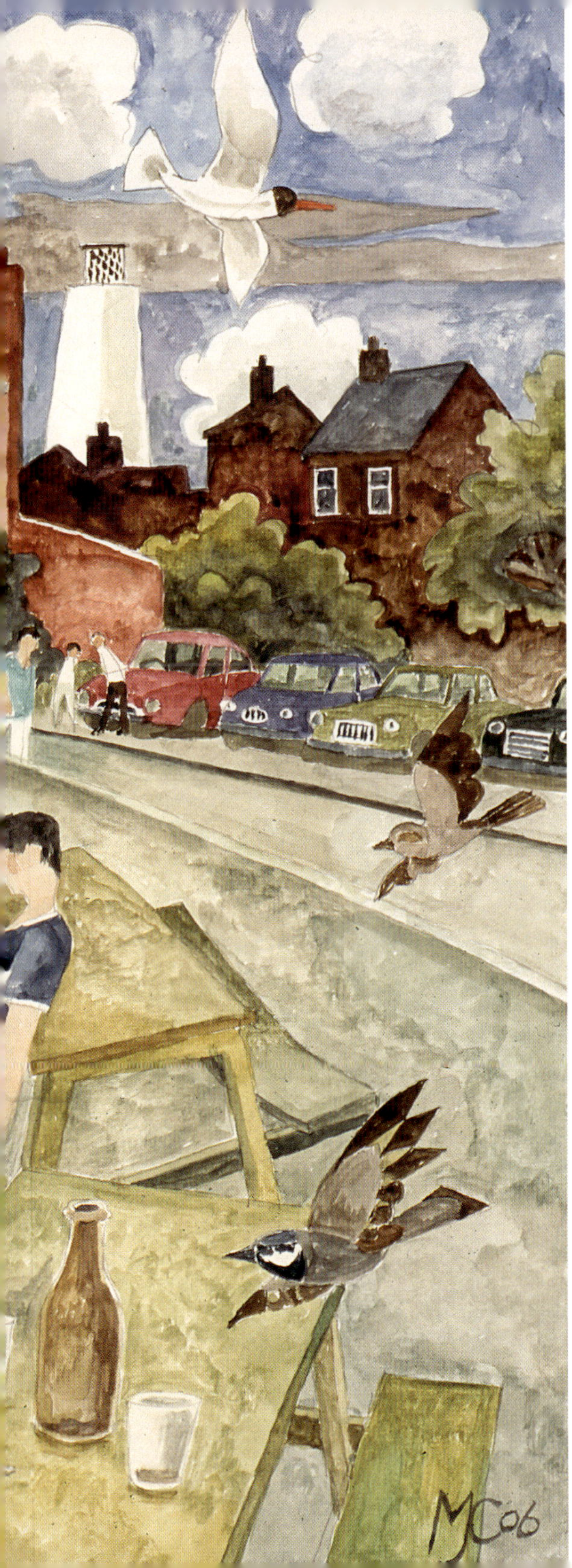

'Punch and Judy on the Promenade' (2006) "This is Southwold with a little artistic licence. Features of the town are included, but not necessarily in the right order. Southwold never fails to delight. The pier is an inspiration, the gentle entertainment, the Punch and Judy, the promenade and the beach huts. Good walks and plenty of good eating places. It's delightful, at least for a day."

'View from Table 17' (2009)

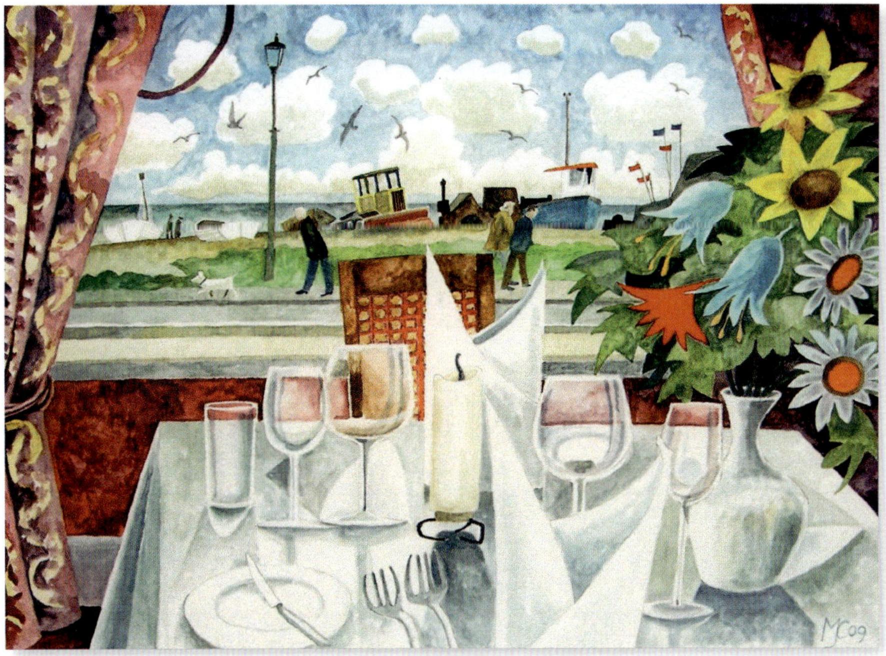

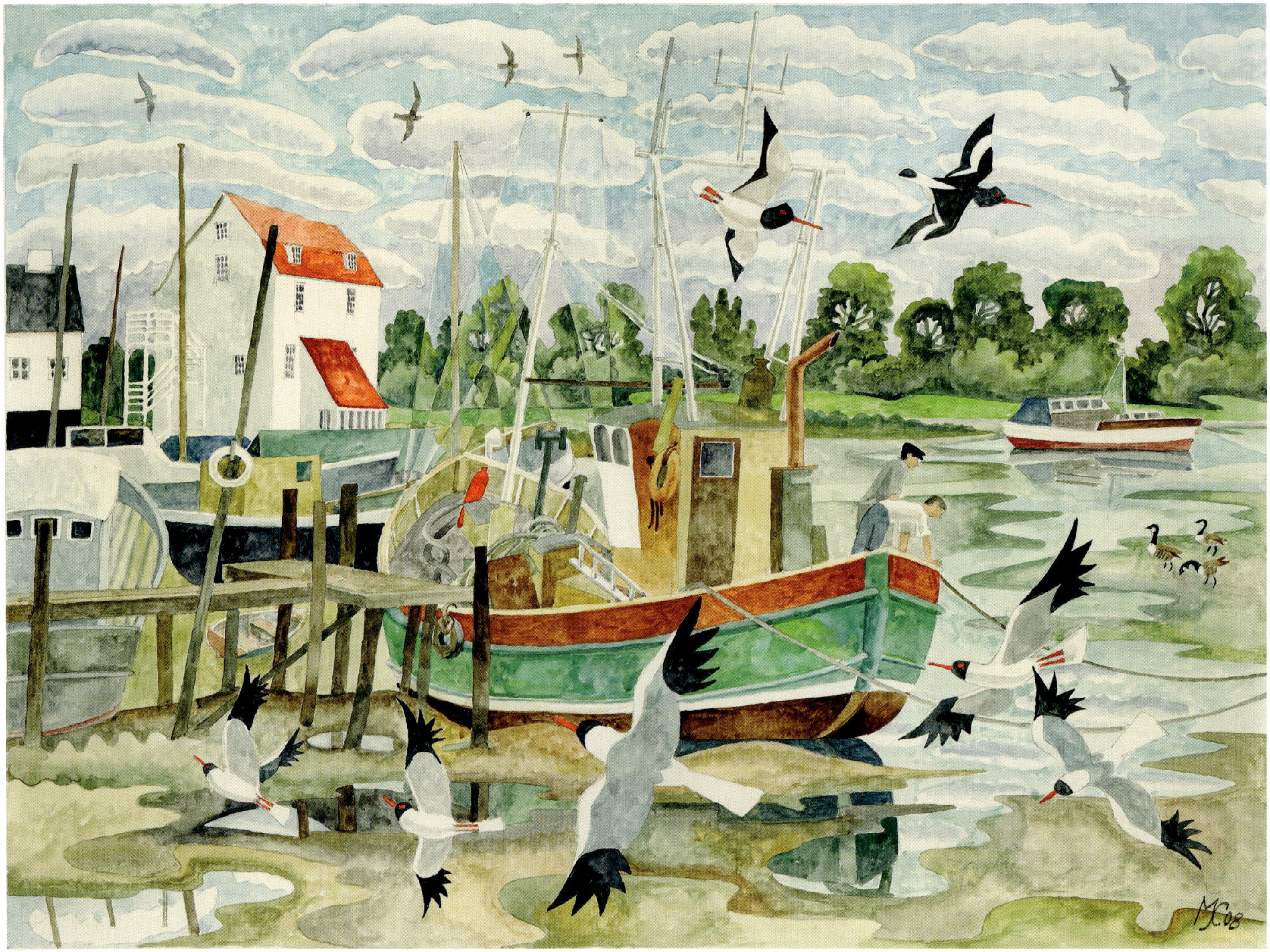

'Woodbridge at Low Tide' (2008) Yes, we know that this isn't strictly the coast, but the artist's adopted home town simply cannot be ignored. Here we've travelled up the Deben to encounter a fishing boat marooned temporarily in the mud by the departing tide, with the famous tide mill in the background and the sea just 13km away.

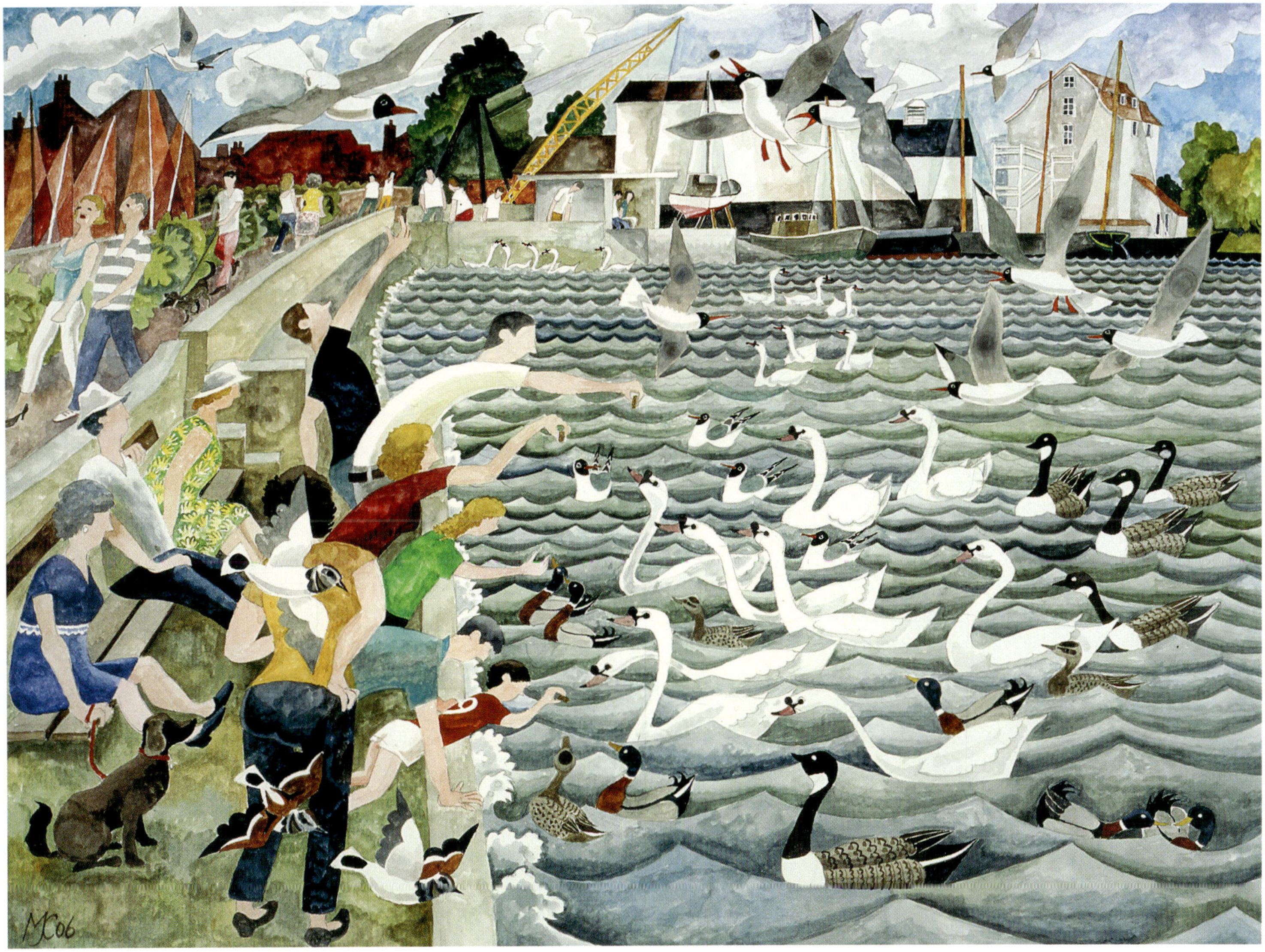

'High Tide, Woodbridge' (2006) A familiar sight at Woodbridge, with the tide mill representing a backdrop to the mass bird feed from the river path. Here the inevitable Mute Swans are accompanied by visiting Canada Geese and local Mallards – all competing for bread with the marauding Black-headed gulls.

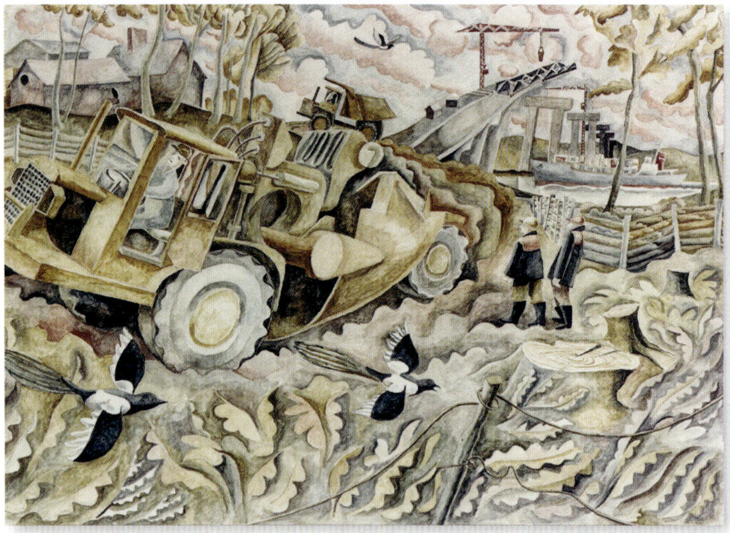

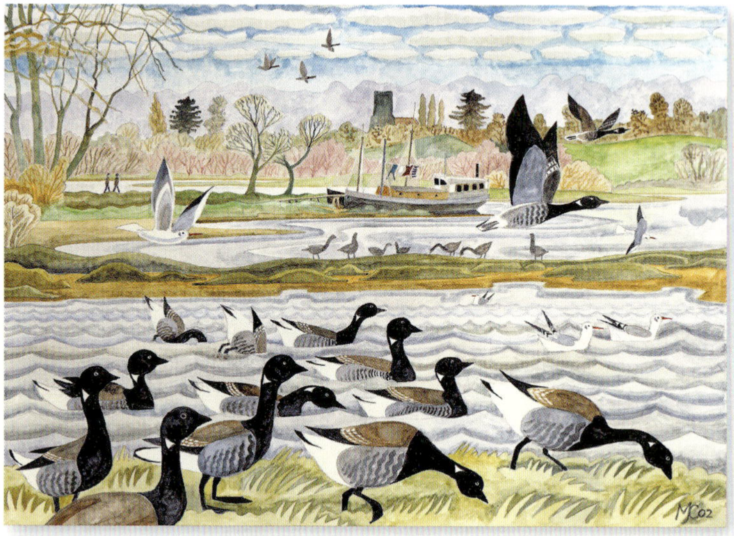

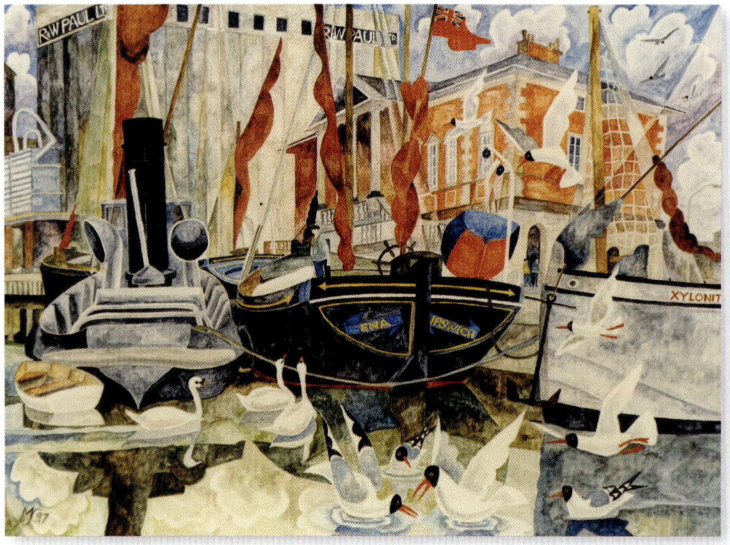

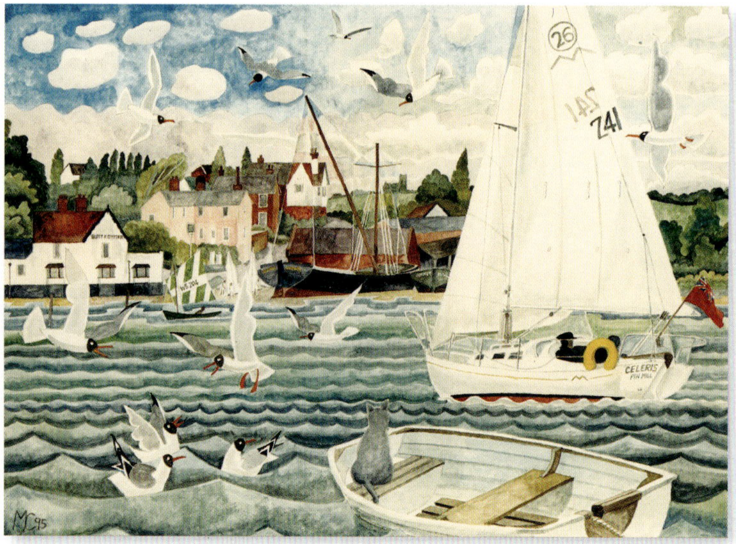

Clockwise, from top left: 'Magpies and Machines' (1983); 'Brent Geese' (2002); 'Celeris at Pin Mill' (1995); 'In Ipswich Docks' (1997)

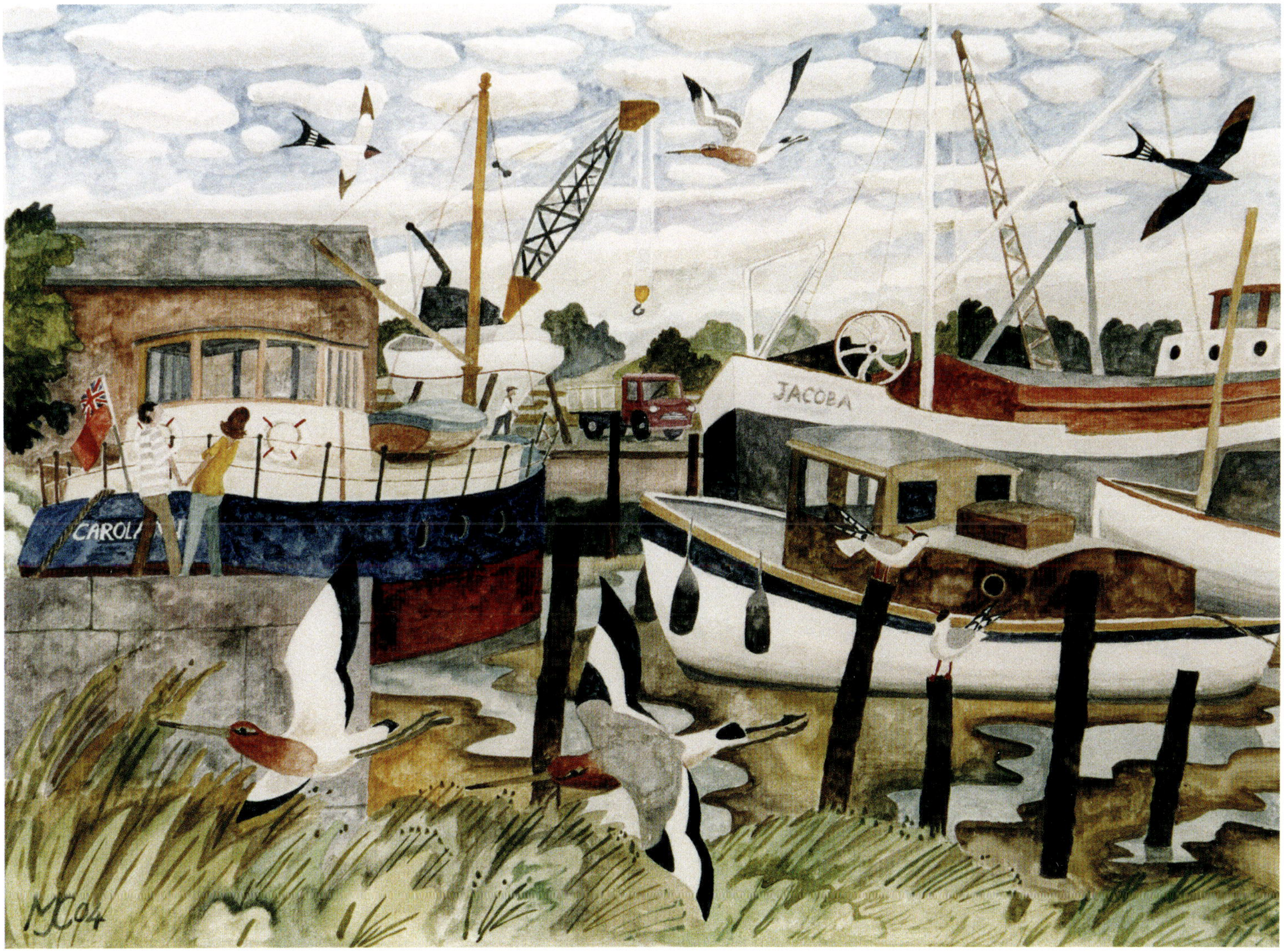

'Dock at Low Tide' (2004) "A small dock along the Deben near Woodbridge. Houseboats and sailors come and go..."

NORFOLK & ESSEX

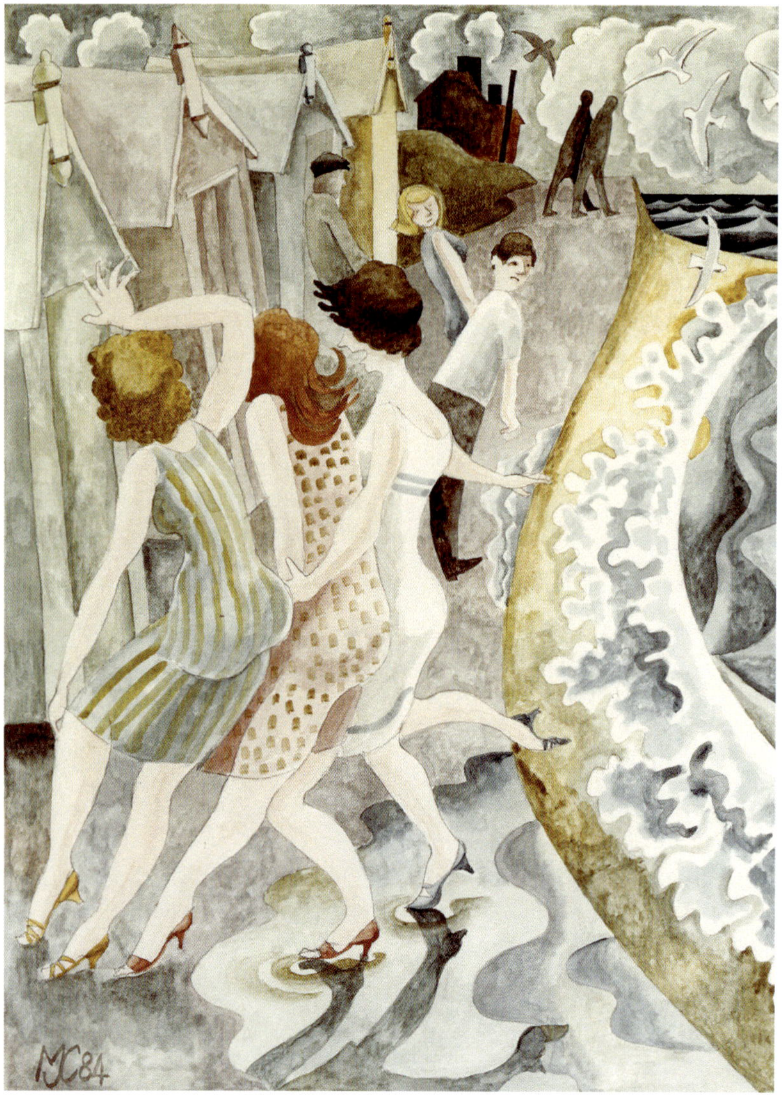

Norfolk has approximately twice the length of coastline of its southern neighbour Suffolk, often more remote and unspoilt, but with a handful of resort towns and some spectacular beaches. Michael's paintings take in King's Lynn to the west, via Thornham, Brancaster, Wells-next-the-Sea and Cley-next-the-Sea to Cromer at the north-eastern edge of the county. Essex has a more seamless border with Suffolk, with rivers providing the main boundary and the landscape changing little on either side. Harwich features both as a busy port and a sleepier town; Walton-on-the-Naze oozes seaside glamour; and the likes of Maldon, Mersea Island, Manningtree and Wivenhoe provide opportunities for boat-themed compositions.

Left: detail from 'Waves and Girls' (1984), an early work showing Essex girls enjoying their visit to the seaside. The whole of this image can be found on page 90. Facing page, clockwise from top left: 'On the Marshes, Christmastime' (2006); 'Cromer' (2001); 'Wivenhoe' (1999); 'King's Lynn' (1996). Cromer is little changed from this 2001 image, as the small fleet of crab- and lobster-fishing boats still resides on the beach near the pier, and is still hauled back in using rusty tractors. The Custom House at King's Lynn is one of the county's loveliest buildings, while the Essex town of Wivenhoe is expanding fast and some fear it could lose much of its charm.

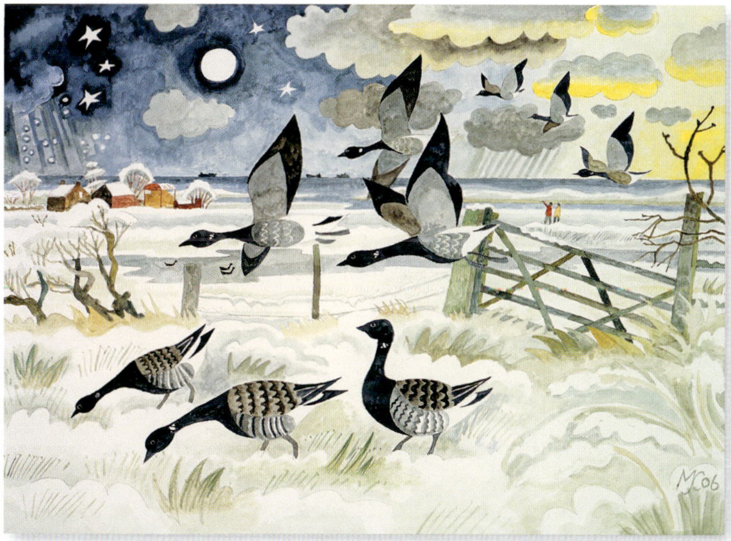

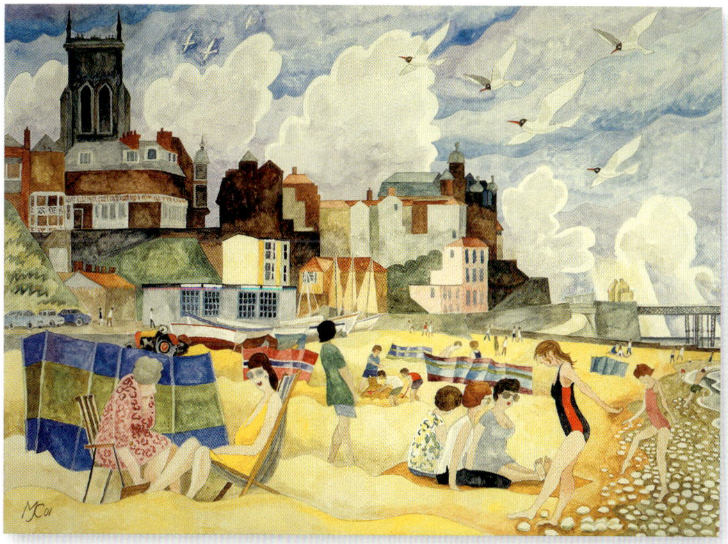

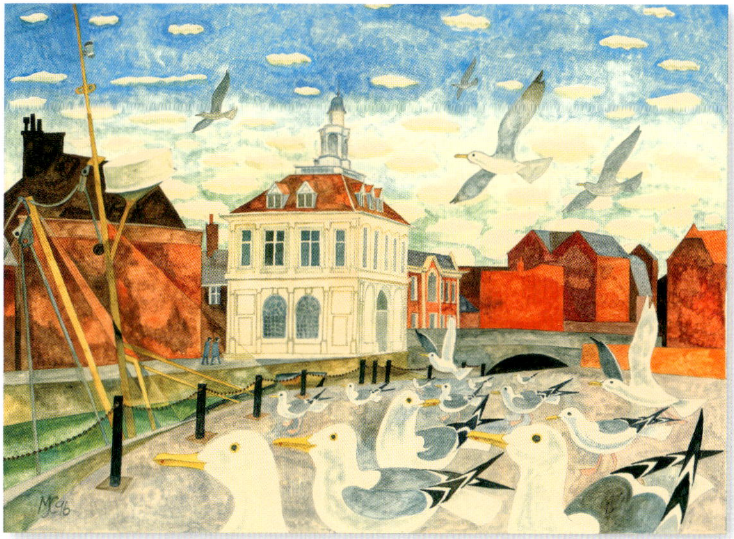

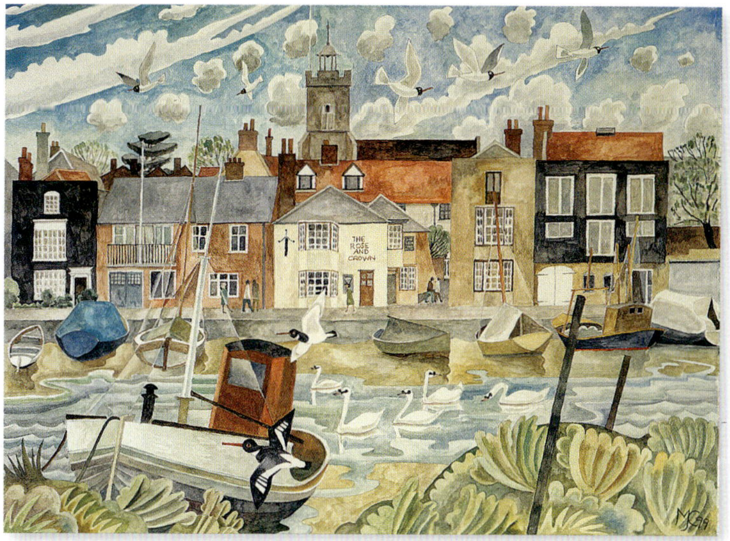
THE ROSE AND CROWN

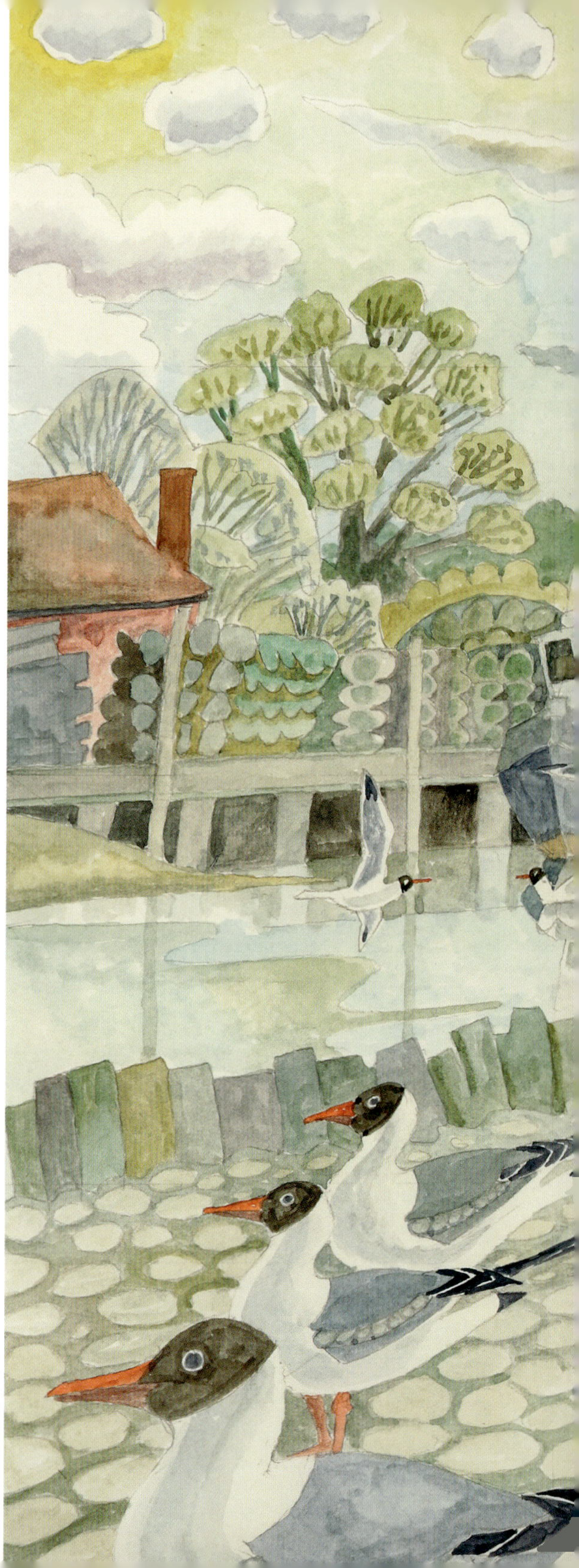

'Thornham, Early Spring' (2014) This north Norfolk harbour boasts birds and boats, so is a popular walking destination. Reed beds abound in the vicinity of the village, some 7km north-east of resort town Hunstanton and close to the RSPB reserve at Titchwell.

'Train Crossing a Creek' (1988)

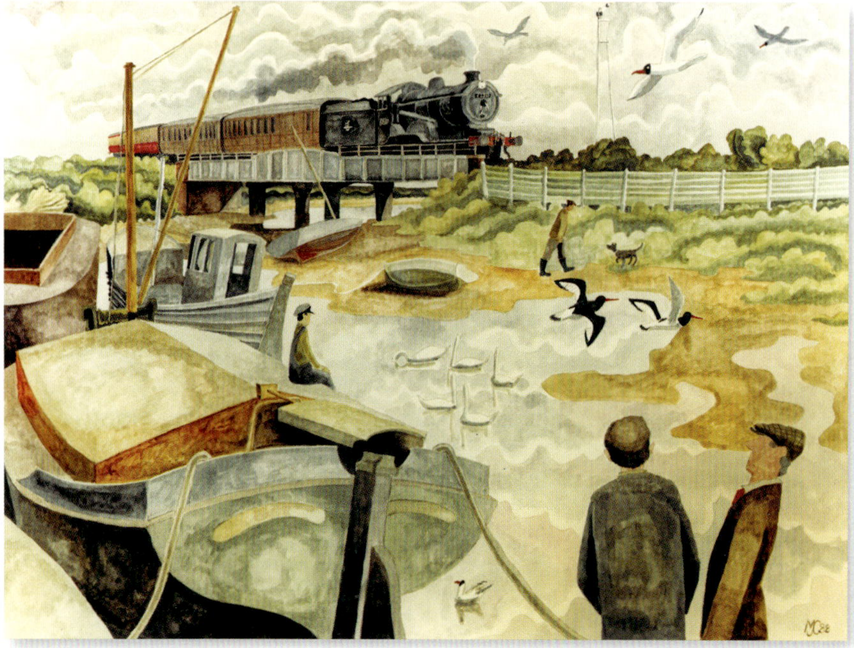

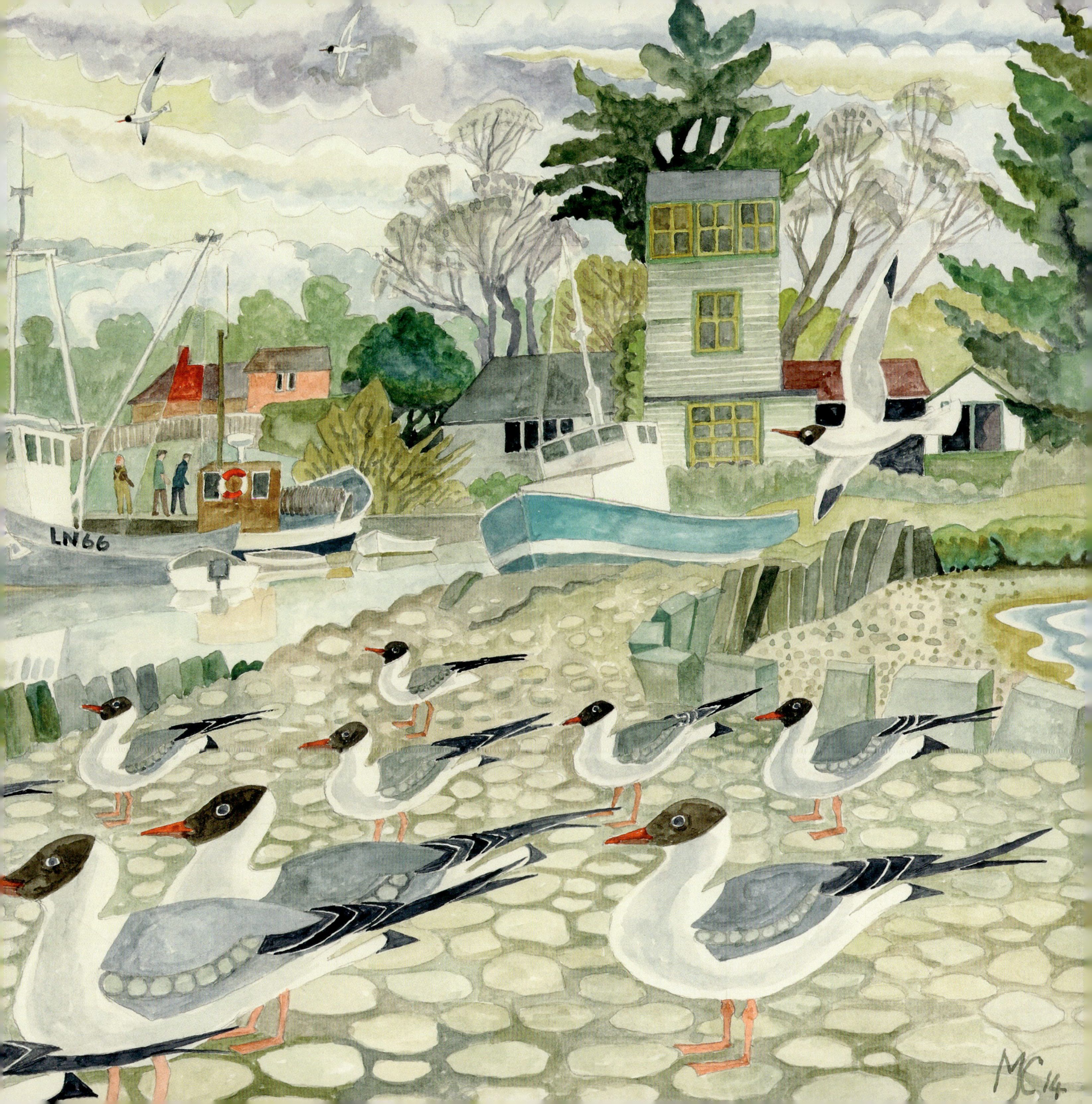
LN66
MC 14

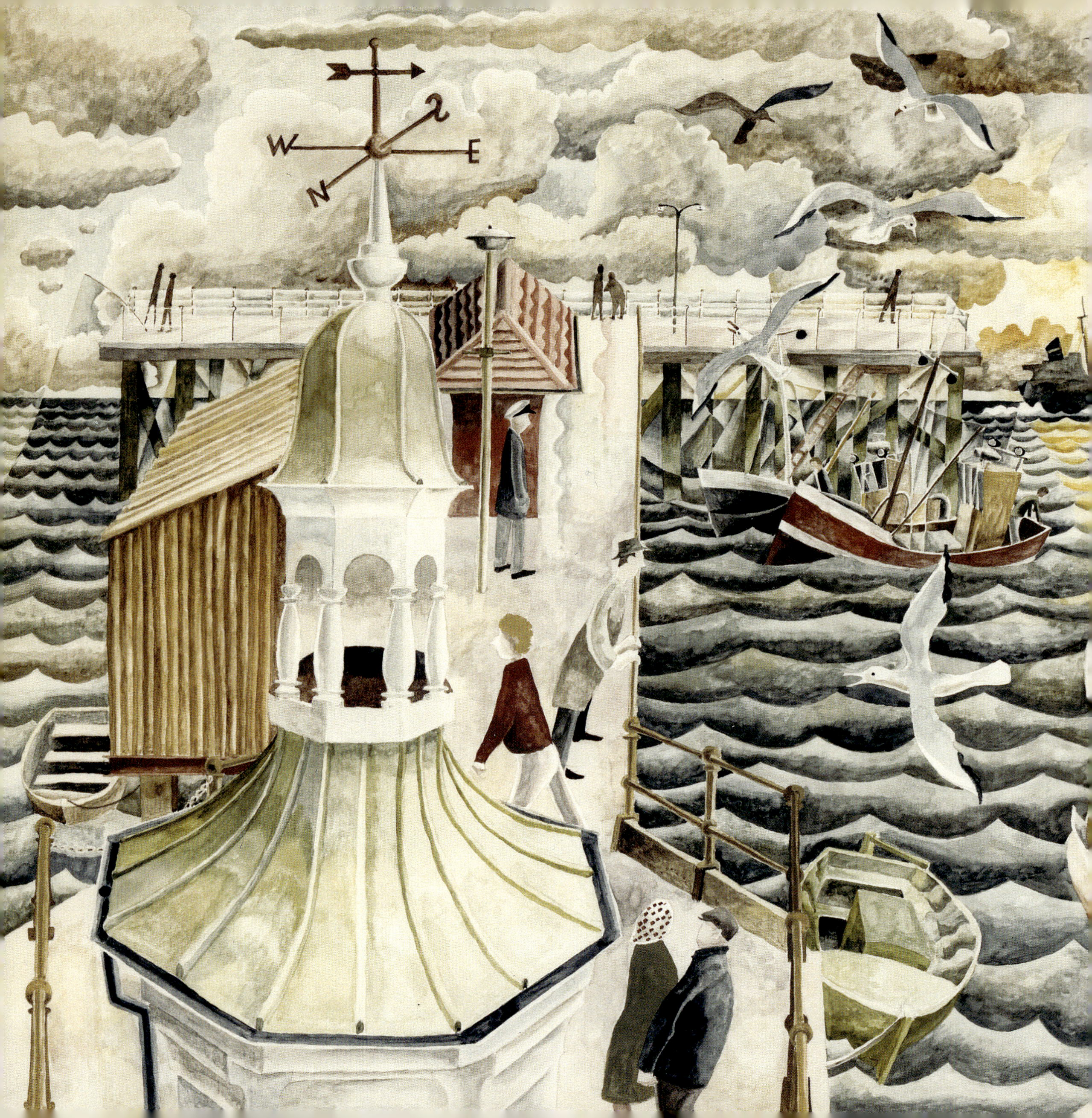
W
E
N

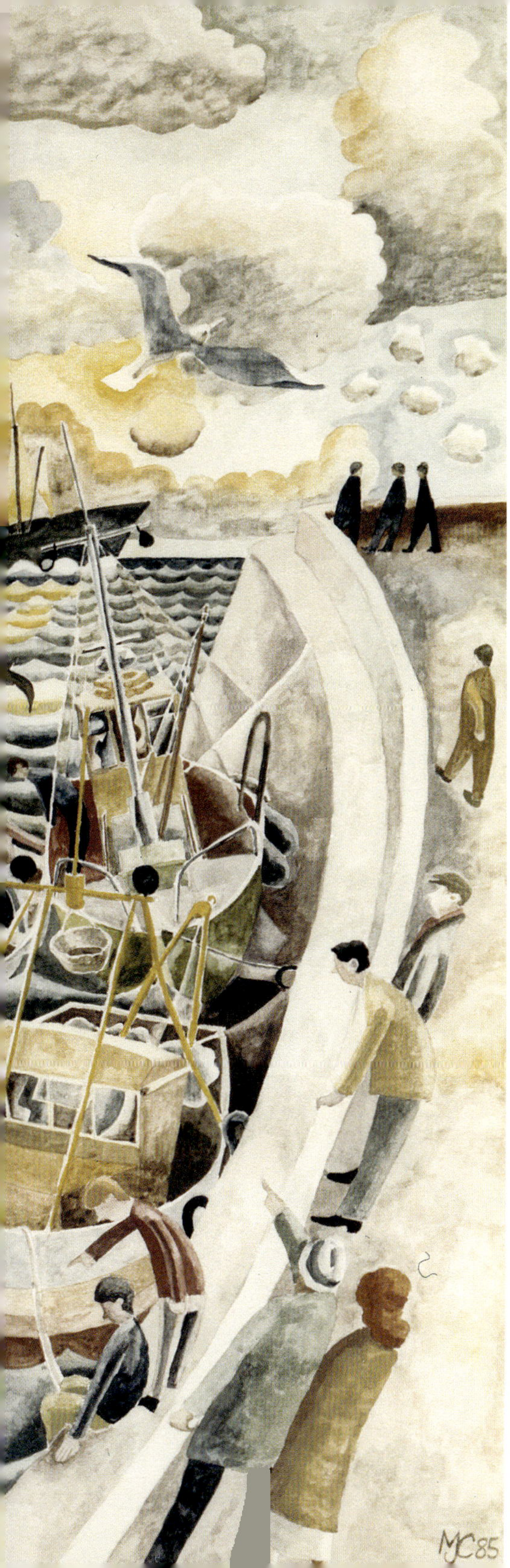

'The Pier, Harwich' (1985) "Harwich is still quaint; the pier is good for a cup of tea and a stroll. The town is unfortunately rather neglected. I often wish someone would take the place over and make it into something rather special. It has great potential."

'Anglers at Sea' (1989)

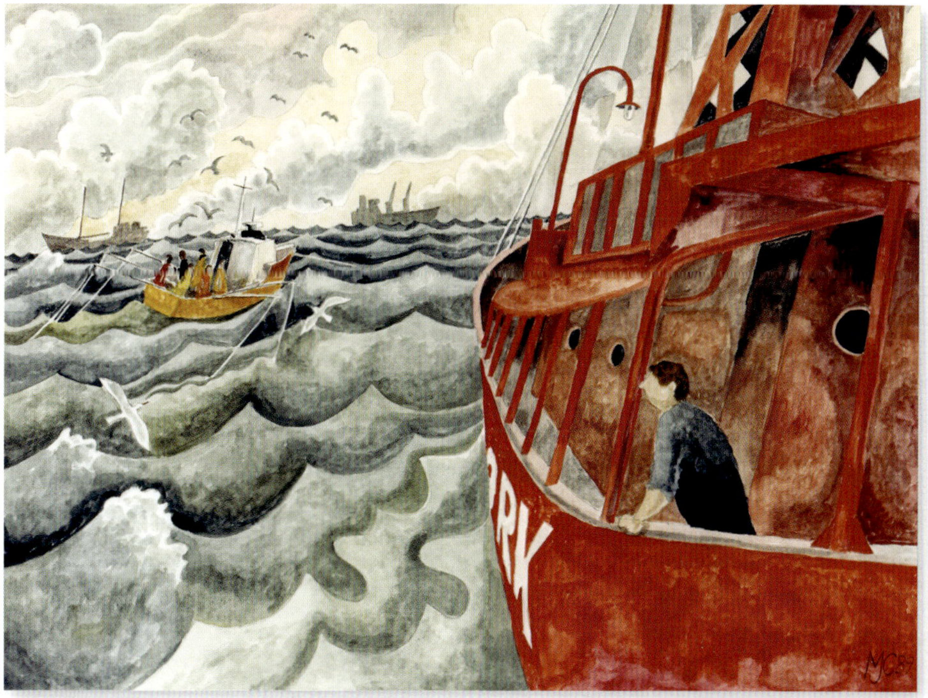

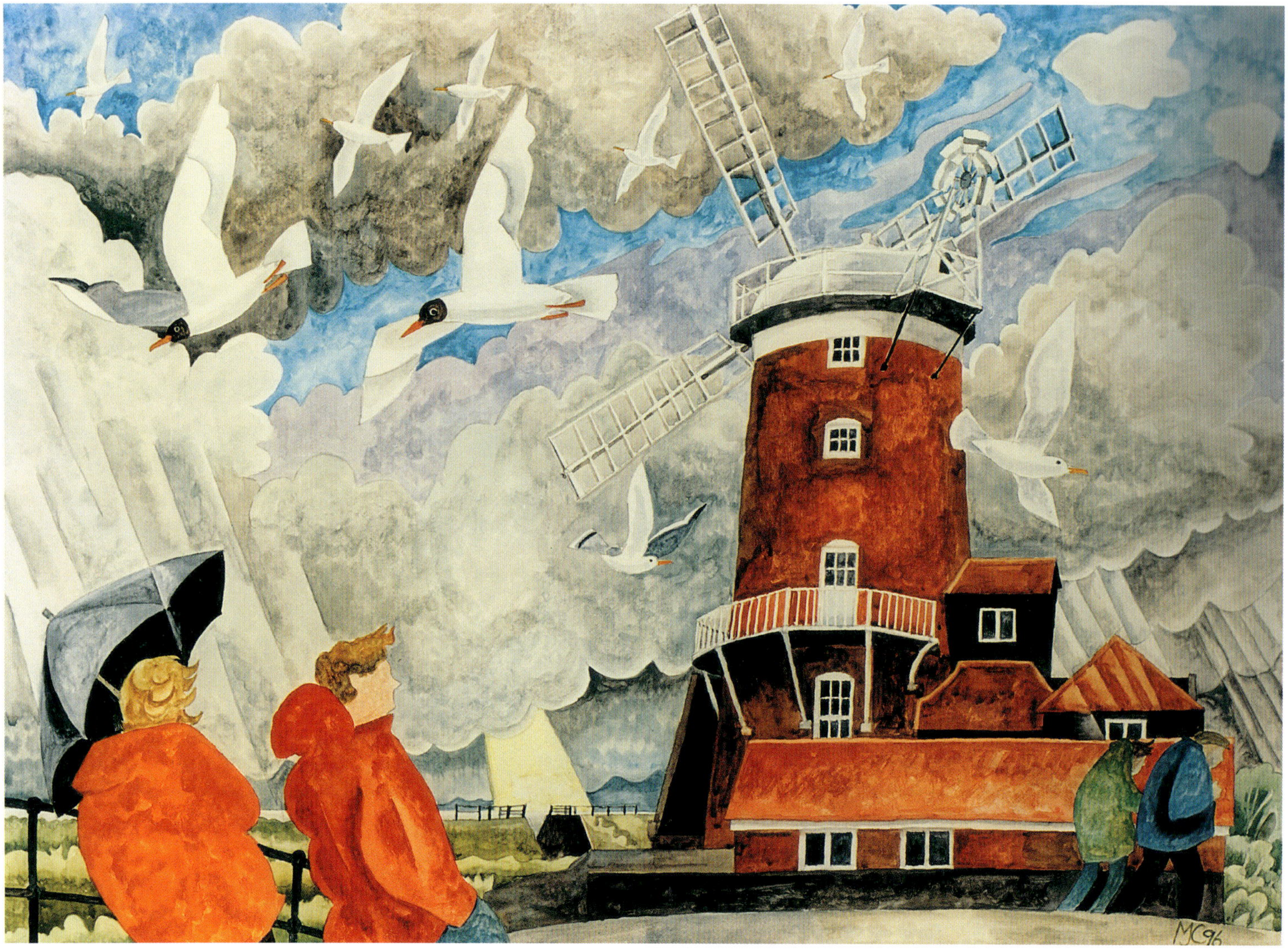

'Cley Mill' (1996) Nowadays a mile from open water, Cley was once a major port. The main trade now is tourism, with the village a magnet for bird watchers. The 18th-century windmill is well preserved and provides memorable B&B accommodation, with views over the reedbeds to the shingle beach beyond.

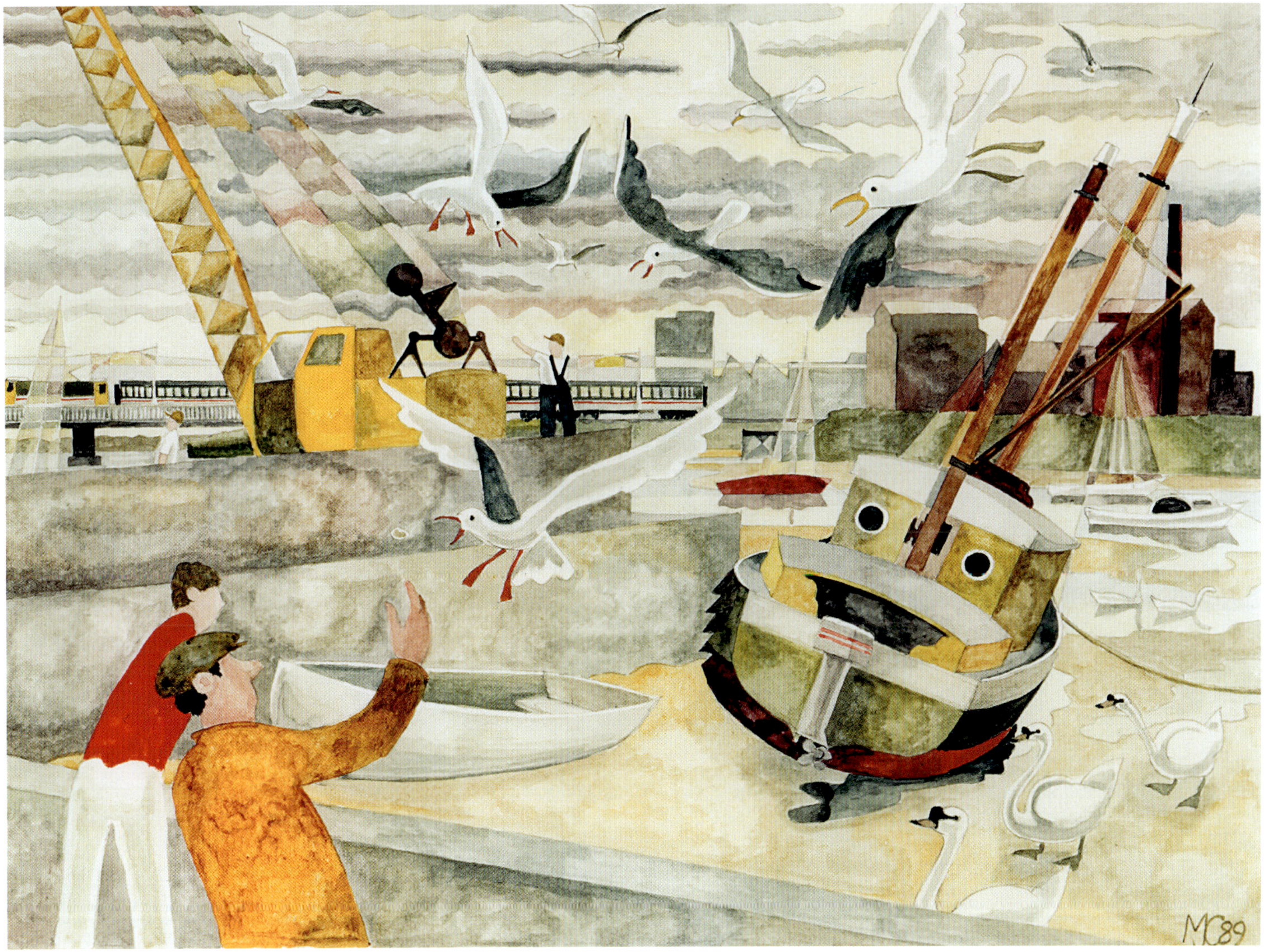

'Low Tide at Manningtree' (1989) Manningtree is one of several English towns claiming to be the country's smallest, located in the Tendring district of Essex on the River Stour. It adjoins Mistley to the east and is glimpsed by rail travellers heading into Colchester from Ipswich on the main Norwich-to-London line.

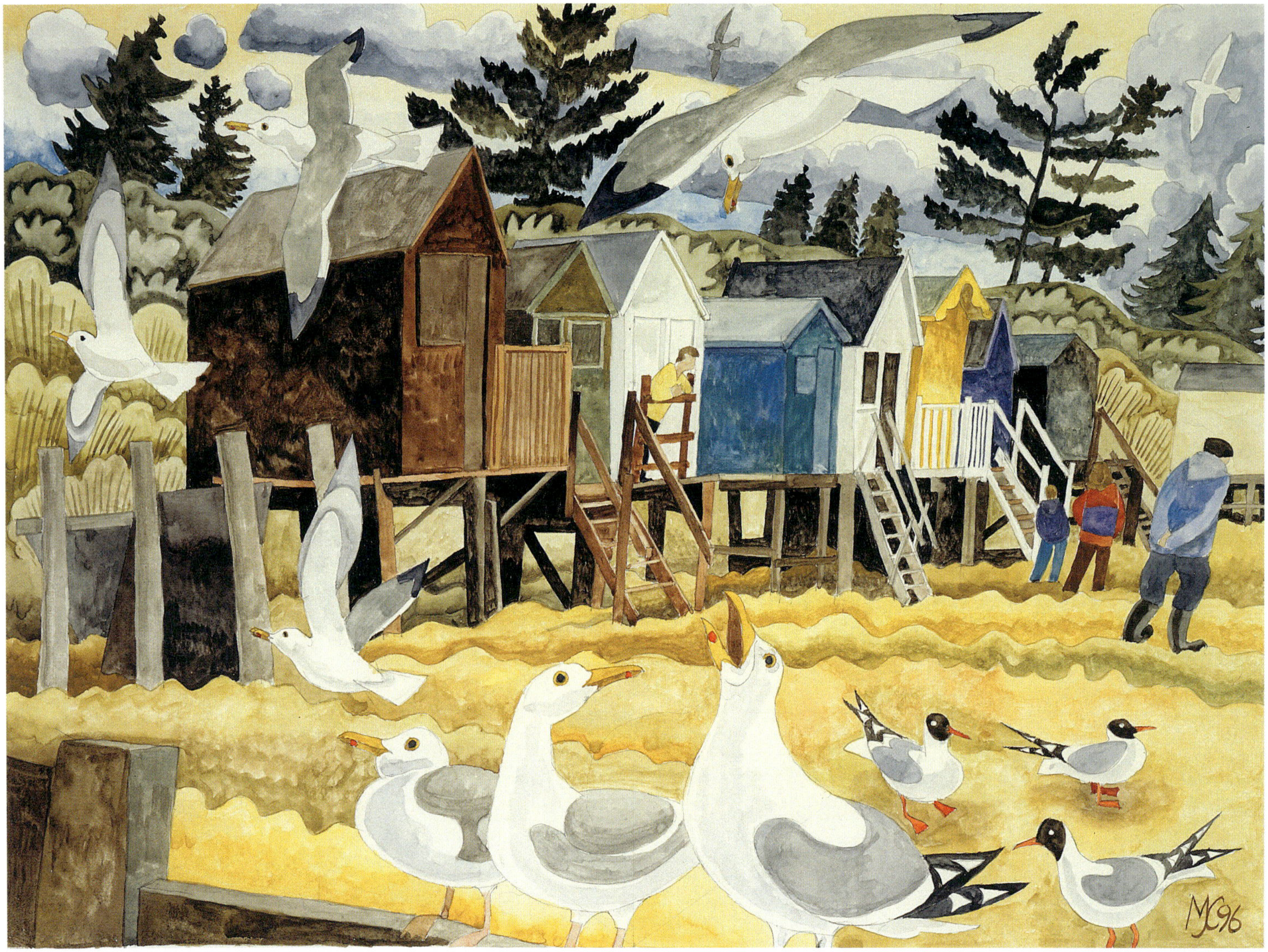

'Beach Huts, Wells-next-the-Sea' (1996). Both this and the painting opposite are from the same year, when Michael tackled some popular Norfolk subjects. King's Lynn, opposite, isn't viewed with the same delight as Wells (above), although it has pockets of charm. Wells-next-the-Sea, however, is an absolute gem, as brightly coloured wooden huts nestle between the pines and the sand, while the town's harbour provides a spectacular outlook. Head past the huts and around the headland to reach Holkham Beach, featured in the film 'Shakespeare in Love'.

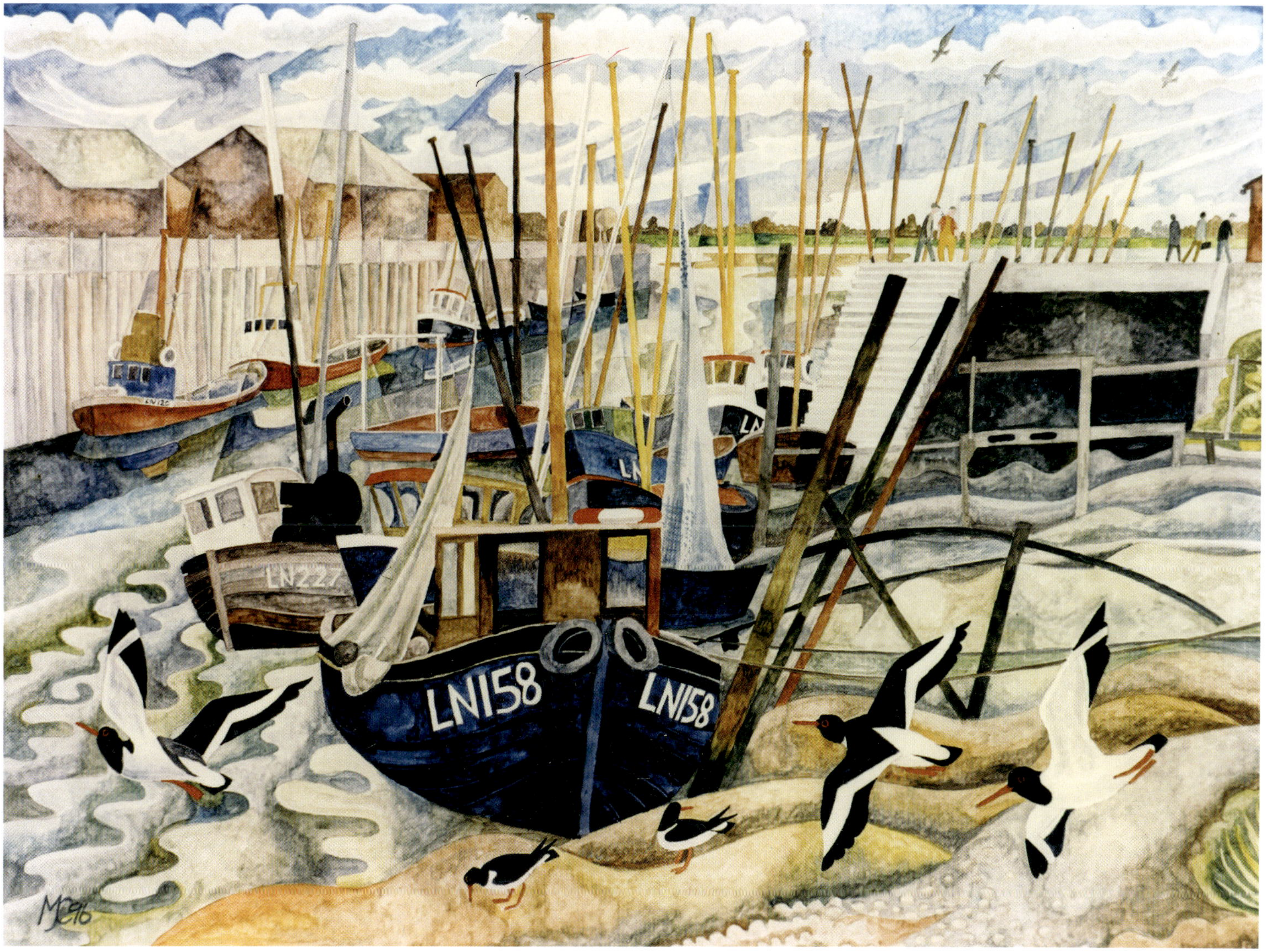

'The Fisher Fleet, King's Lynn' (1996) During the 14th century, Lynn ranked as England's most important port. Sea trade with Europe was dominated by the Hanseatic League of ports, and the town retains two former Hanseatic League warehouses. By the 17th century fishing was the key remaining industry, and Daniel Defoe just a few years later described the town as "beautiful, well built and well situated". Fishing is nowadays limited to a few boats, providing interest here with the local Oystercatchers.

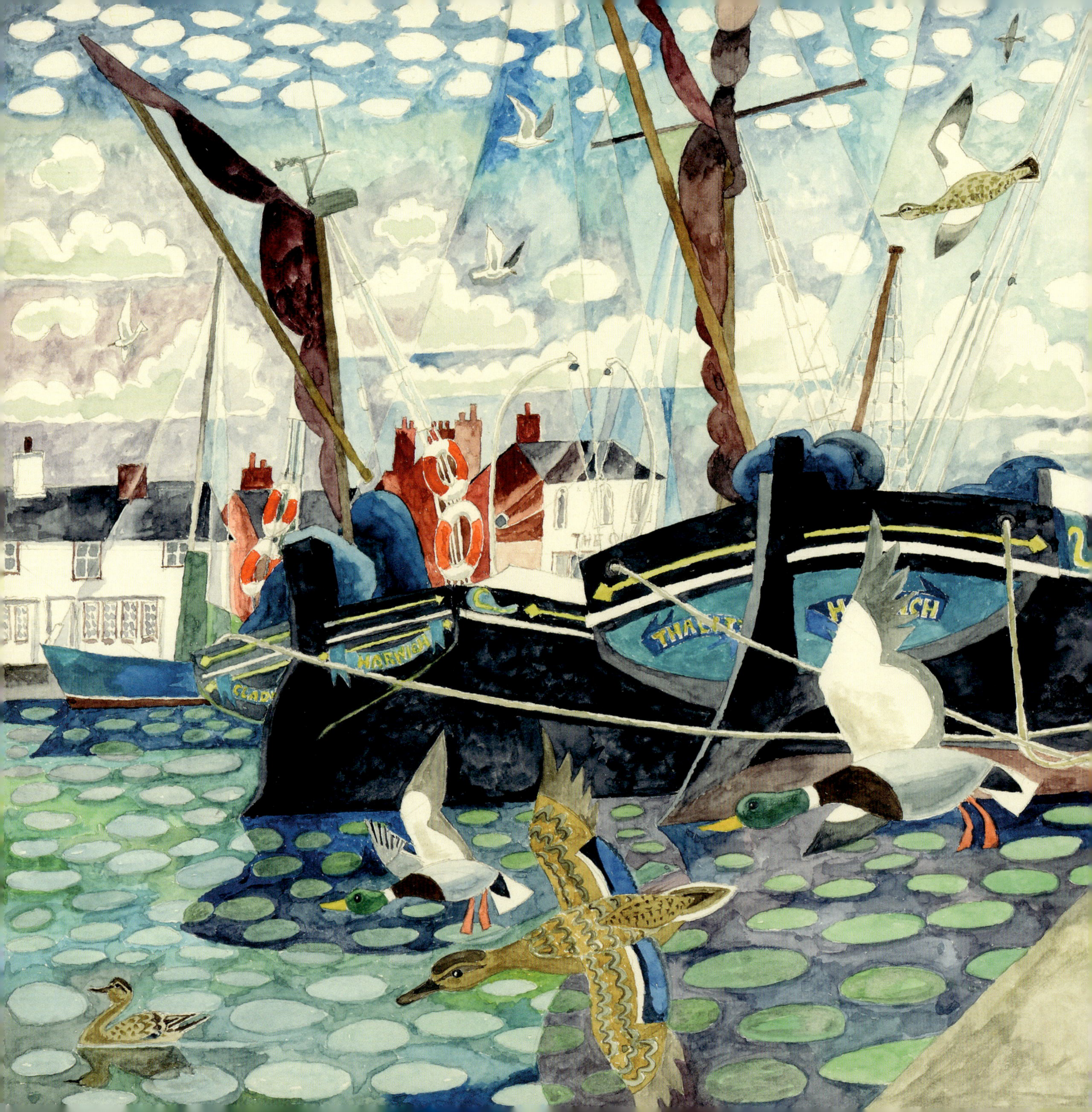
HARWICH

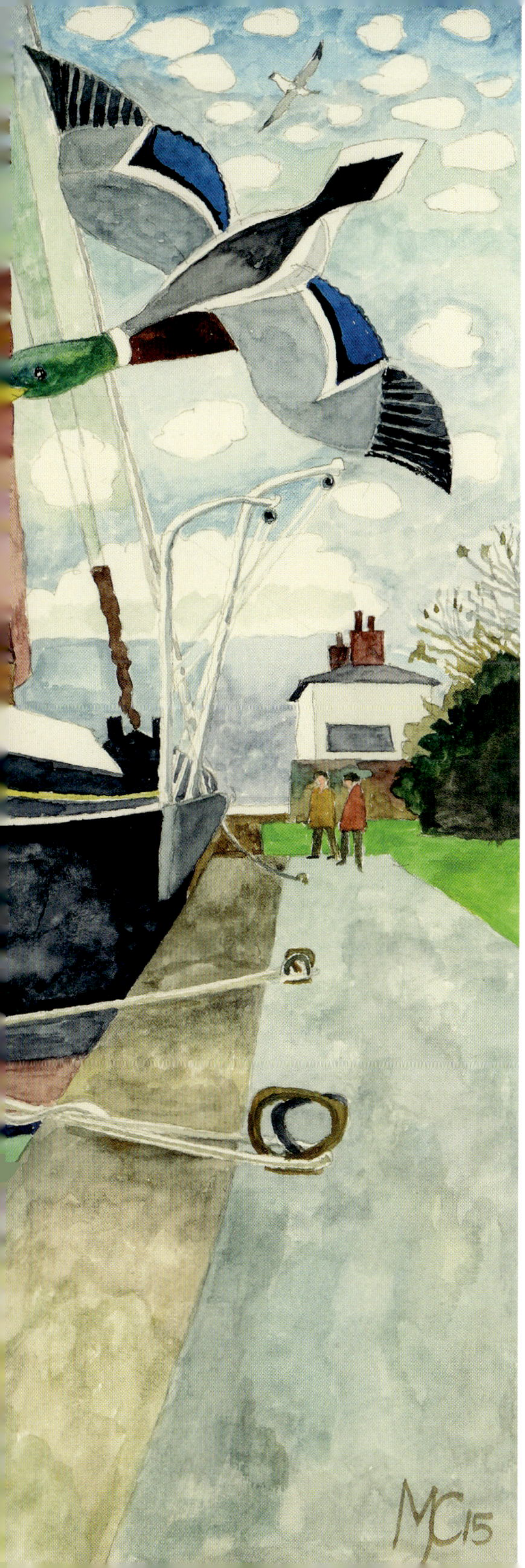

'Gladys and Thalatta, Heybridge Basin' (2015) Thalatta is a Thames sailing barge, built in Harwich in 1906 and rebuilt in St Osyth in 2012. She is 27 metres long and almost 8 metres across the widest part of the deck. She is now permanently spritsail rigged, and has a mainmast and topmast that, together, are about 27 metres high, plus a mizzen mast. Gladys is another spritsail barge, built in 1901 at Harwich. In 1912 she was sold to Cranfield Flour Mills of Ipswich, which operated her as a bulk grain cargo vessel until 1972. During the 1970s Gladys was converted to a pleasure yacht, and the 26-metre vessel was used for corporate entertainment before a full restoration programme began.

'The Low Lighthouse, Harwich' (1999)

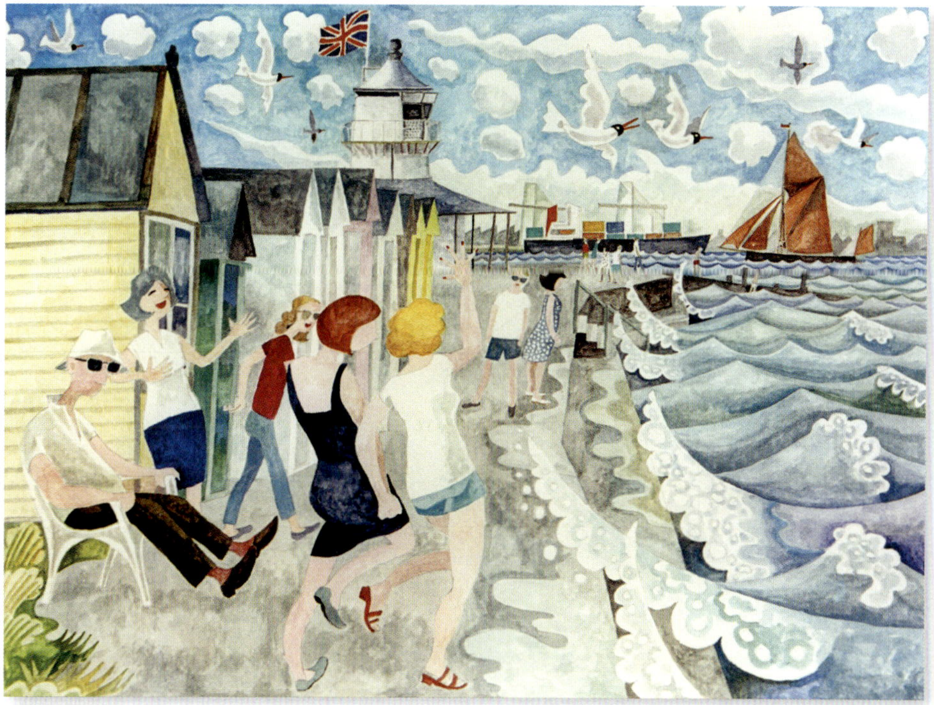

'At The Coal Barn' (2013) A remnant of Thornham in Norfolk from the time when it was an important harbour, the old coal barn has been through many owners and changes of use. "A bleak building on the marshes near Brancaster. A very important structure in its day. Barges delivered their cargo and unloaded their coal here."

'Watching the Barges' (1998)

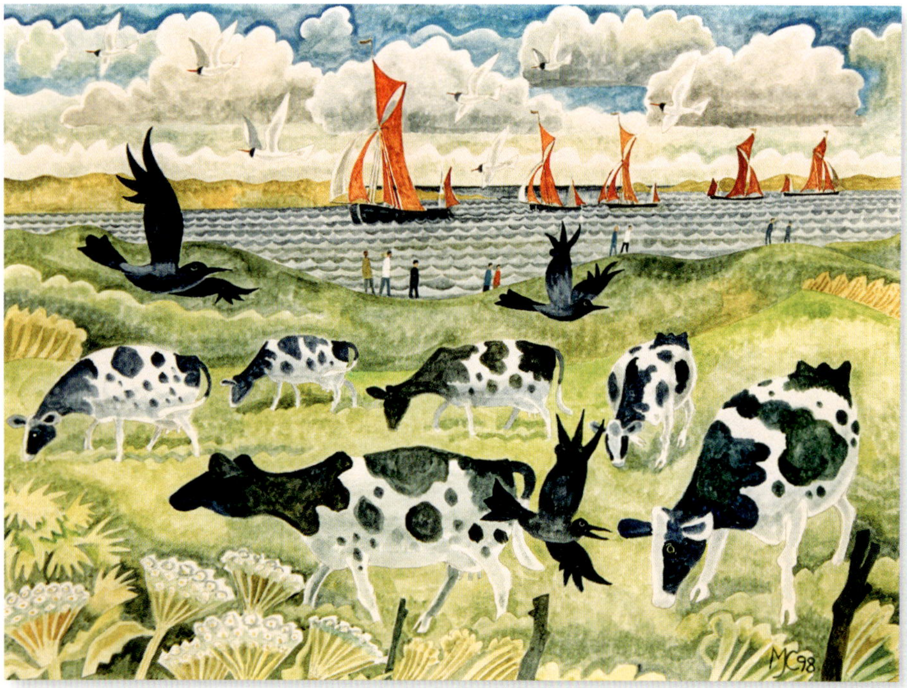

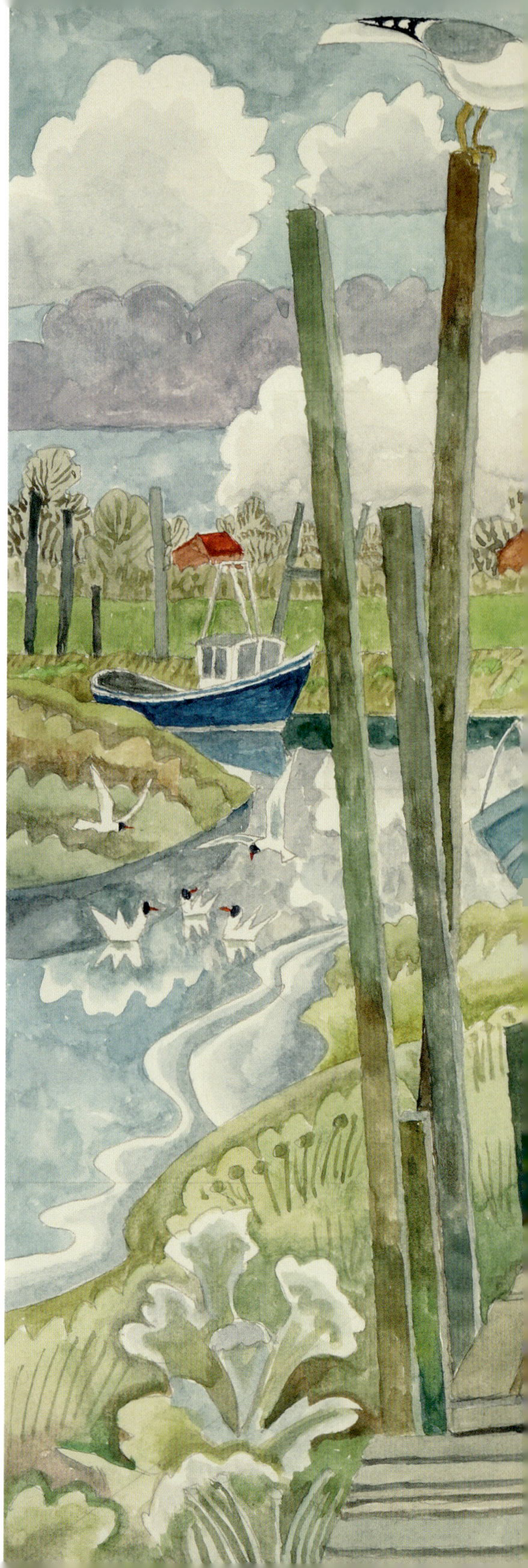

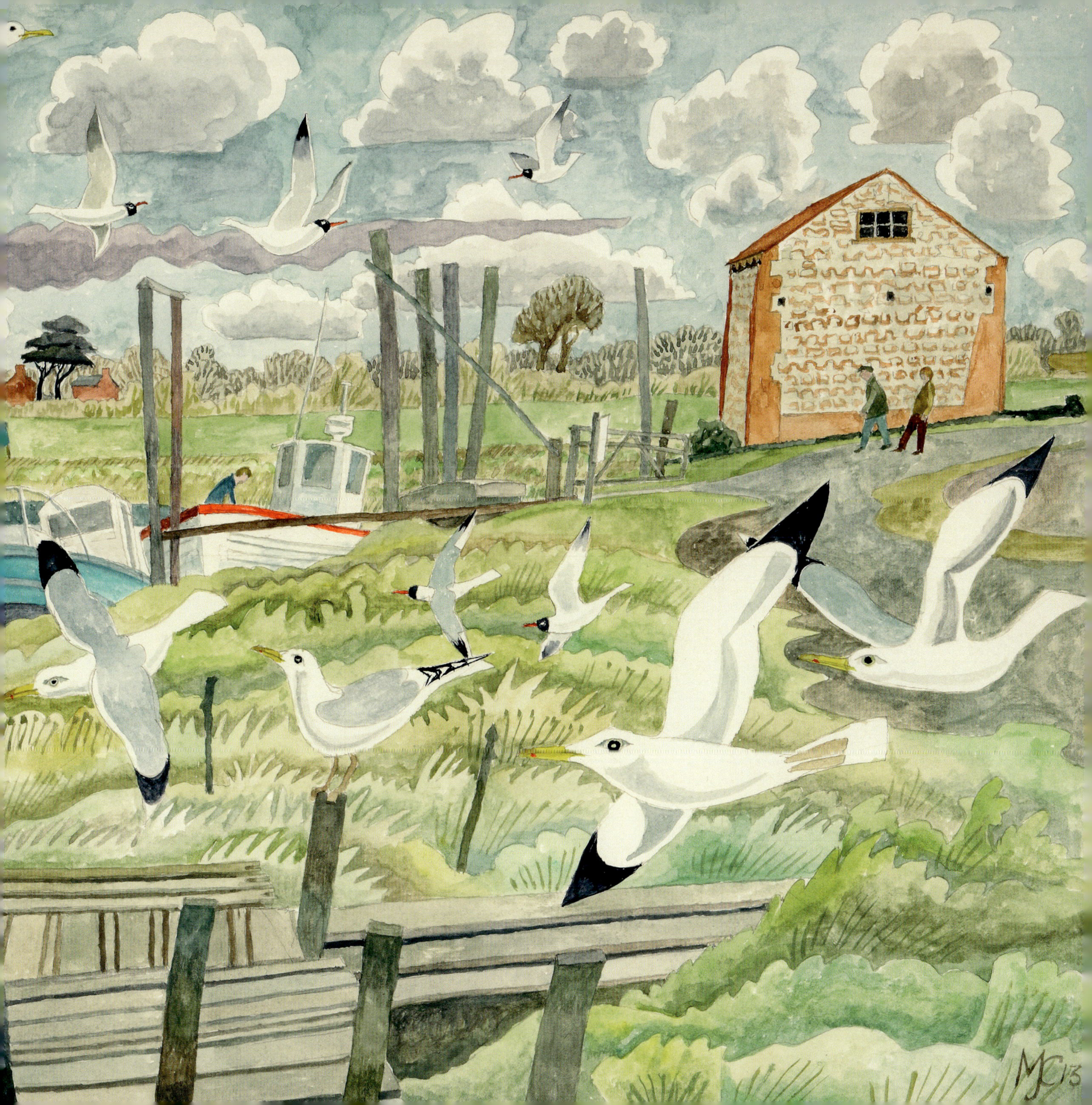

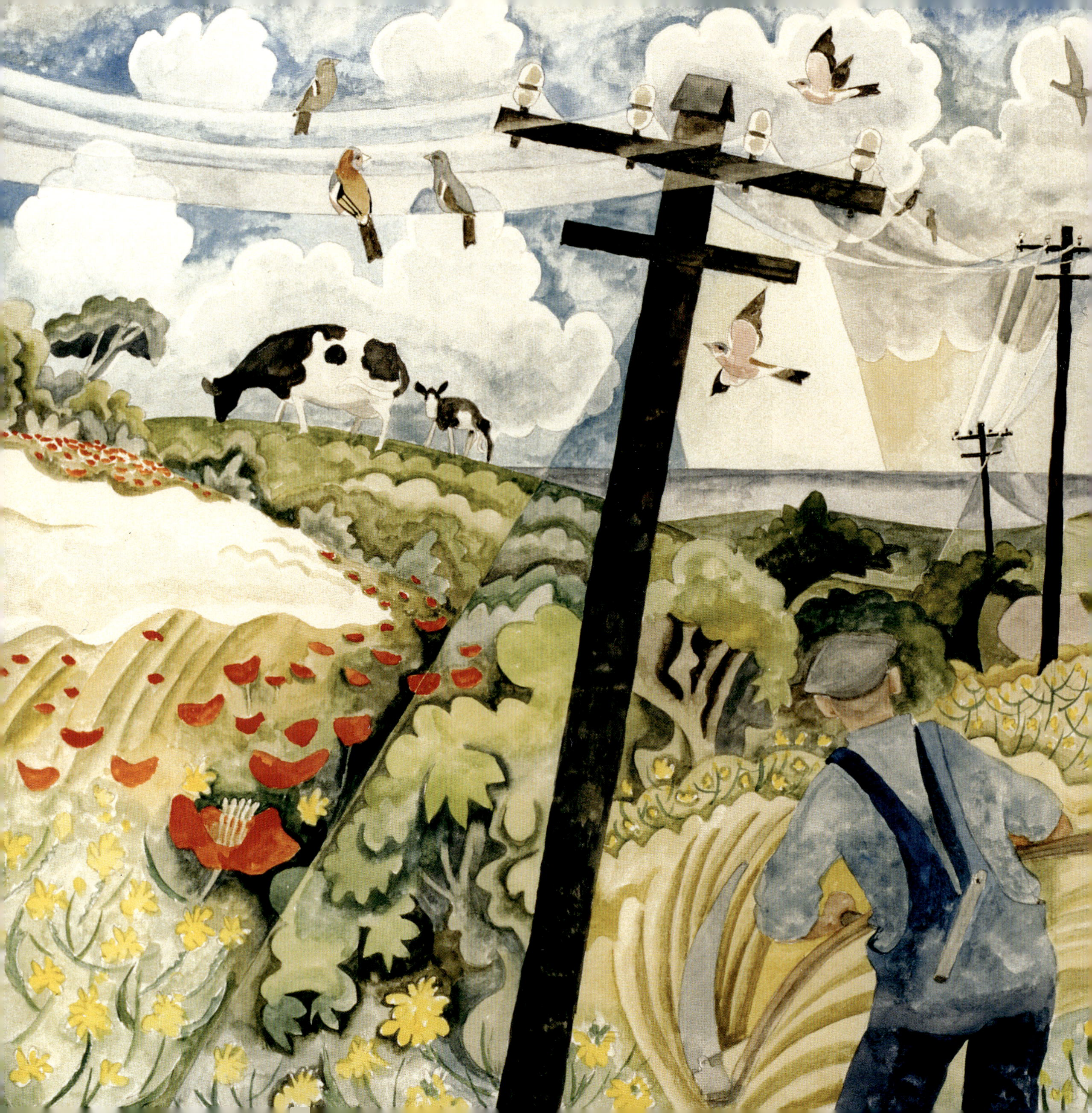

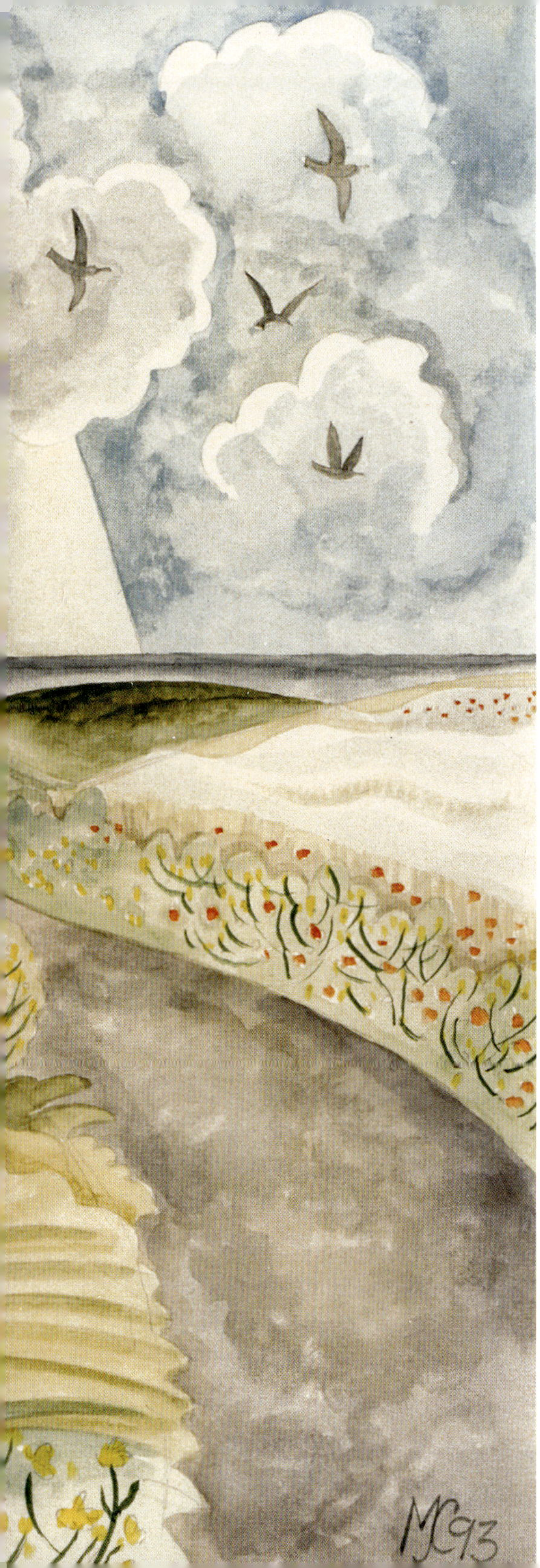

'The Coast: Norfolk' (1993)

As on the highway's quiet edge
He mows the grass beside the hedge,
The old man has for company
The distant, grey, salt-smelling sea,
A poppied field, a cow and calf,
The finches on the telegraph.
Across his faded back a hone,
He slowly, slowly scythes alone
In silence of the wind-soft air,
With ladies' bedstraw everywhere,
With whitened corn, and tarry poles,
And far-off gulls like risen souls.

Frances Darwin Cornford (1886-1960)

Frances Cornford (granddaughter of Charles Darwin) published a number of collections of poetry including 'Travelling Home' in 1948, which contains her delightful short poem entitled 'The Coast: Norfolk' and inspired this painting.

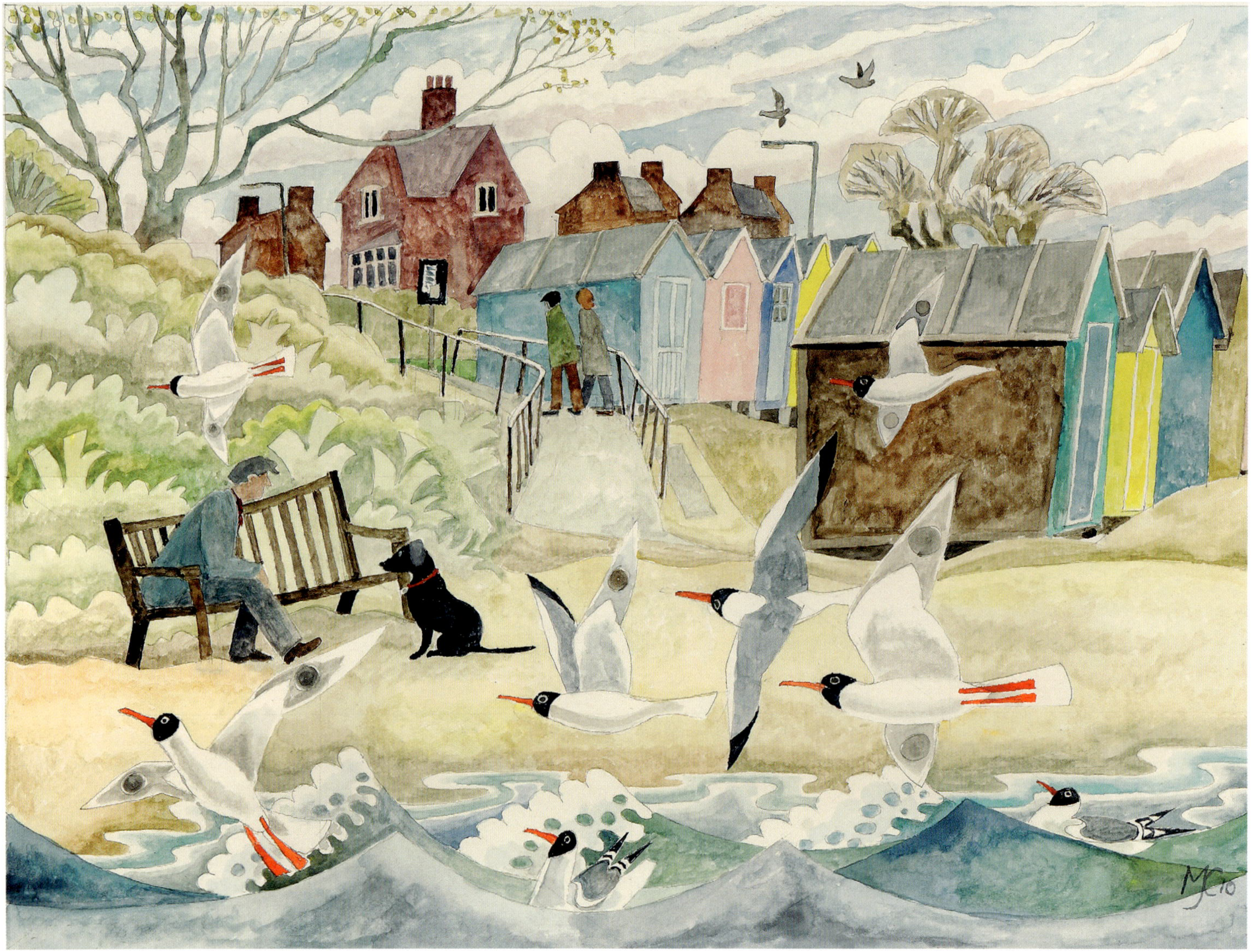

'Down on the Beach, Mersea Island' (2010) Mersea Island in Essex is located in the Blackwater and Colne estuaries to the south-east of Colchester. The island is split into two main areas, West Mersea and East Mersea, and connected to the mainland by the Strood, a causeway that can flood at high tide. Fishing has been a key industry since Roman times, particularly oysters. Along with tourism, this makes up a significant part of the island's economy. "Too many people have now discovered the gentle joy of sand, boats, birds and the stillness of this small fishing village. The man was a local and oblivious of his surroundings, talking quietly to his dog. The soul of the place was perhaps captured here."

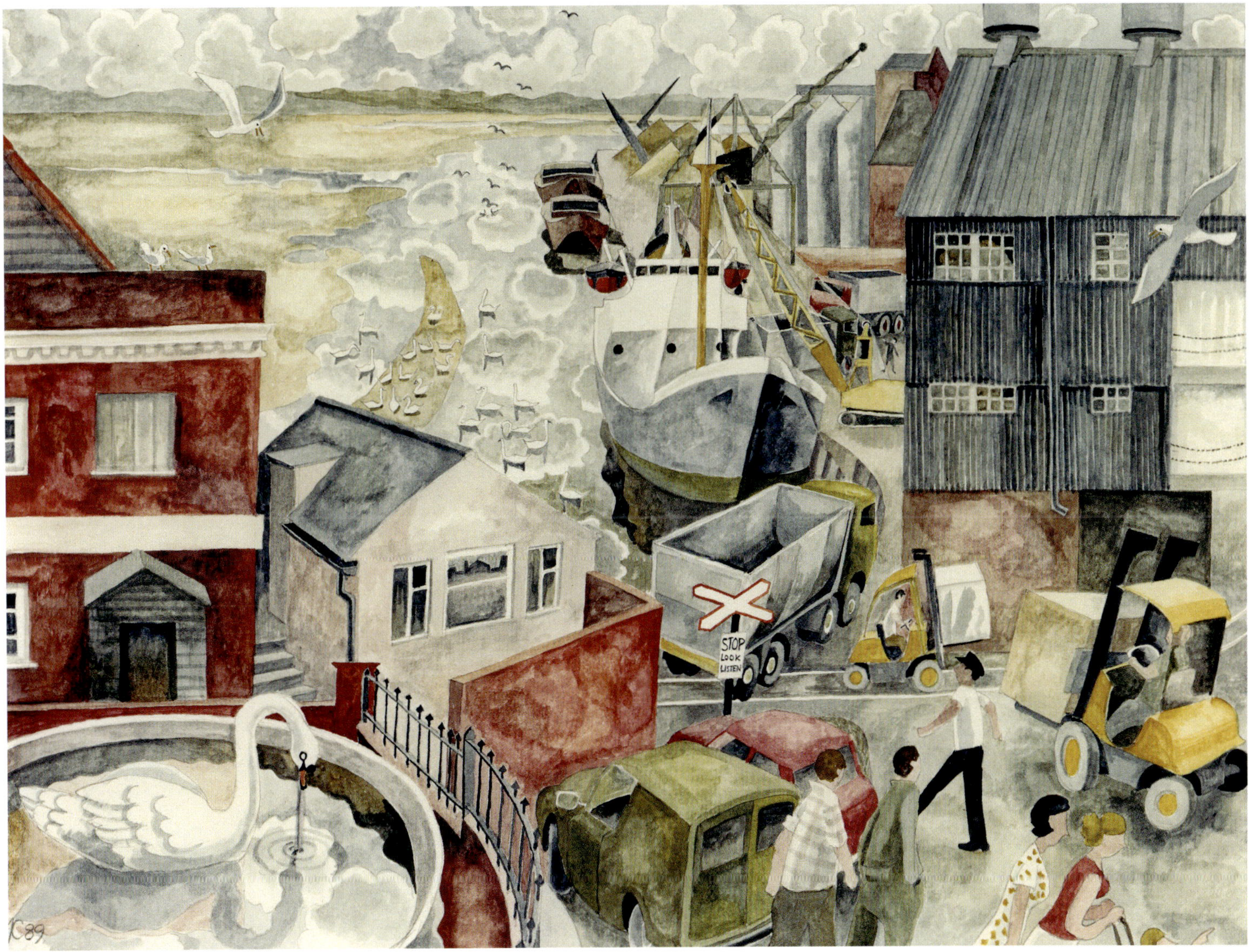

'Mistley Quay' (1989) Mistley is an Essex village around 15km north-east of Colchester, lying beside the Stour estuary. The first quay was built around 1720 and trade went up to Sudbury in Suffolk. Around 1770 the quay was enlarged and was known as Port of Mistley. Small-scale shipbuilding took place, including the production of modest warships for the Royal Navy. Controversially, in 2008 a safety fence was built along the quay, triggering protests from locals and visitors, with the 'Free the Quay' campaign gaining the support of various celebrities. An Appeal Court hearing took place in July 2018, and at the time of writing the judgment was awaited.

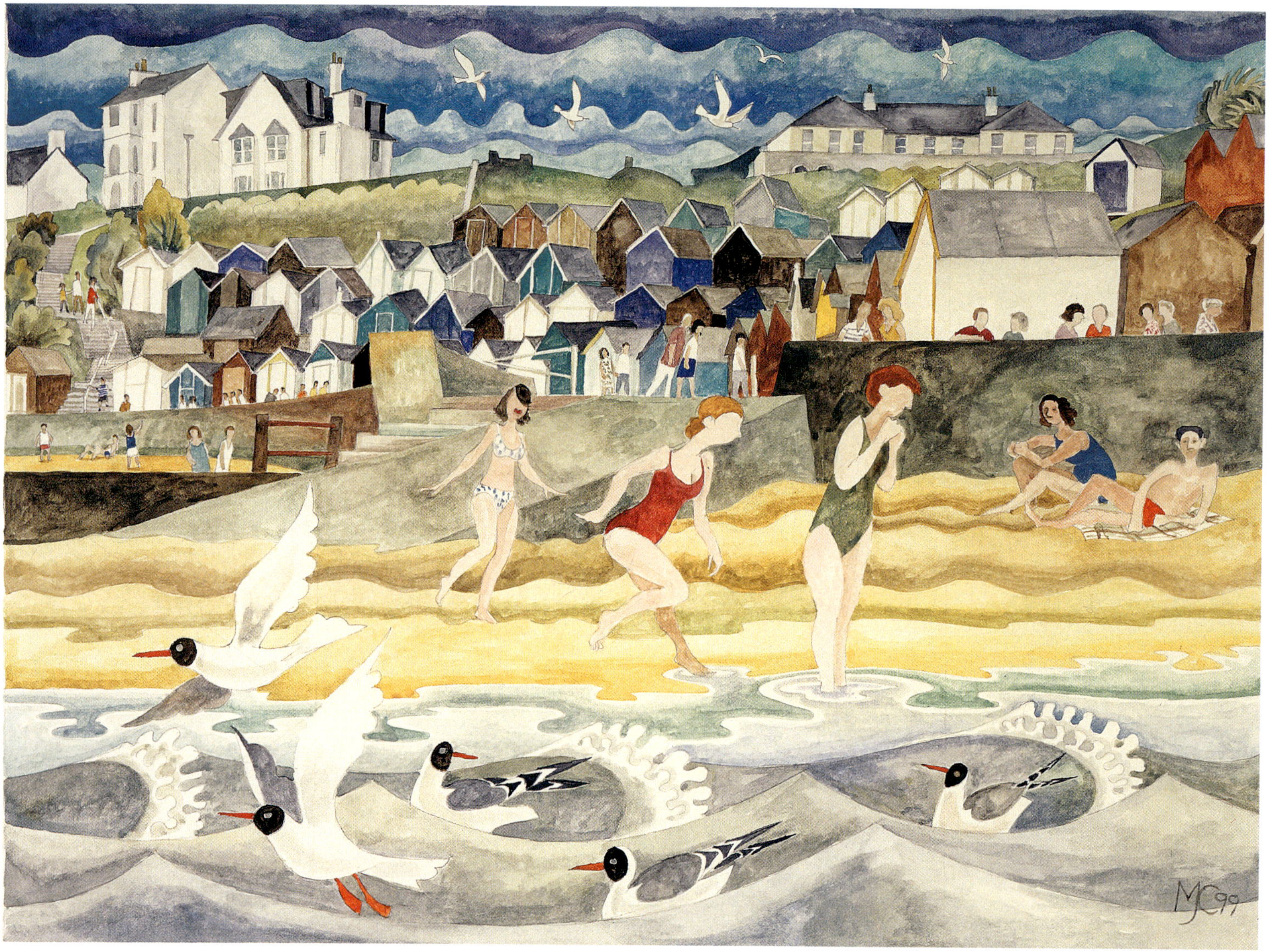

'Walton-on-the-Naze' (1999) This small Essex town and holiday resort is north of Clacton and south of Harwich. It neighbours the more formal Frinton-on-Sea. "Simple pleasures of dipping in the cold water; couples watching on as the screaming girls dare each other to get wet. Many people live along the cliff and have contacted me to tell me so, pointing out in the painting which house is theirs."

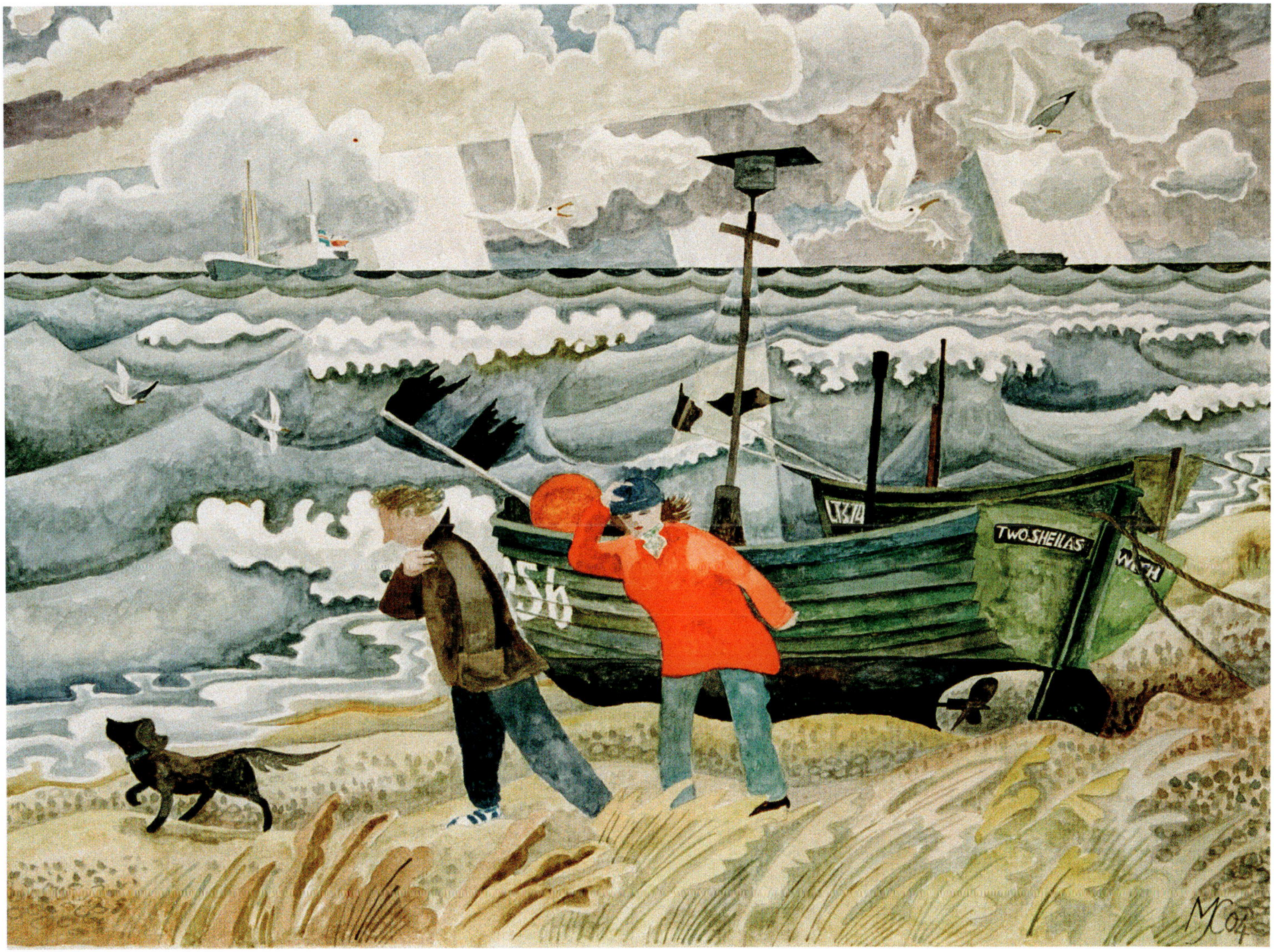

'Stormy Beach' (2004) "A brisk walk along a beach in all weathers is an invigorating pastime. Norfolk, Suffolk or Essex – all feature the same combination of beach, weather, fishing boats and passing ships under big skies."

'Harwich Harbour' (1989) "Taking the foot ferry from Felixstowe over to Harwich is an enjoyable trip for a summer's day. Fresh fish, lunch and a walk to the lighthouse."

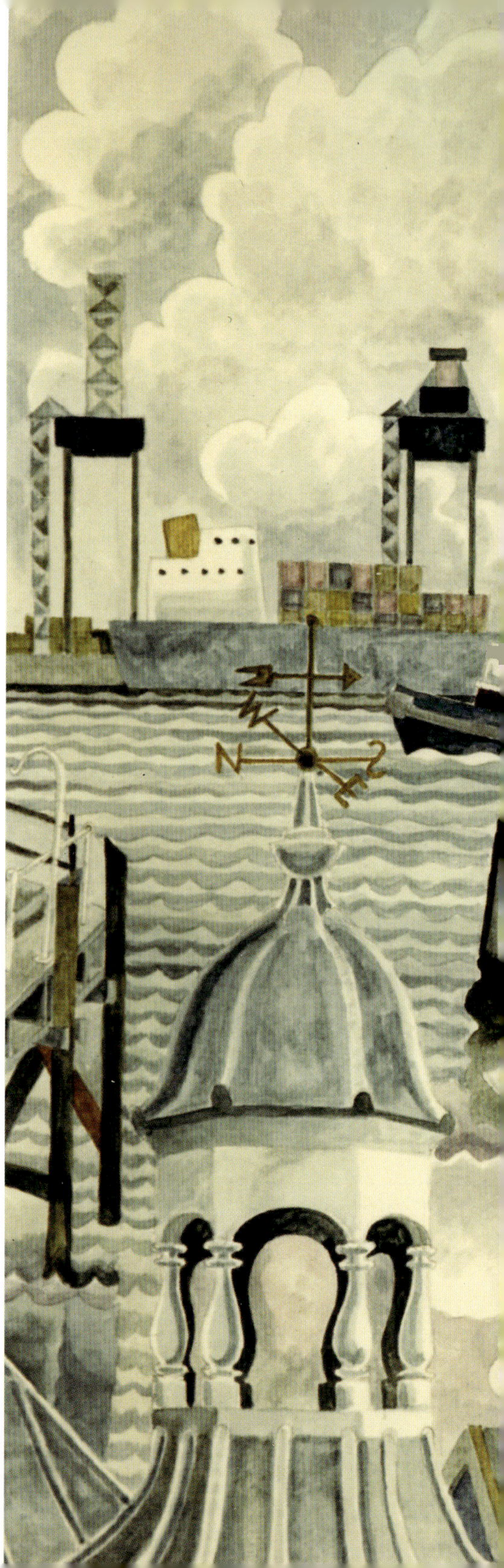

'Redundant Lightships' (1988)

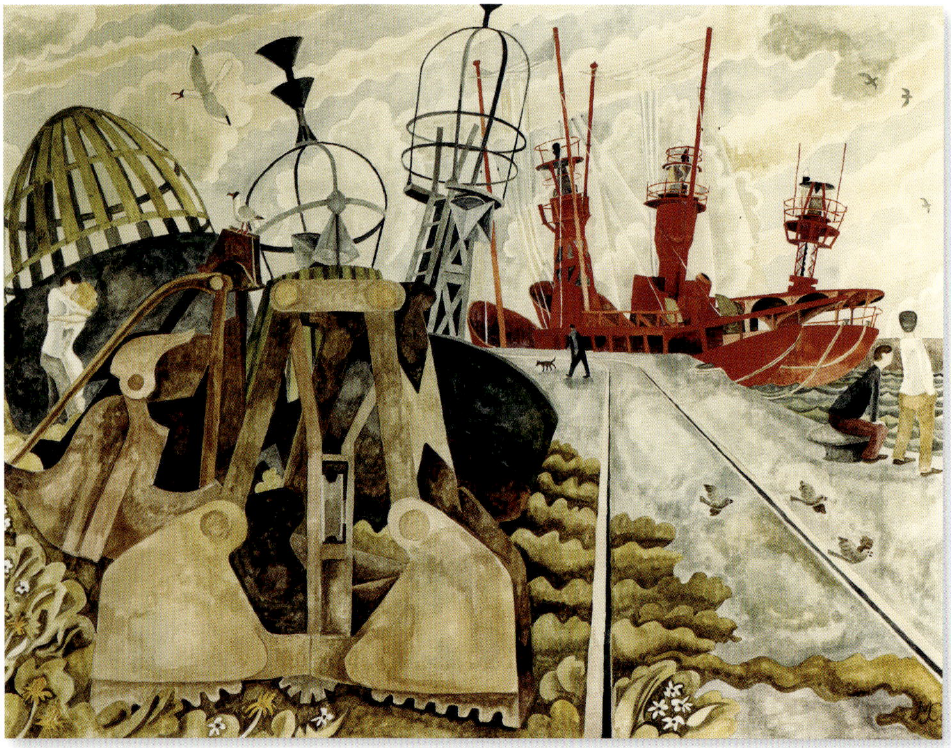

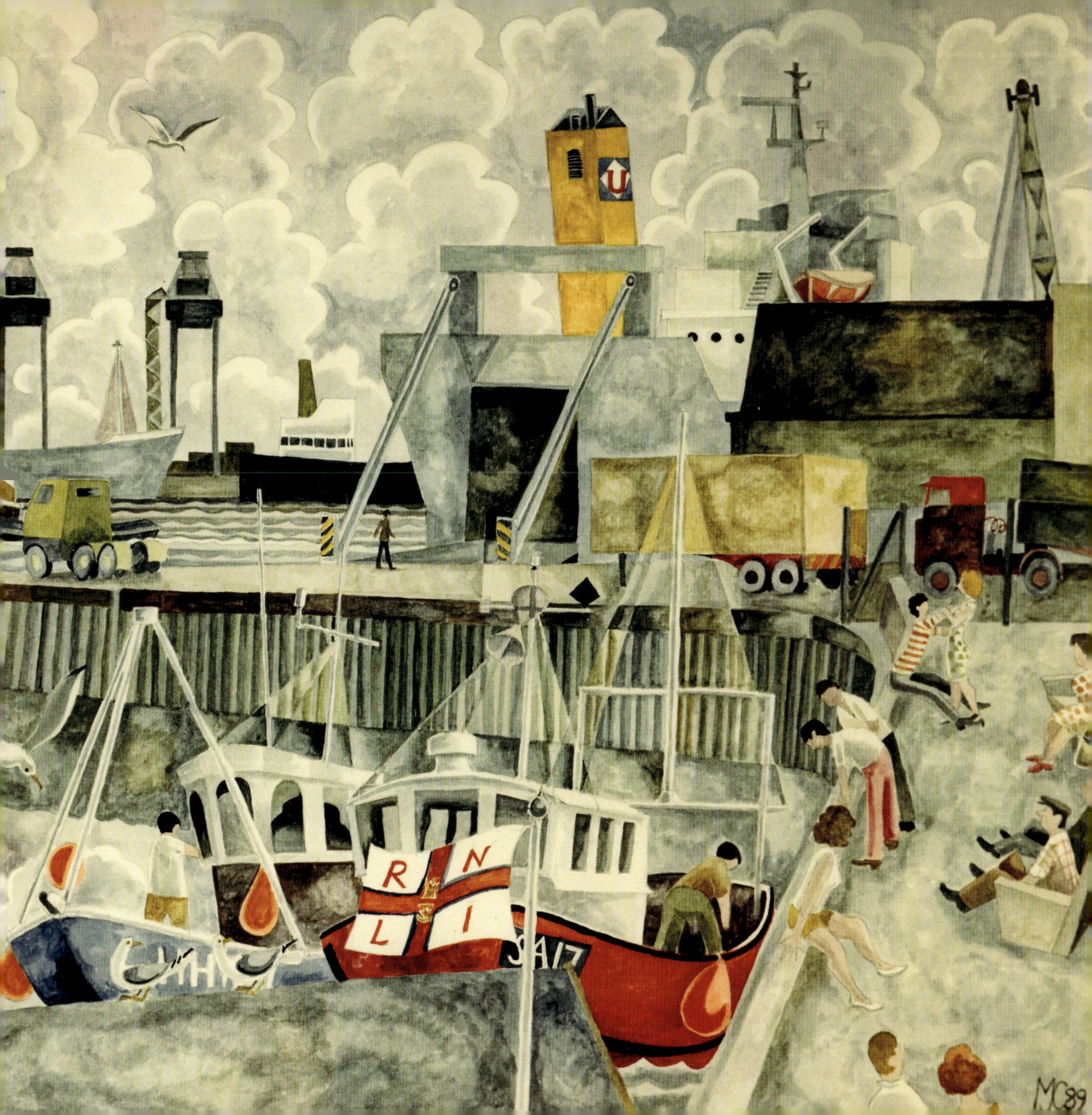
U
R N
L I
MC89

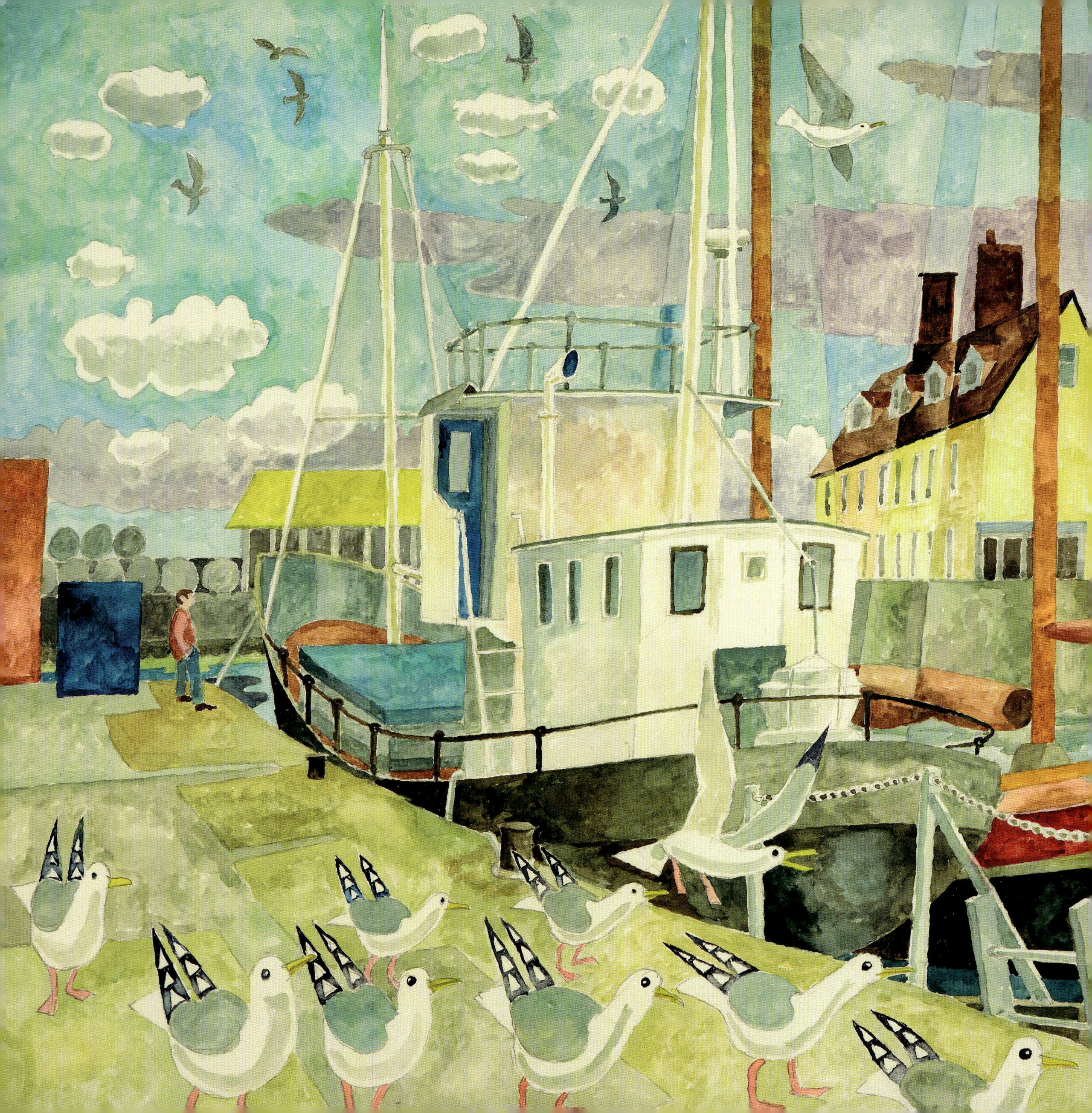

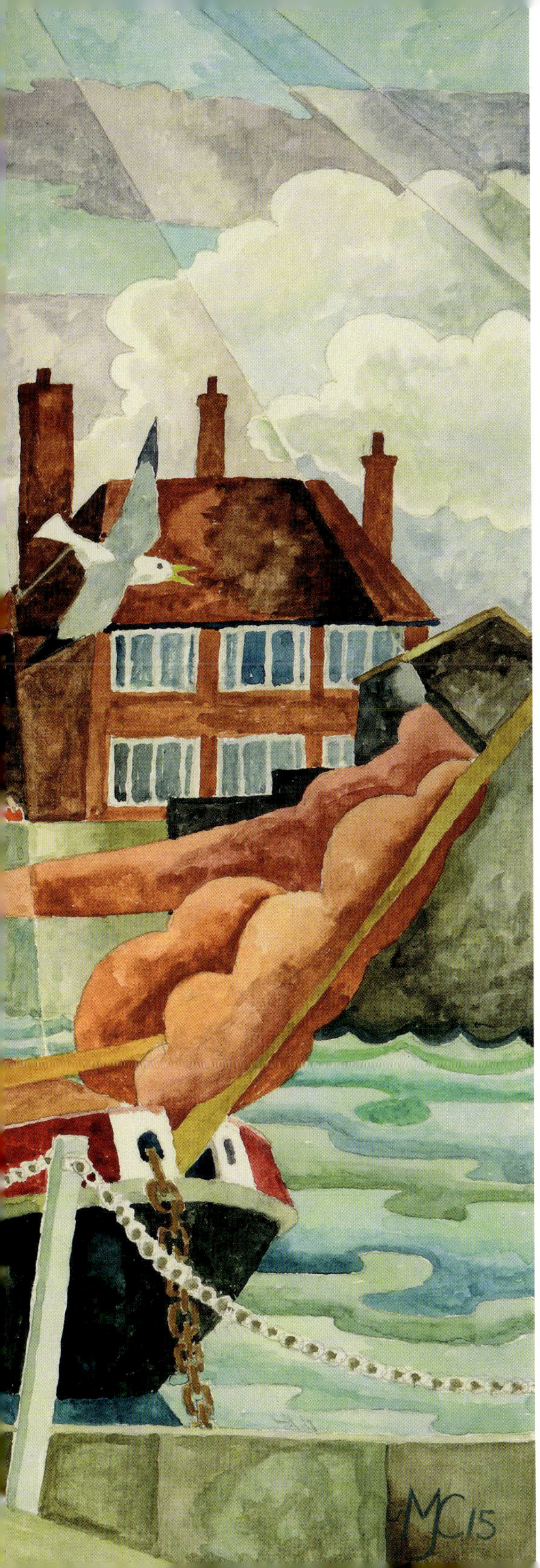

'Maldon Quayside' (2015) Maldon is on the tidal River Chelmer by the Blackwater estuary in Essex. Hythe Quay at the confluence of the Chelmer and Blackwater, which flanks the northern edge of the town, was an important port – and Cooks Yard remains significant for Thames sailing barges. The Blackwater re-emerges into the Blackwater estuary, through locks at the Heybridge Basin.

'March Maldon' (2000)

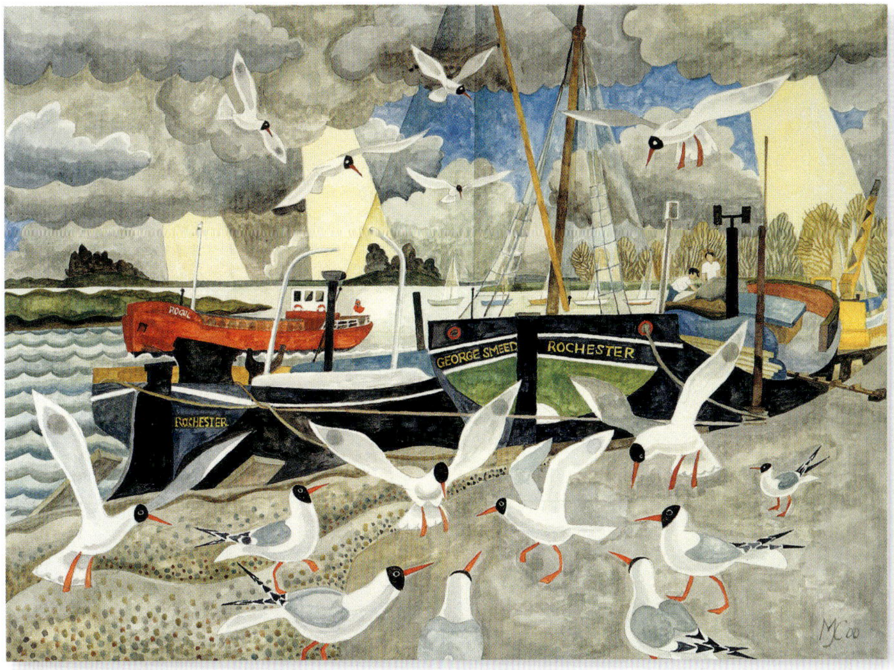

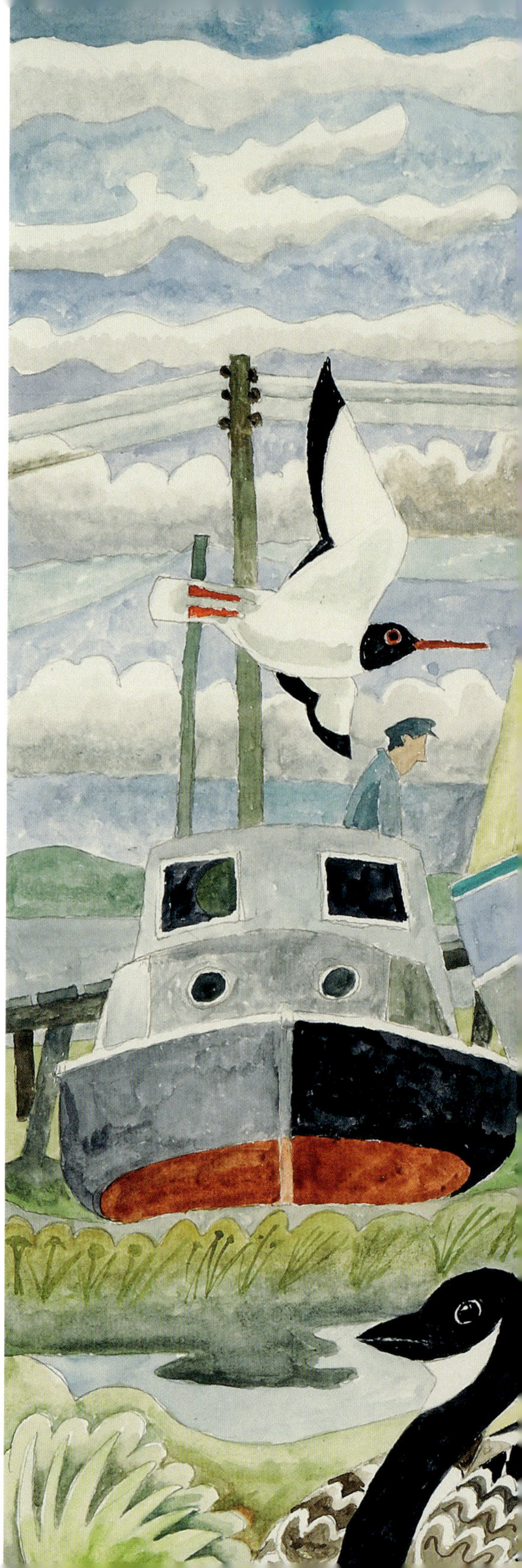

'Houseboats and Oystercatchers' (2010) "A day on Mersea Island provided a cacophony of ideas for a picture. This looked quirky and interesting; the birds performed very well."

'Waves and Girls' (1984)

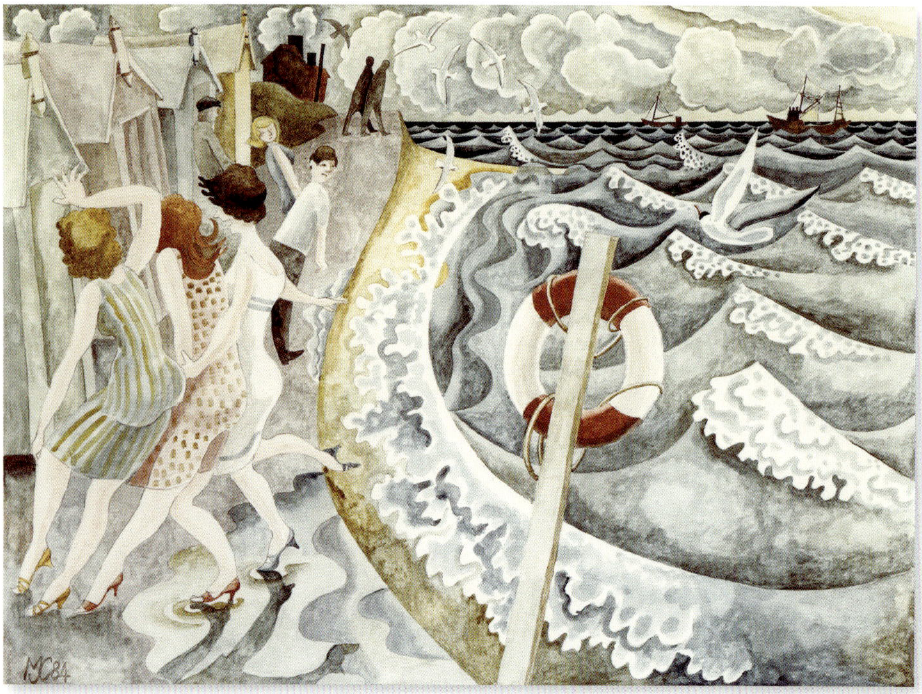

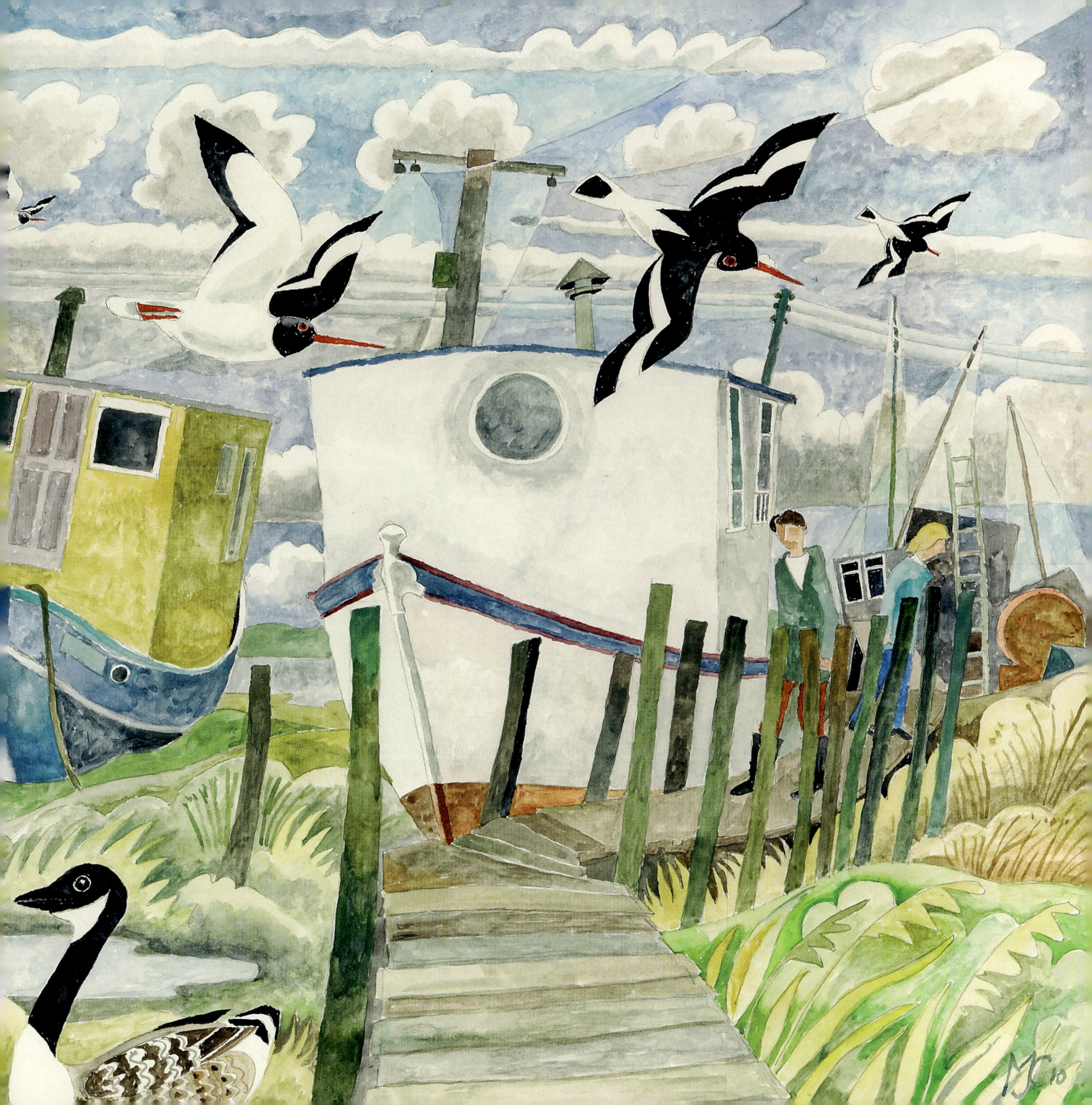

SOUTH & SOUTH-WEST

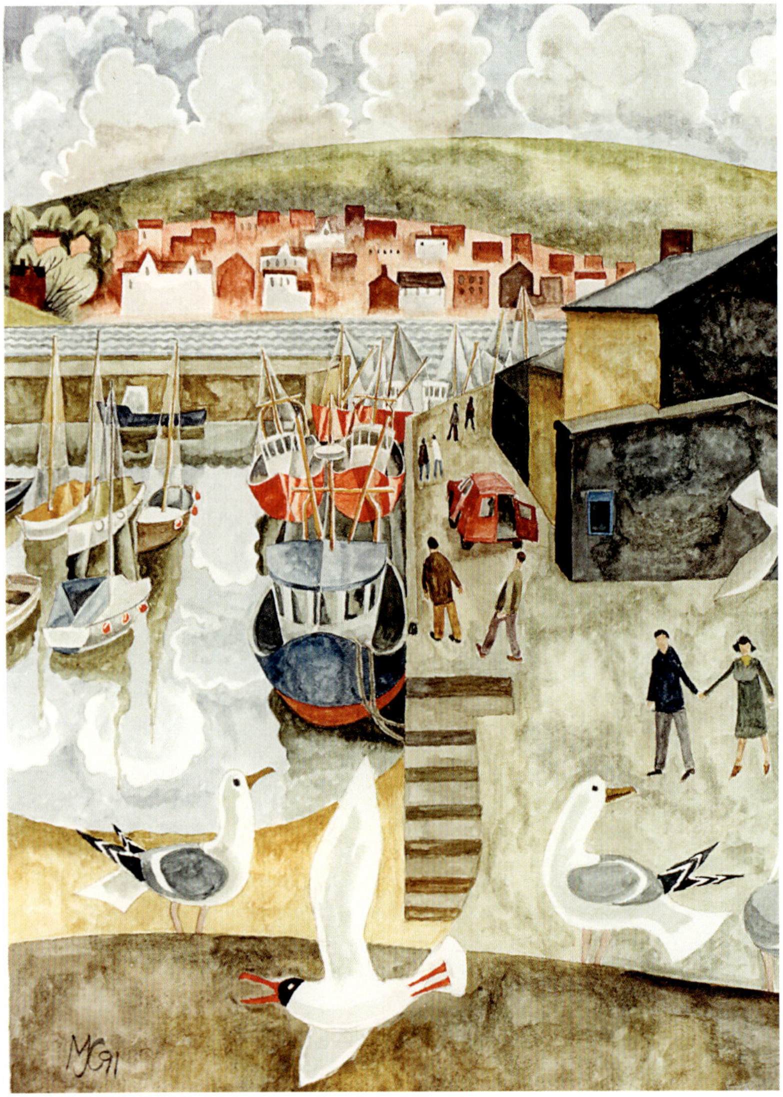

Expeditions to Kent and Sussex gave Michael the chance to paint some southern wildernesses and landmarks, with several locations sharing similarities with his Suffolk and Essex favourites. Exhibitions in Dorset took the artist south-west, exploring elements of the Jurassic Coast and the pretty towns and villages lying just inland. A more undulating and varied landscape than found on his home patch, Dorset provided the basis for a large portfolio of attractive and occasionally surprising pictures. This section also takes in a few Cornish beauty spots, extending as far as Tresco in the Scillies, as well as a glimpse of Ireland and the Irish Sea.

Left: detail from 'Lyme Regis' (1991). This picture in its entirety can be found on page 116. Always popular, Lyme Regis benefited greatly from the filming of 'The French Lieutenant's Woman', with the Undercliff and the Cobb (harbour wall) becoming familiar to millions who had yet to visit the so-called 'Pearl of Dorset'. Facing page, clockwise from top left: 'Puffer and Puffins' (1997); 'Weymouth Beach' (1991); 'Port Godwit' (2008); 'Lighthouses, Portland Bill' (1991). The Dorset town of Weymouth makes several appearances in this section, located midway along the Jurassic Coast, close to Portland Bill. It has an excellent harbour providing ferry services and hosting the 2012 Olympic sailing events.

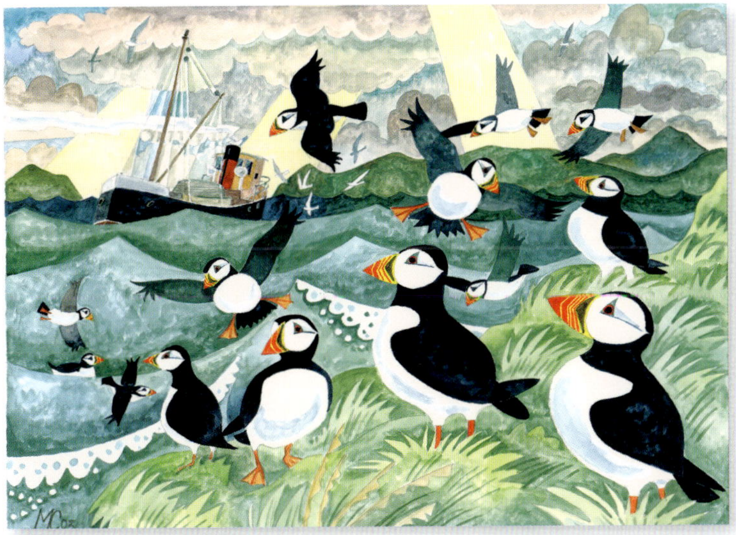

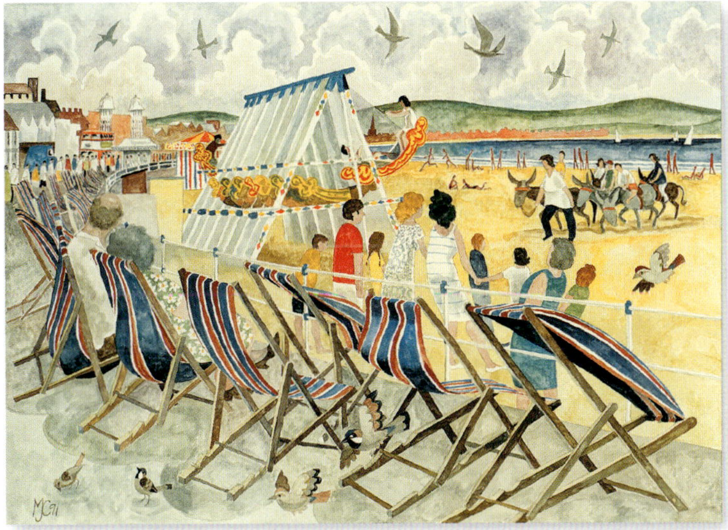

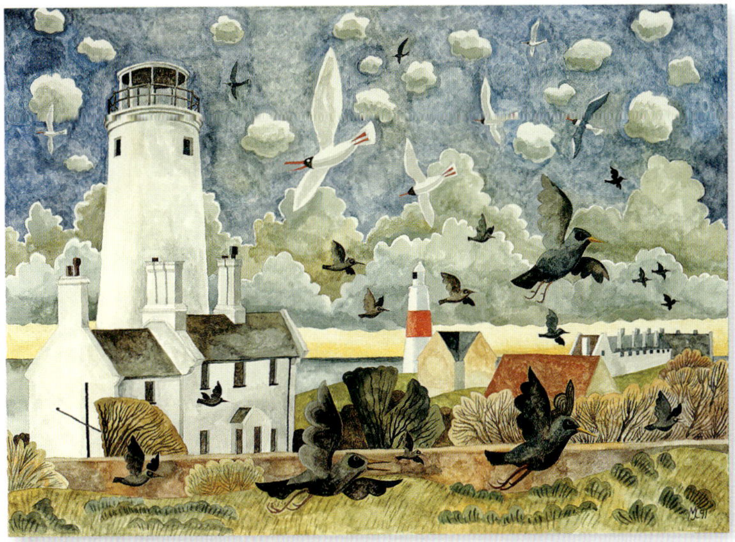

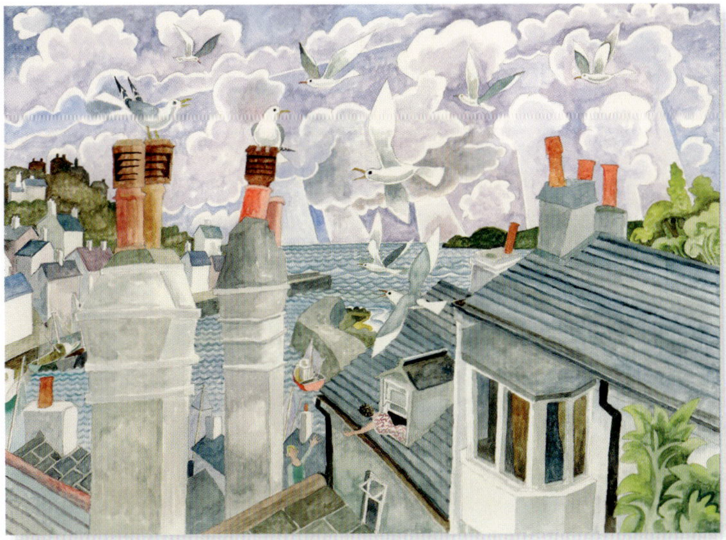

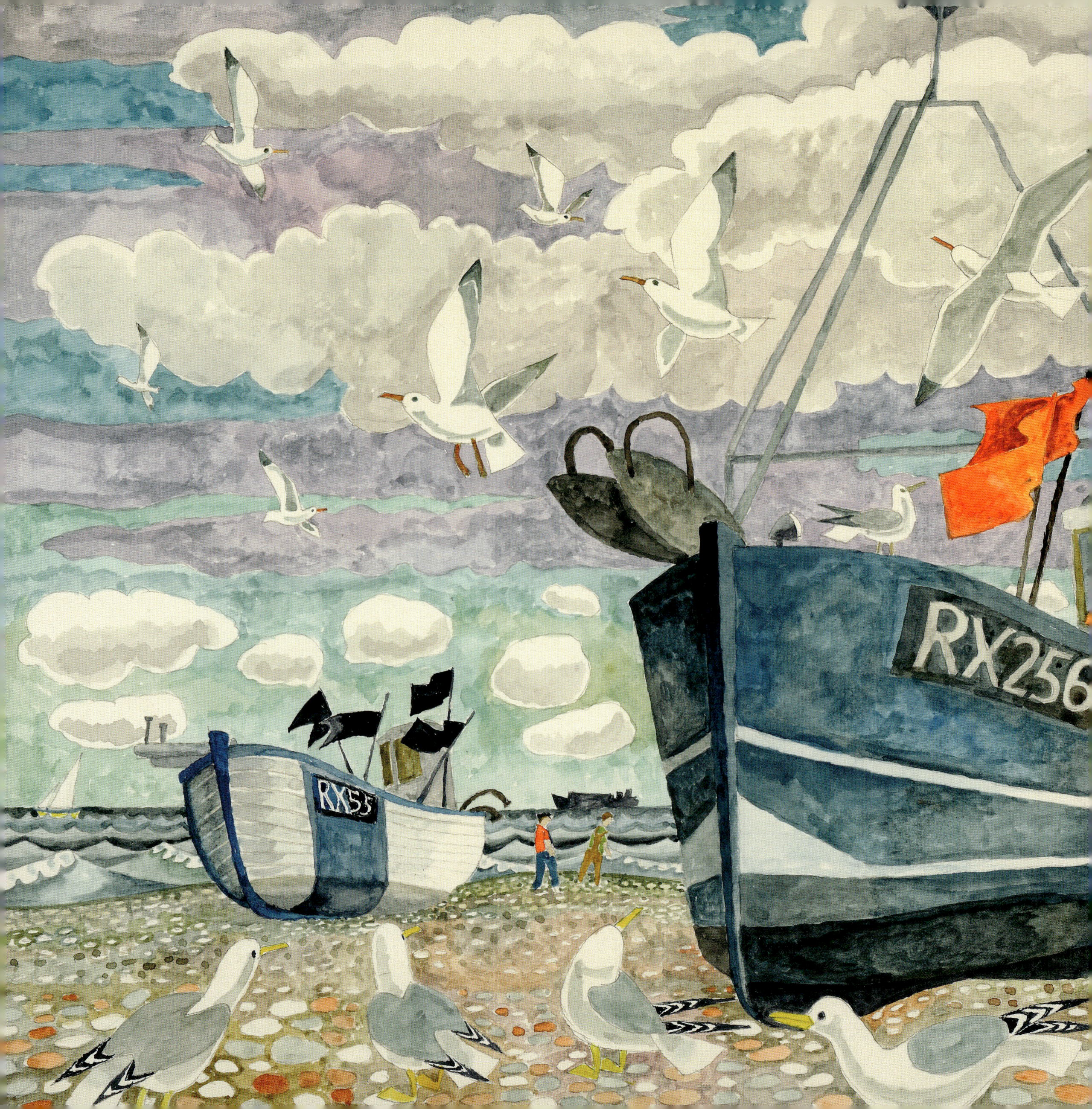
RX256
RX55

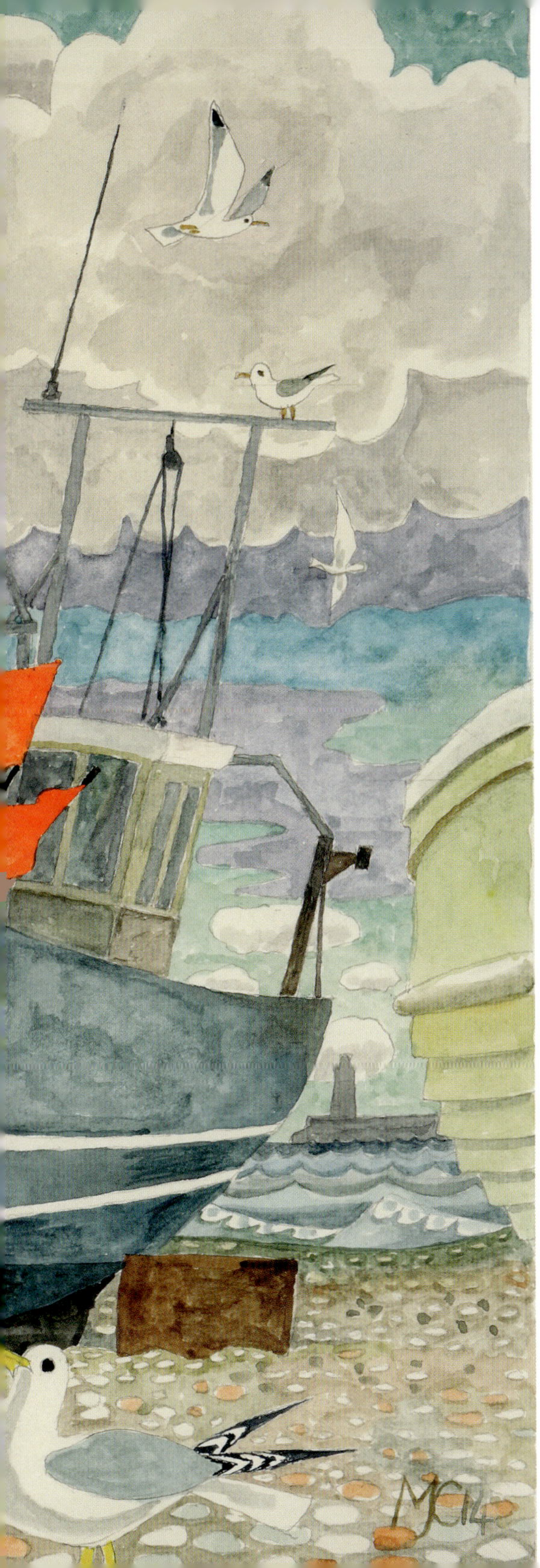

'A Sussex Beach' (2014) Hastings in Sussex was one of the medieval Cinque Ports and later became a popular seaside resort with the coming of the railway. Fishing boats continue to operate from the beach, as they do along parts of Suffolk's shingled shoreline, which made the artist feel quite at home. "Part of an attractive line of fishing boats along Hastings beach."

'Shag Rocks' (2008)

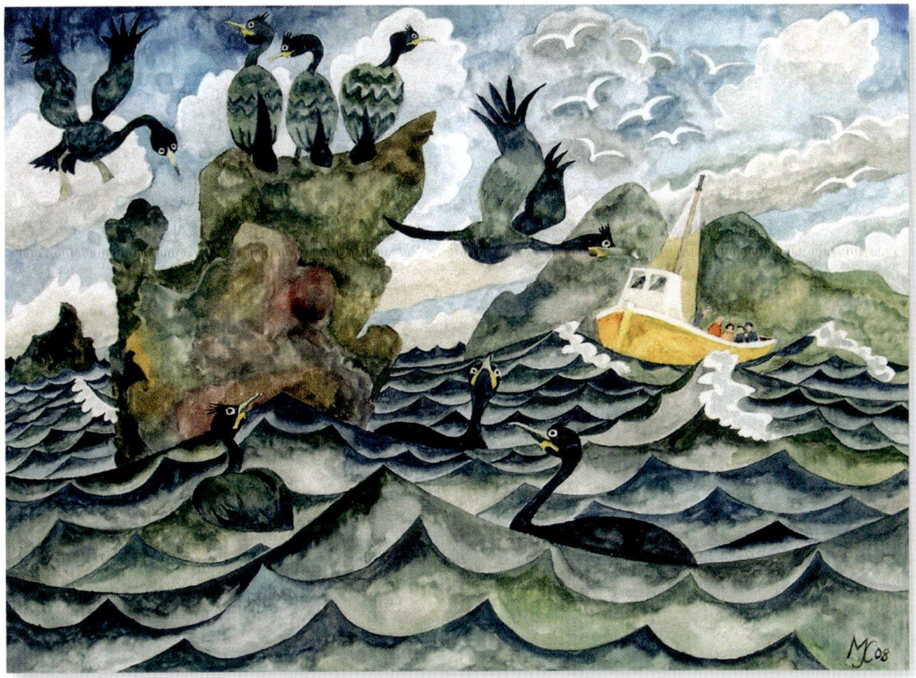

'Tresco' (2012) "Quite often rough seas prevent landing on Tresco. When it is good, it is very good. Gardens cover the cliff with a network of paths and steps. A heavy canopy has created its own mini climate for the more tender plants and trees. A walk around the sandy point back to the ferry boat is worth the effort."

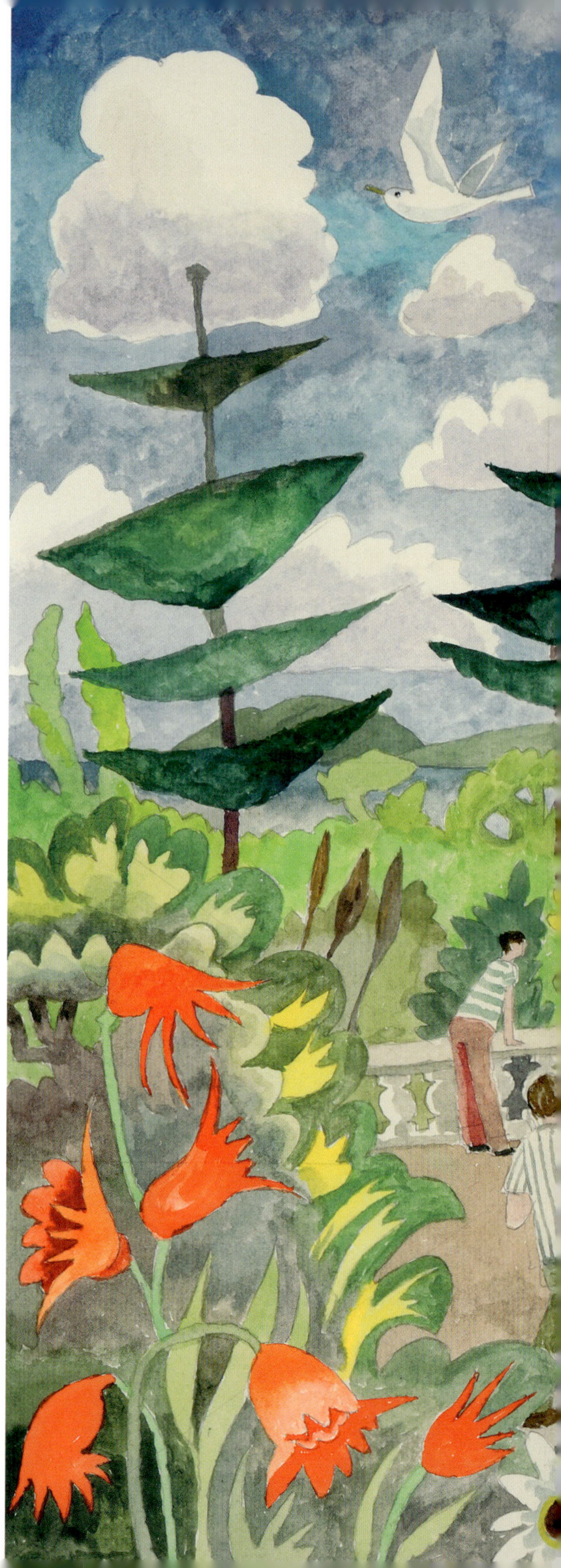

'Seascape with Pink Clouds' (1998)

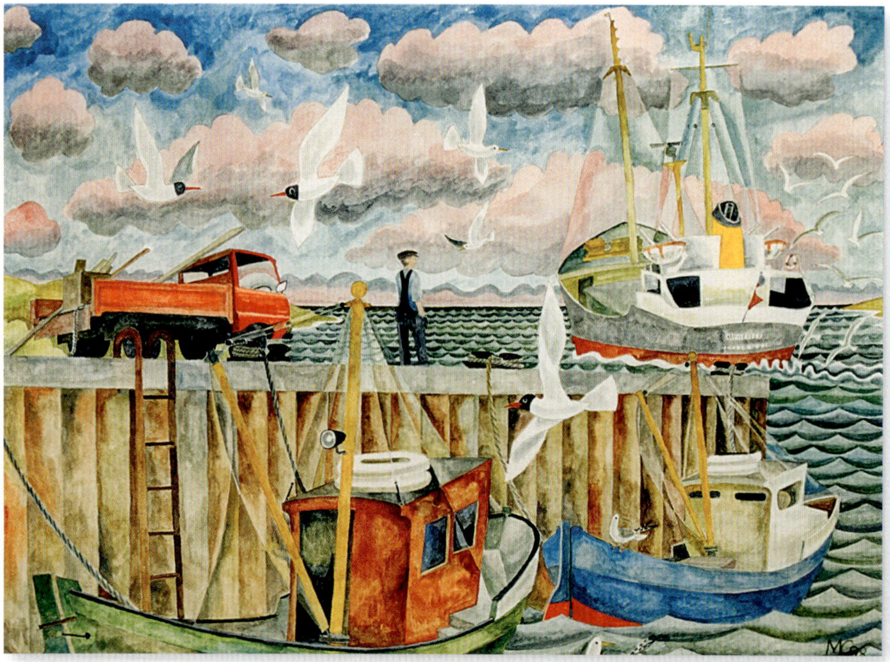

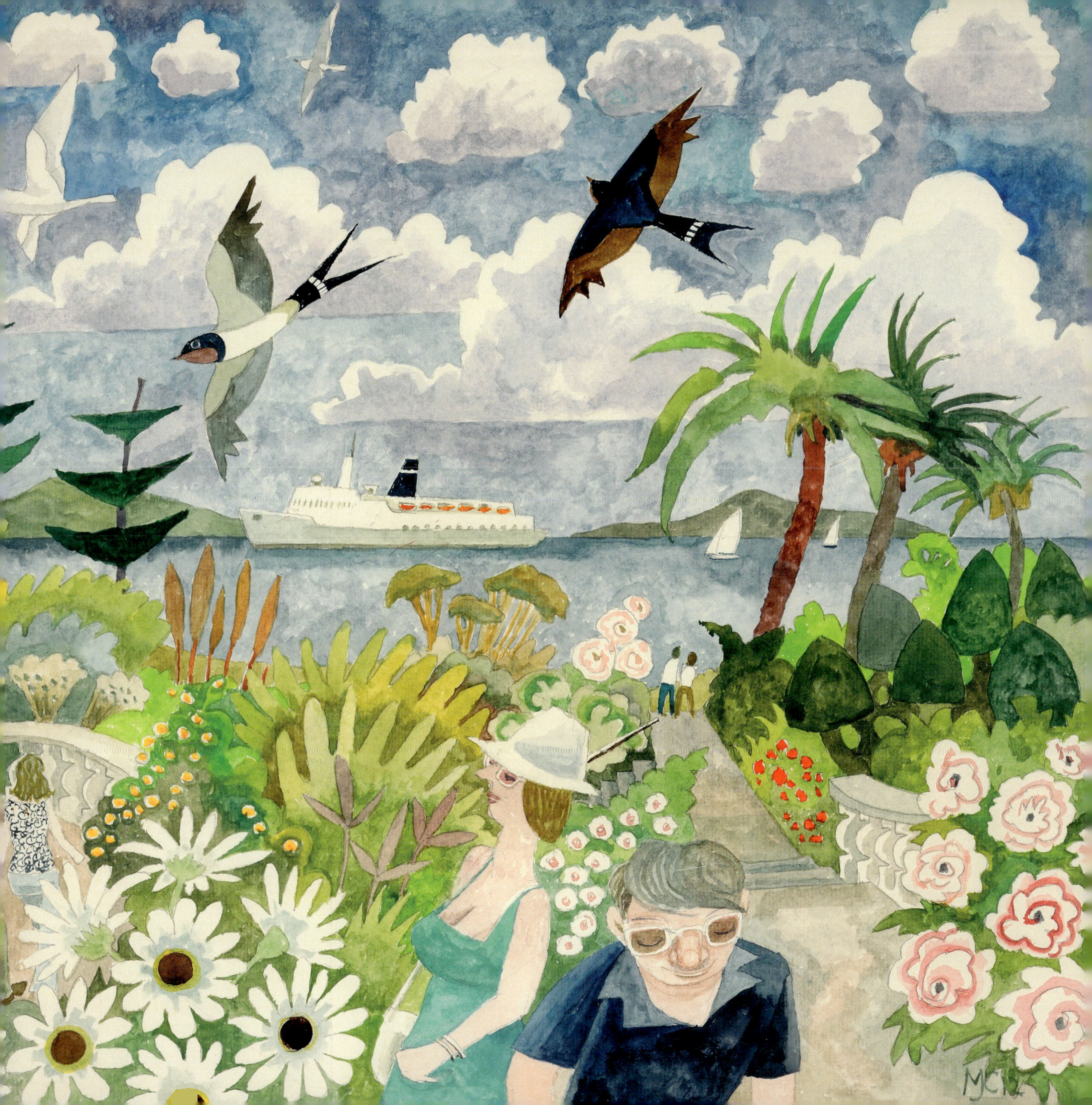

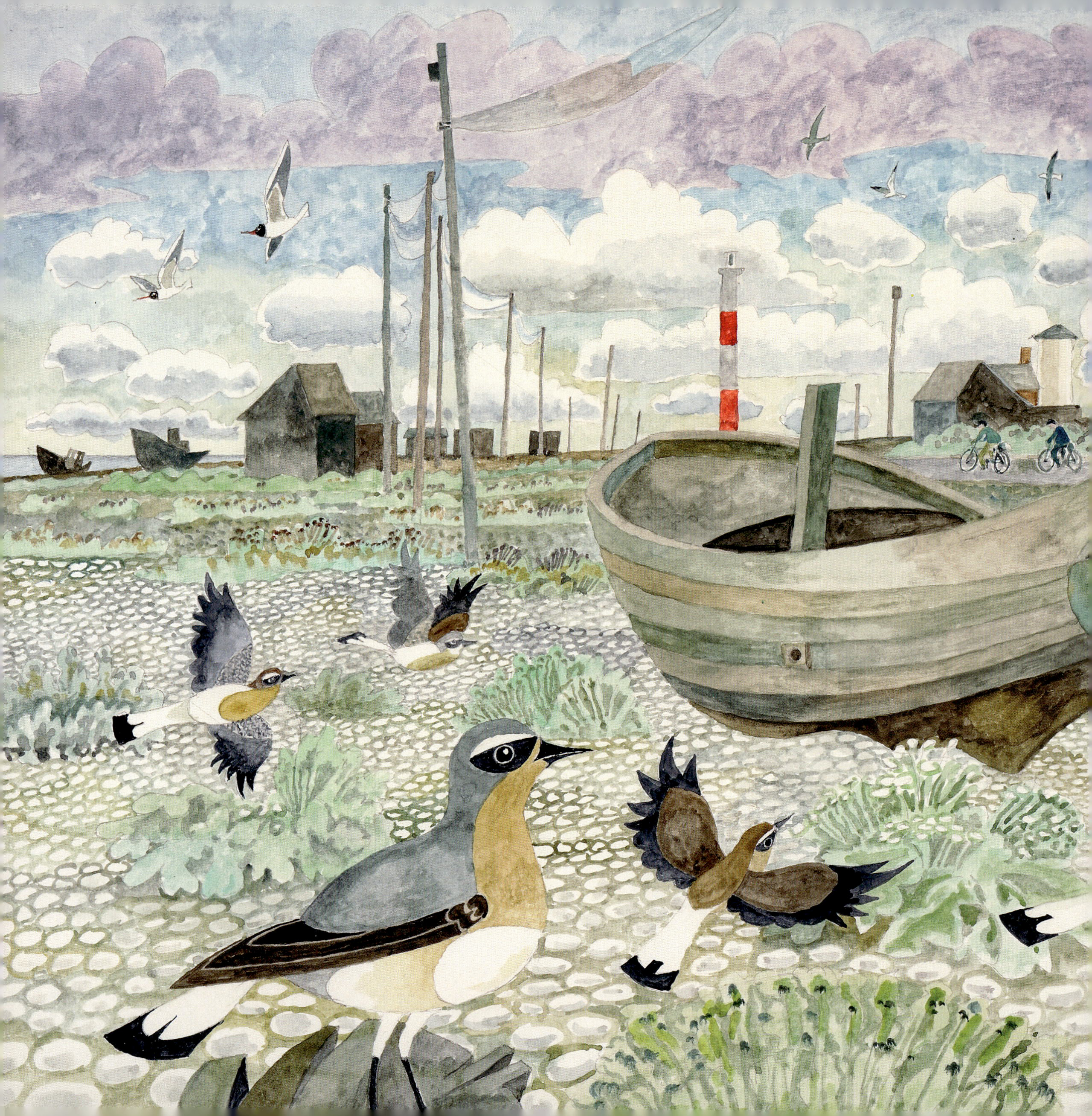

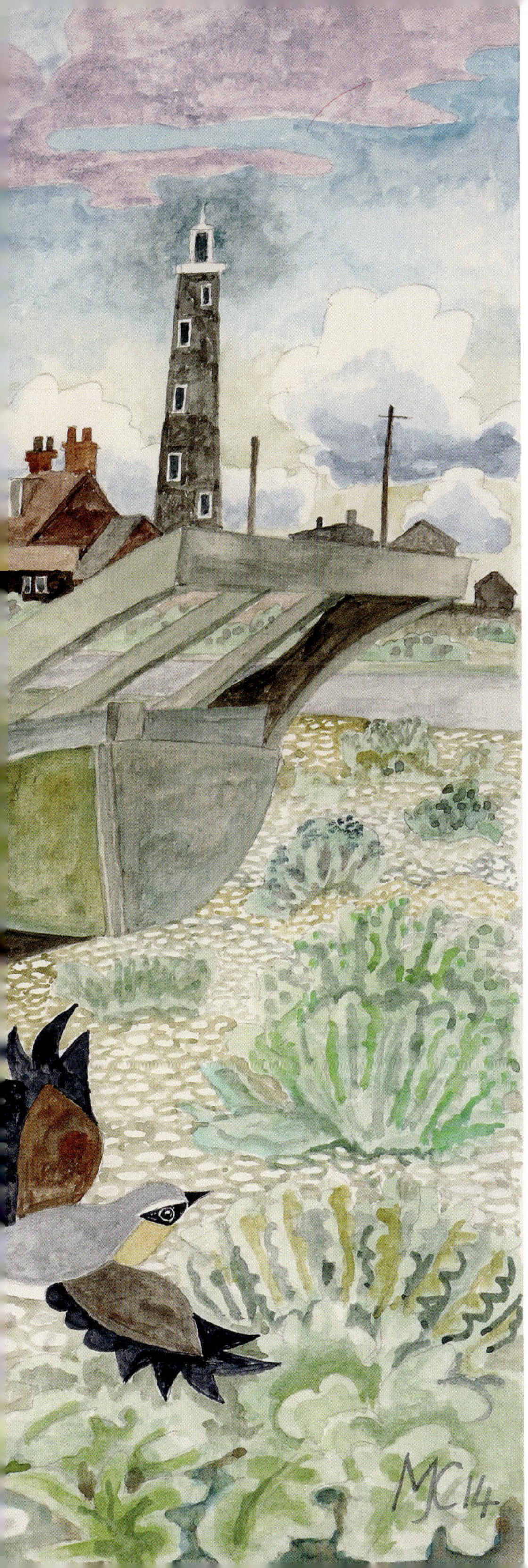

'Wheatears, Dungeness' (2014) "Dungeness, a remote shingle wilderness, dotted with lonely cottages, home to people who like it like that. A haven for seabirds, fauna and flora growing in the windy, salty shingle."

'Godwits and Egrets' (2003)

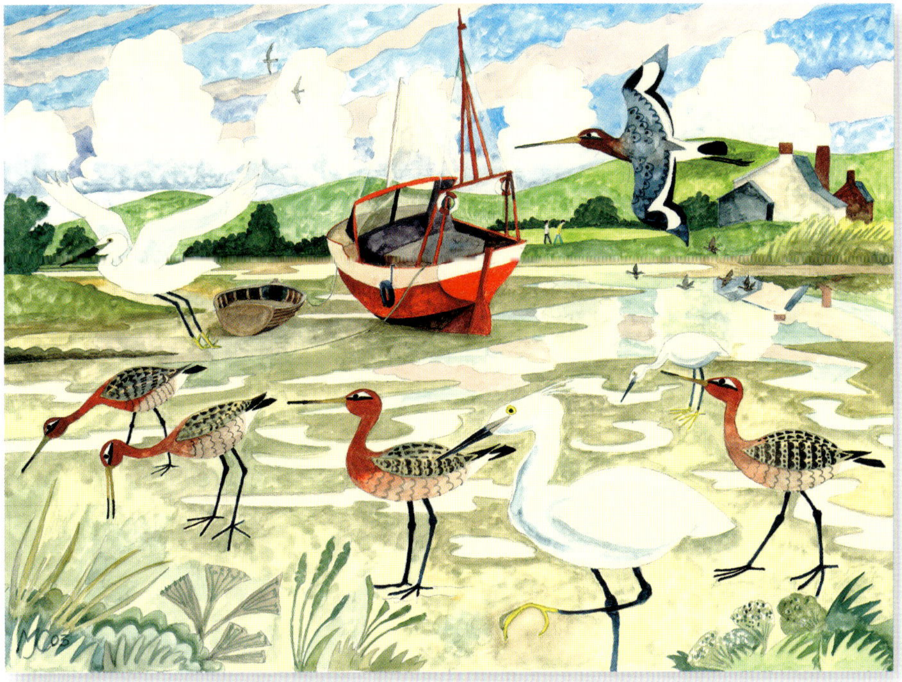

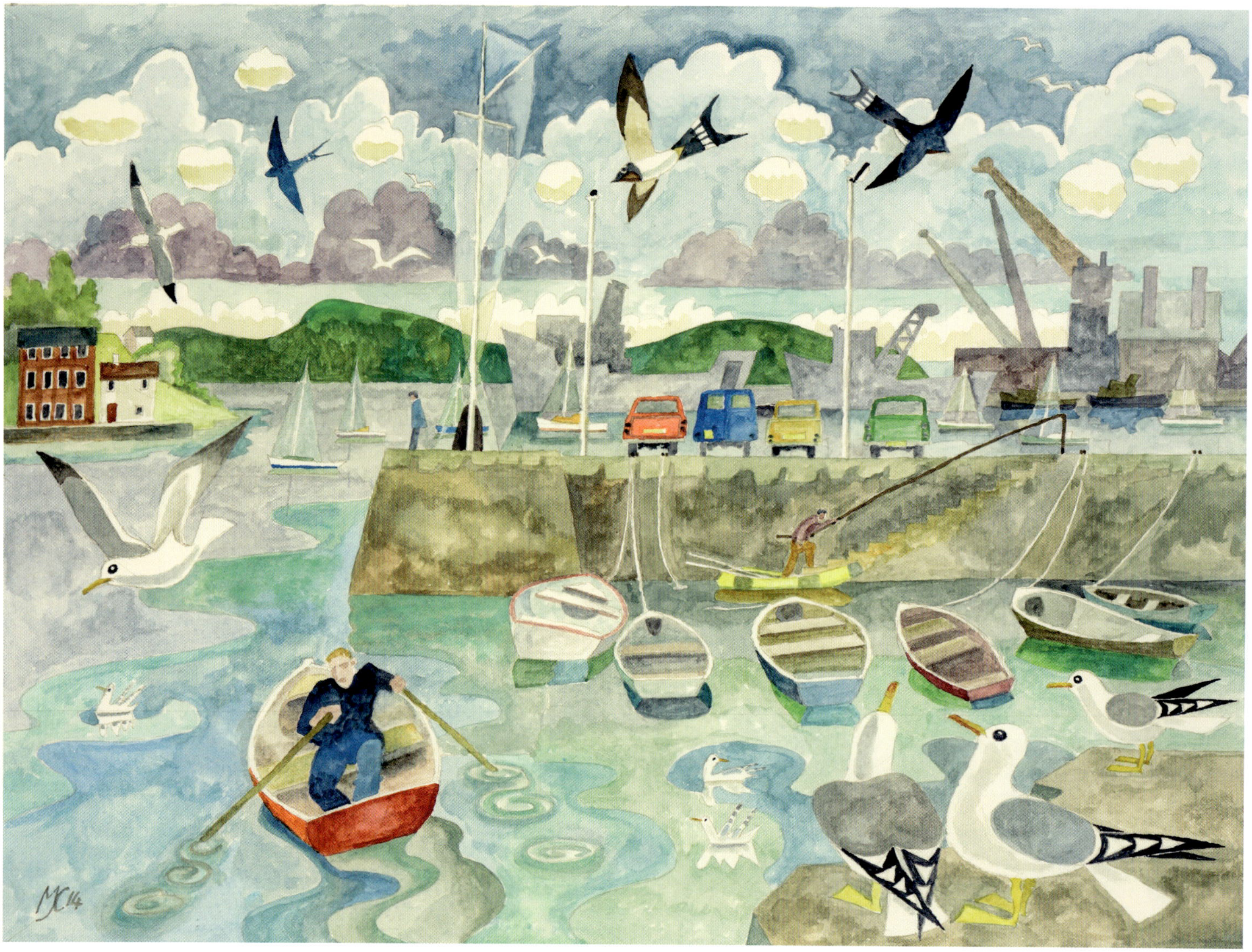

'Falmouth Harbour' (2014) Hard work at the oars, while the gulls watch on. "A view from our hotel window, people digging for worms in the mud beneath. Always something to see, something going on."

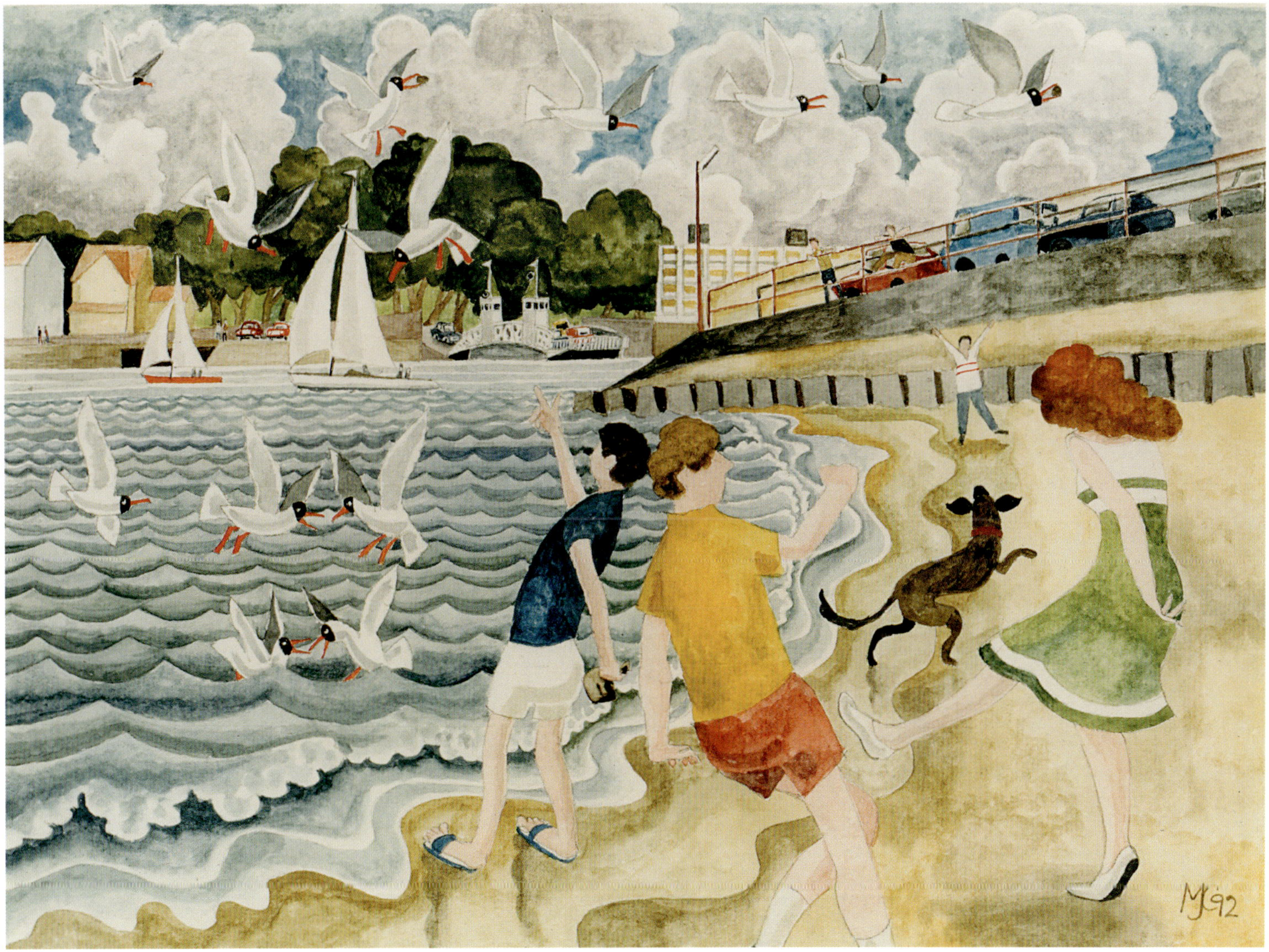

'Sandbanks Car Ferry, Dorset' (1992) Sandbanks is a small peninsula crossing the mouth of Poole Harbour. It is now infamous for property prices at Sandbanks Beach – having at one point soared to the fourth-highest land value in the world.

'On Romney Marsh' (2014) Romney Marsh is a sparsely populated wetland habitat bordering Kent and East Sussex. "Sheep protected by a high sea wall over the road from their field. They were not put off by the wind turbines or the passing traffic."

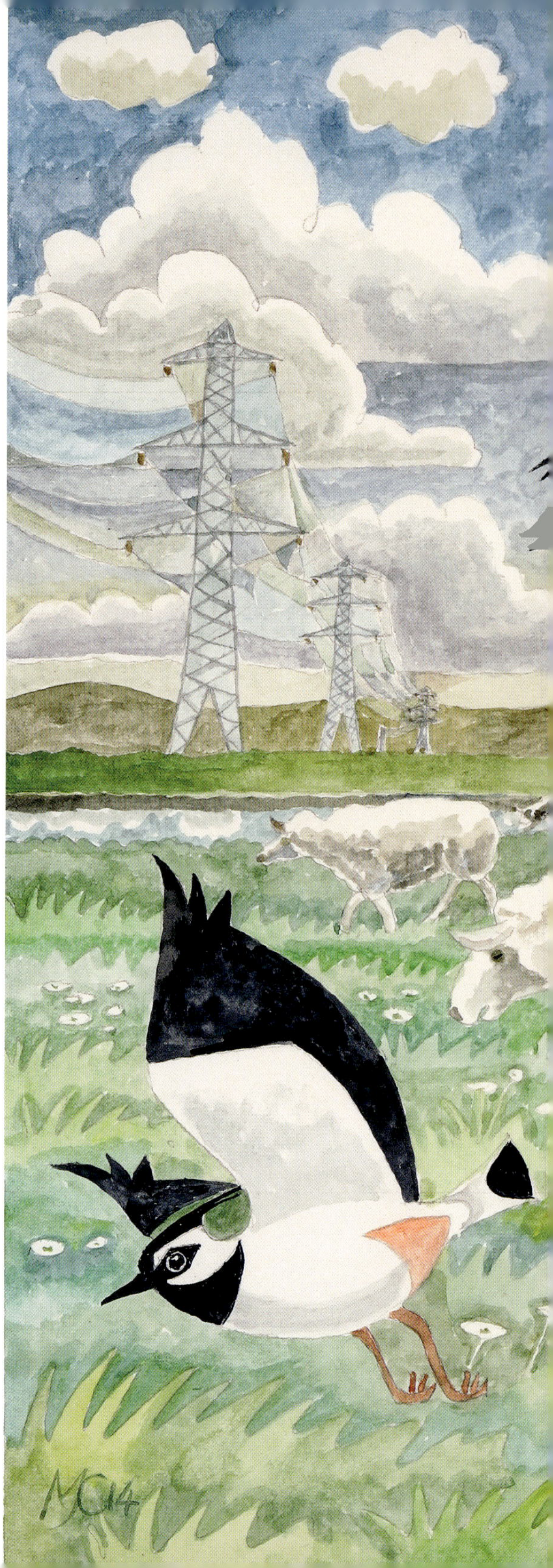

'Purbeck Pastorale' (1991)

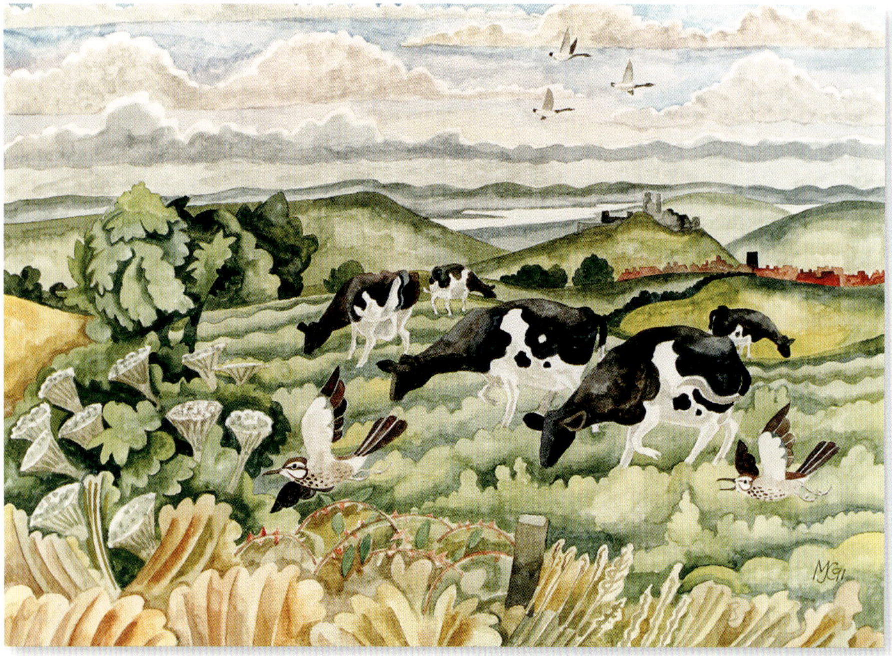

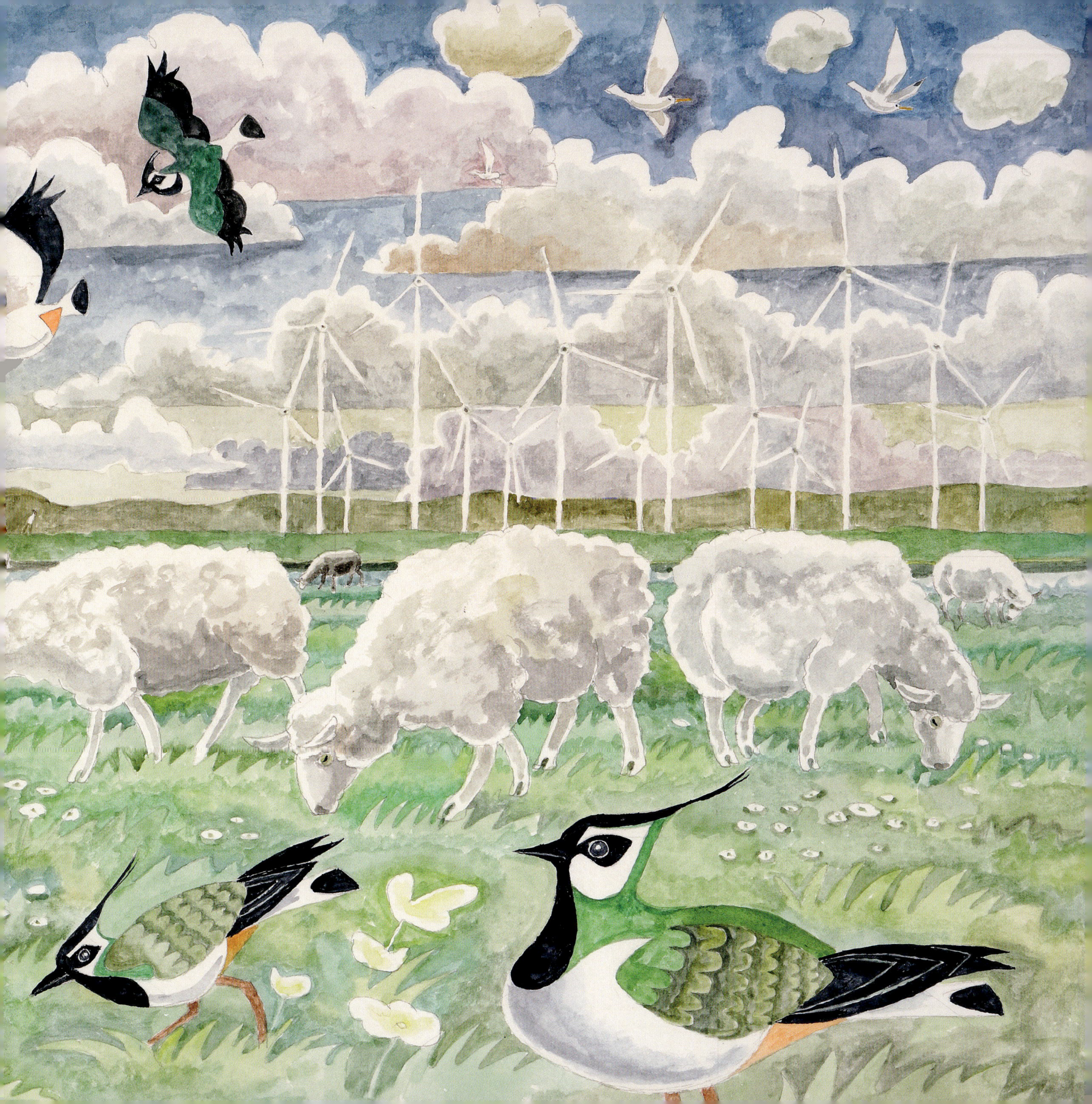

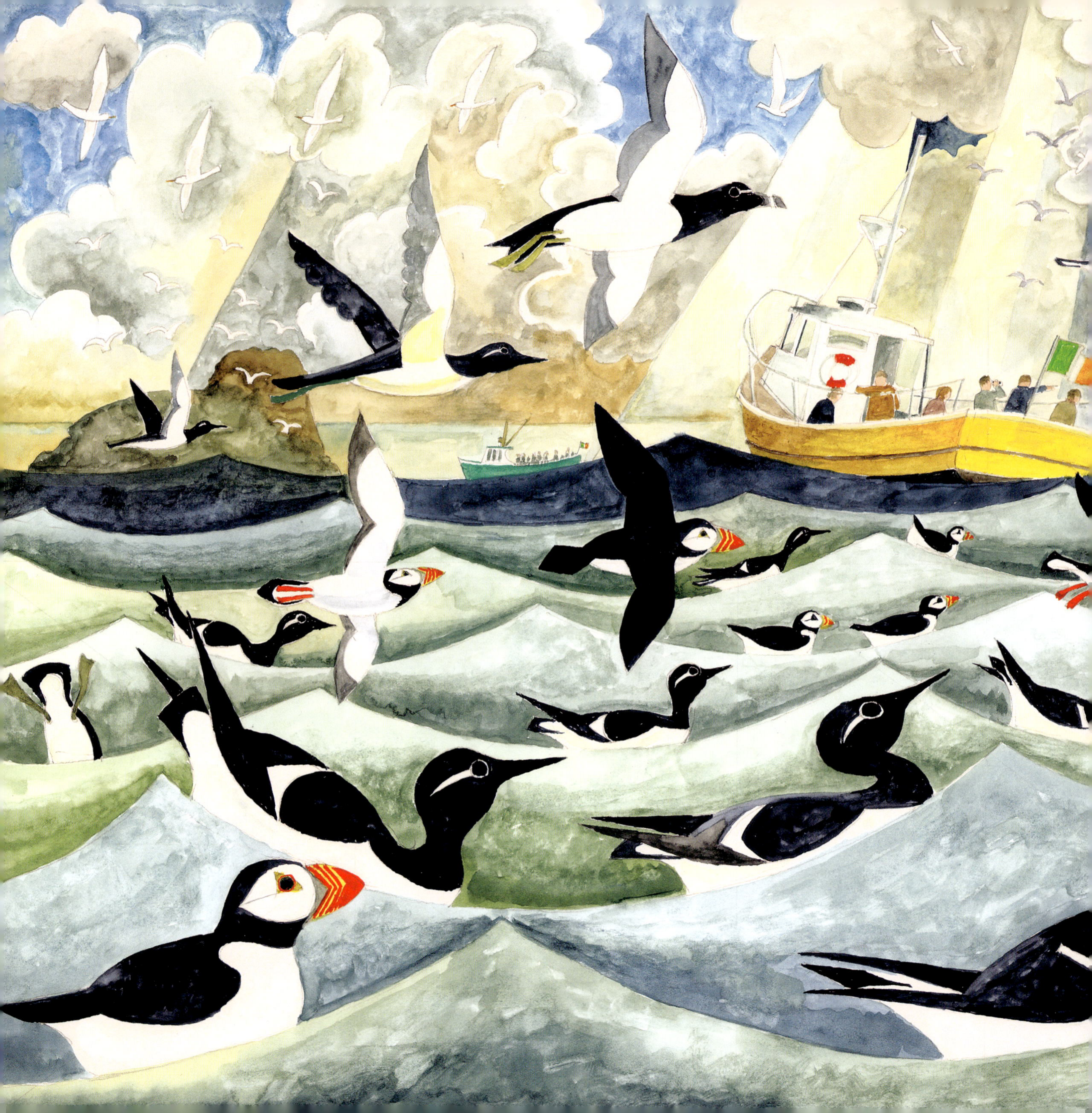

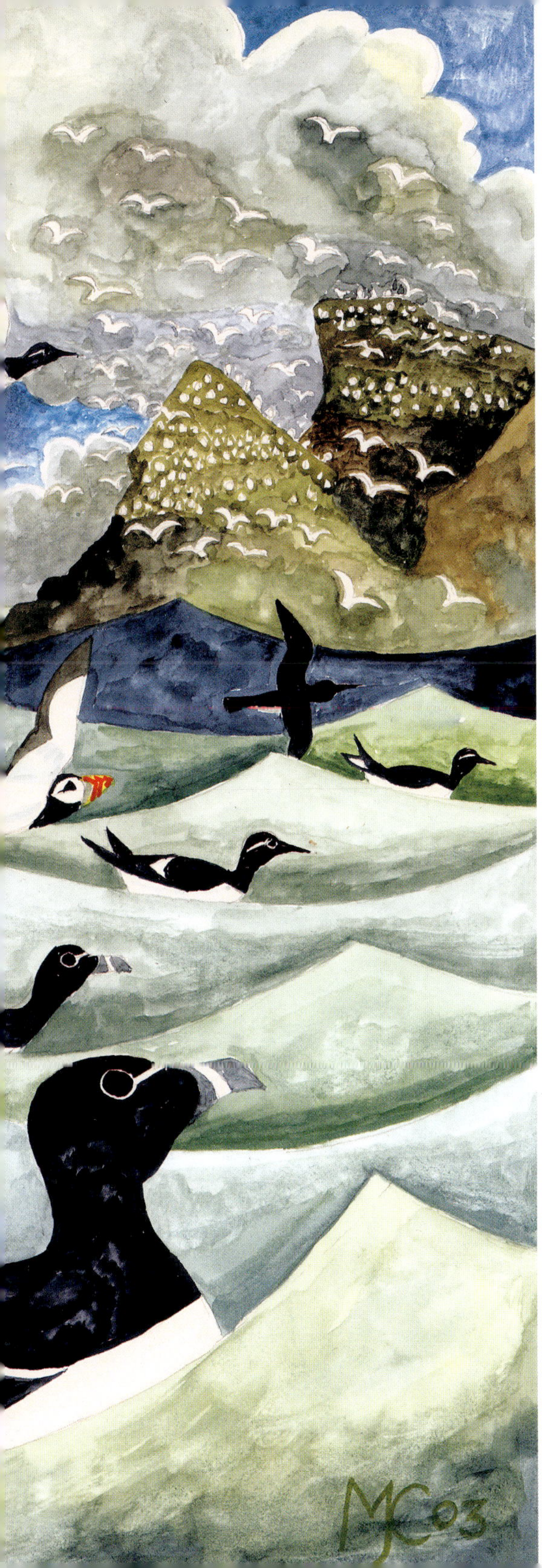

'Auks a fishing' (2003) "Wildlife off the coast of Ireland is plentiful." As evidence, the artist here captures Puffins, Razorbills and Guillemots enjoying the choppy sea before taking food back to their nests onshore.

'The Harbour Ferry, Weymouth' (1991)

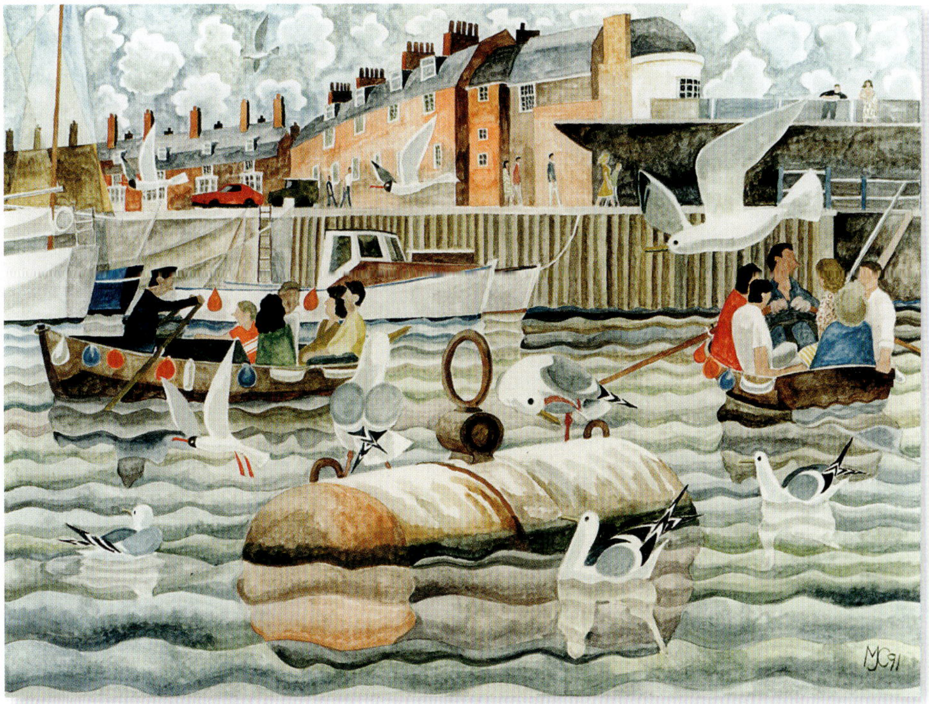

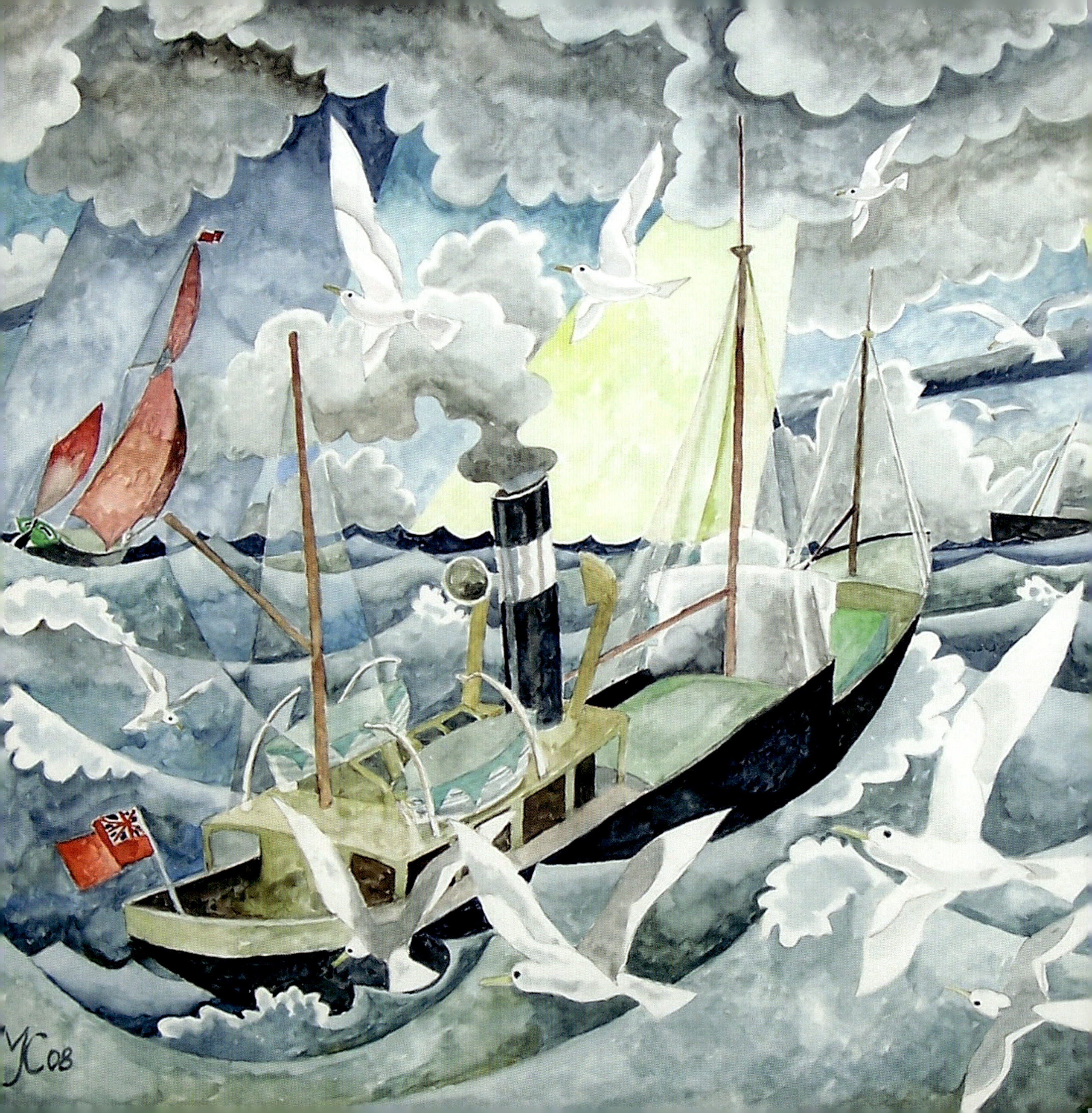

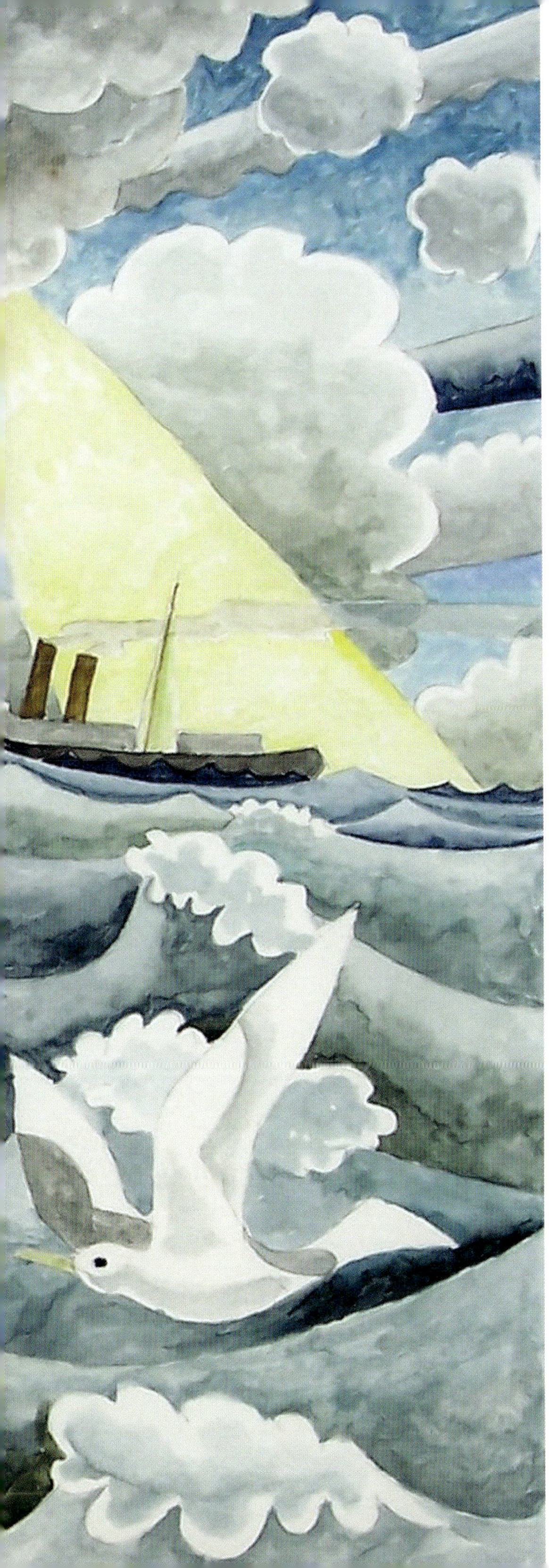

'Mad March Days' (2008)
An illustration of the last verse from the poem 'Cargoes'

Dirty British coaster with a salt-caked smoke stack
Butting through the Channel in the mad March days,
With a cargo of Tyne coal,
Road-rail, pig-lead,
Firewood, iron-ware, and cheap tin trays.

John Masefield (1878-1967)

'West Bay, Dorset' (1991)

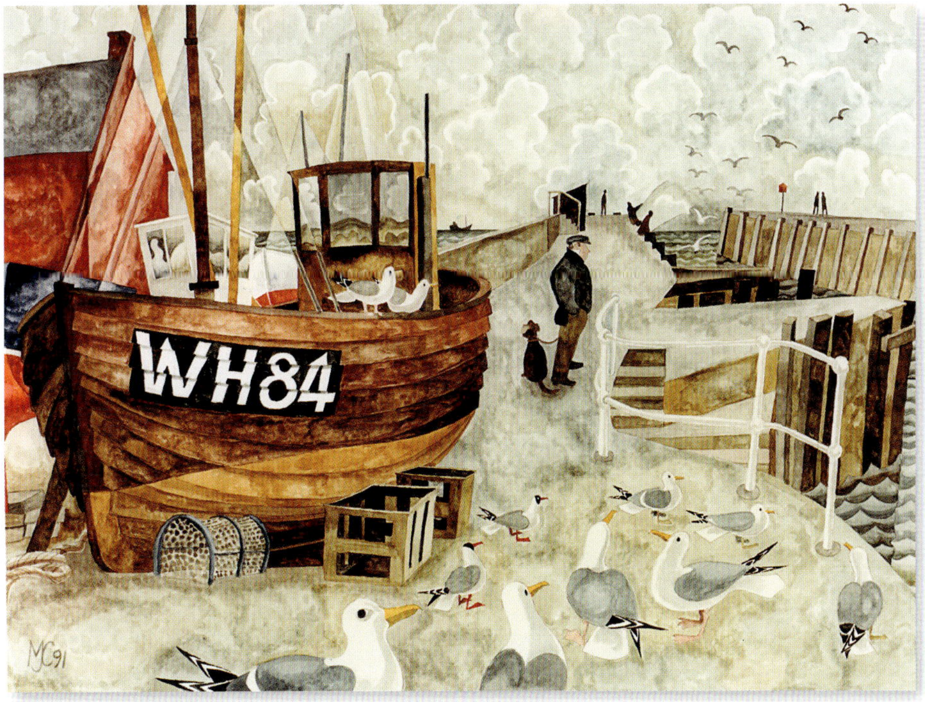

'Tugboats' (2003) "Fowey, Cornwall. A motor boat trip up the river." Located on the River Fowey in south Cornwall, the small town has boasted a natural harbour since the 13th century. River and foot ferry services cross the river to Bodinnick and Polruan. Pleasure boats depart regularly from the Town Quay steps. Cruises take visitors upriver past the docks, where china clay ships are still loaded. Fowey's most famous resident was author Daphne du Maurier.

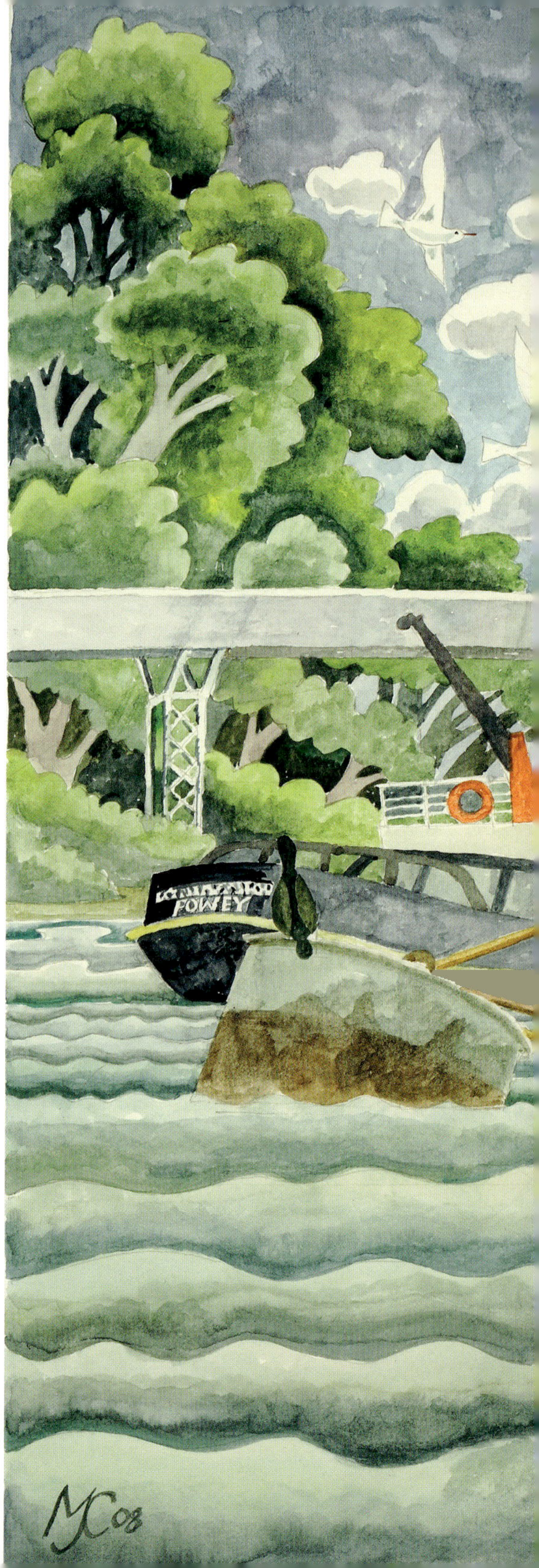

'Indefinitely at Wareham' (2001) "Indefinitely sounded a nice title, so I painted it!"

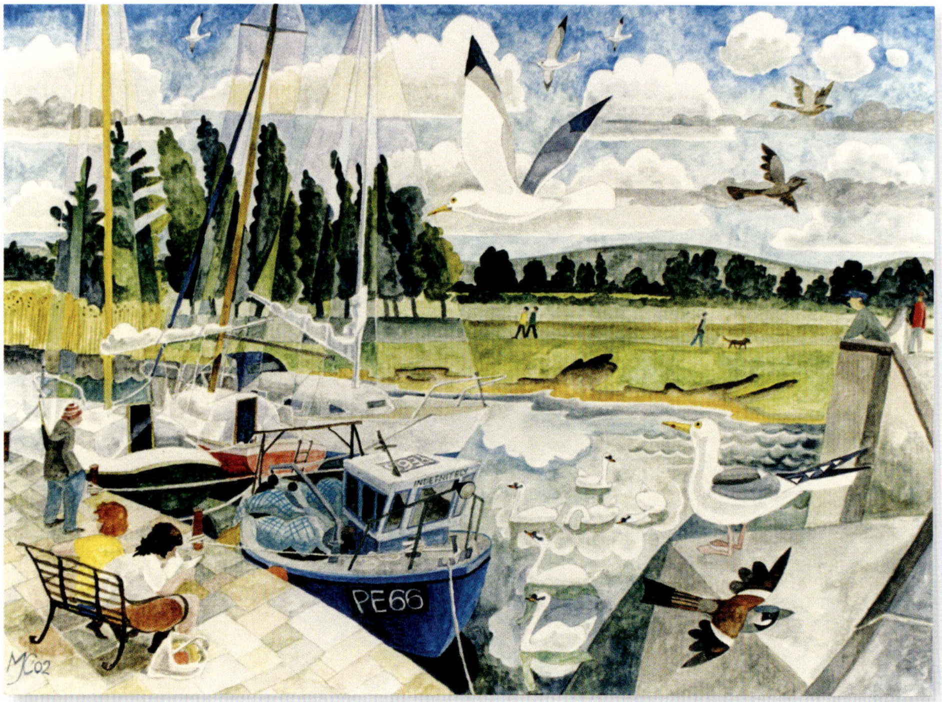

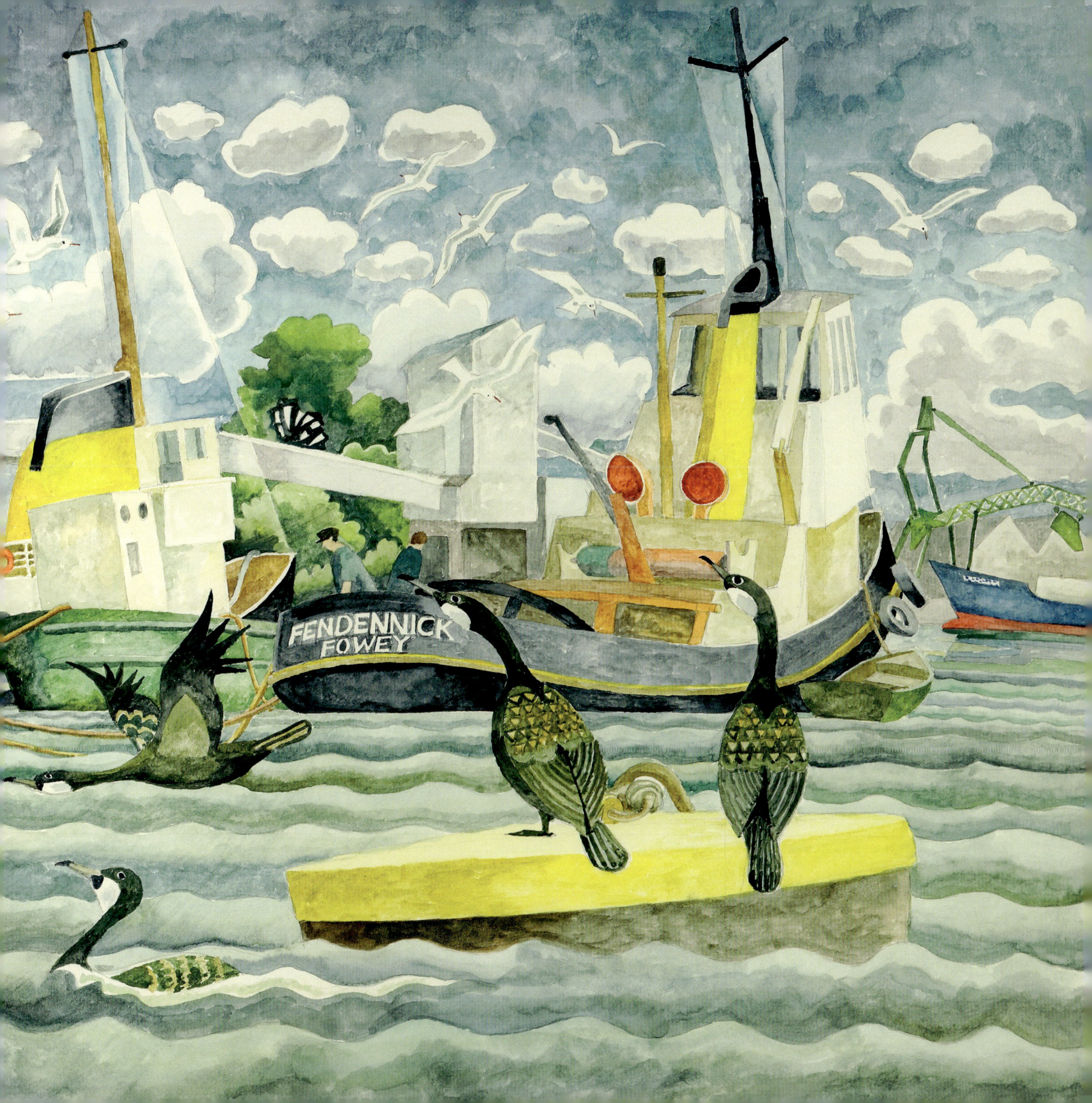
FENDENNICK
FOWEY

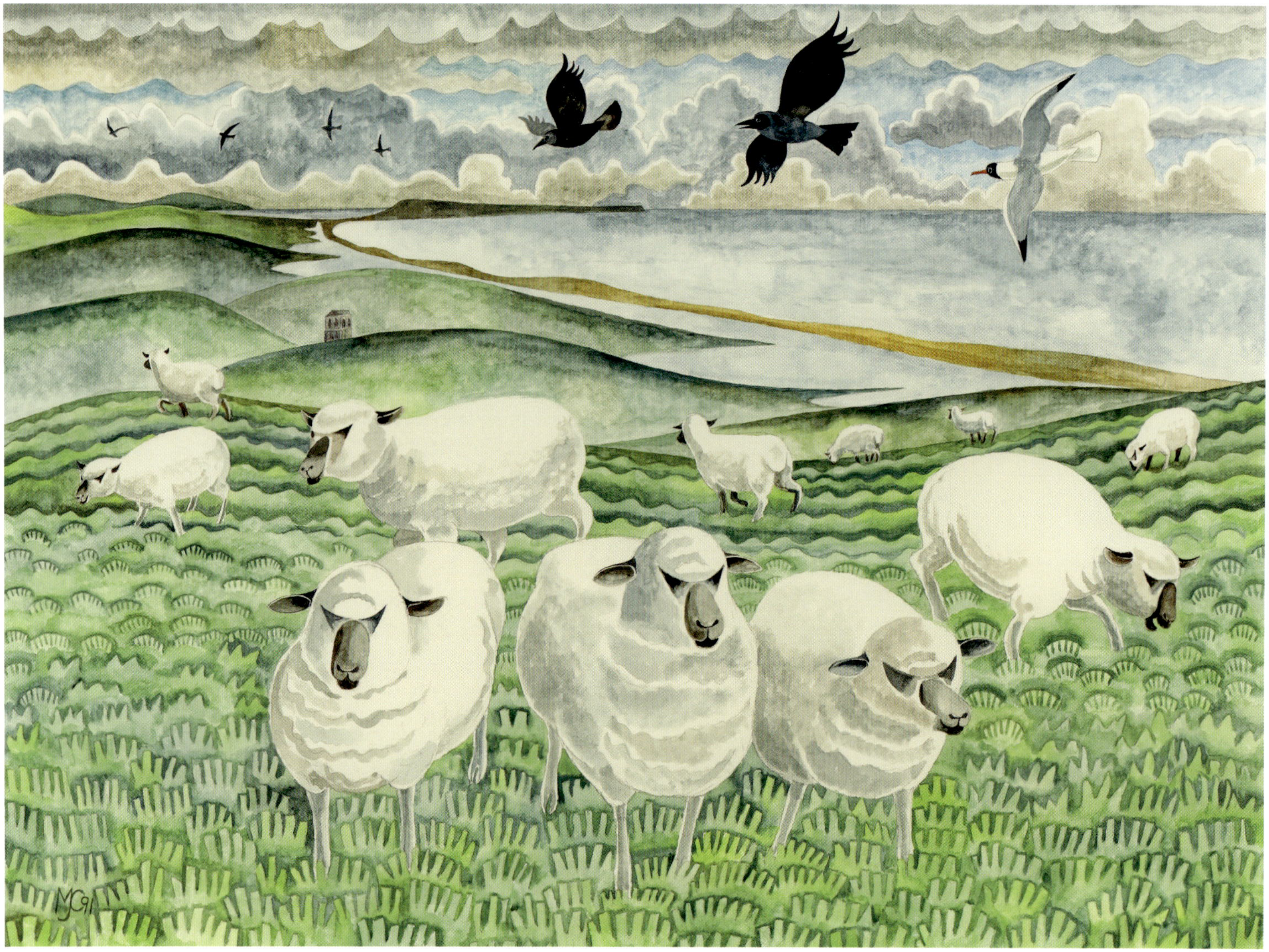

'Dorset Downs' (1991) "A painting produced for the 'Along the Dorset Coast' exhibition at the Peter Hedley Gallery in Wareham."

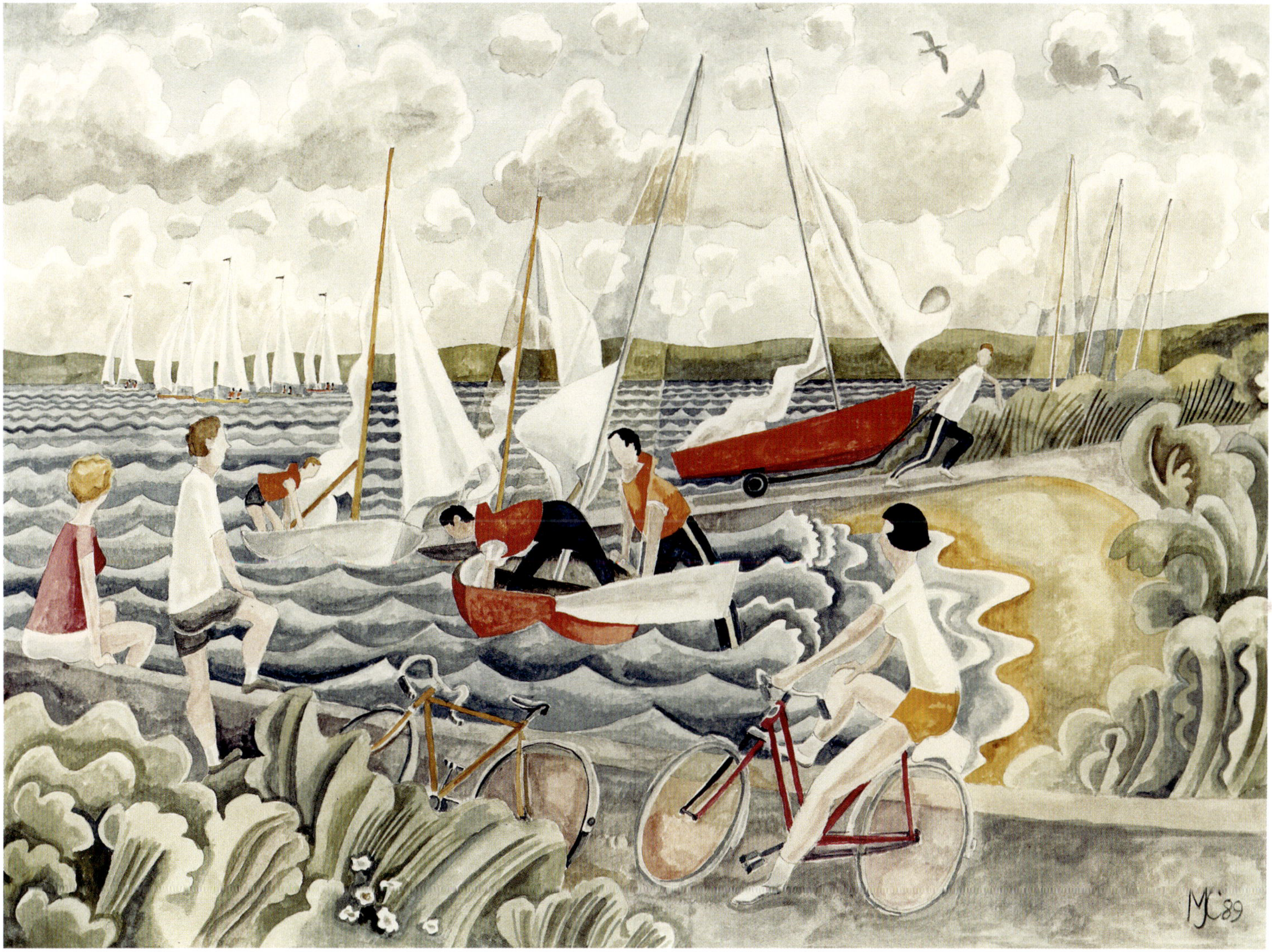

'Cyclists and Sailors' (1989) "An August holiday weekend. Girls watching the boys. A combination of Dorset sights and scenes."

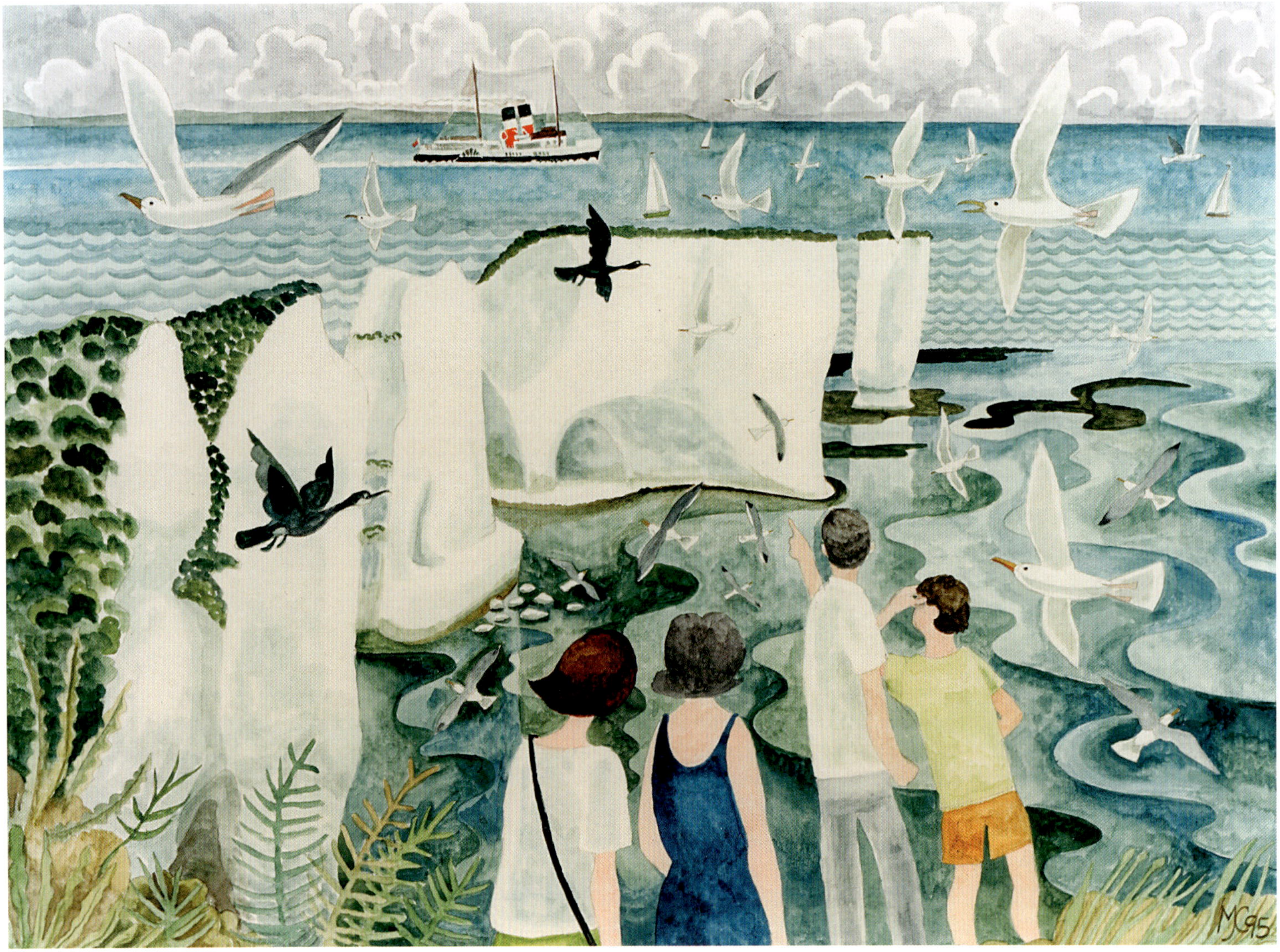

'PS Waverley Passing Old Harry Rocks' (1995) The Waverley is the last seagoing passenger-carrying paddle steamer in the world. Built in 1946, she sailed from Craigendoran on the Firth of Clyde to Arrochar on Loch Long until 1973. Bought by the Paddle Steamer Preservation Society (PSPS), she was restored to her 1947 appearance and began operating passenger excursions around the British coast. Old Harry Rocks are three chalk formations, including a stack and a stump, located at Handfast Point, on the Isle of Purbeck in Dorset. They mark the most easterly point of the Jurassic Coast.

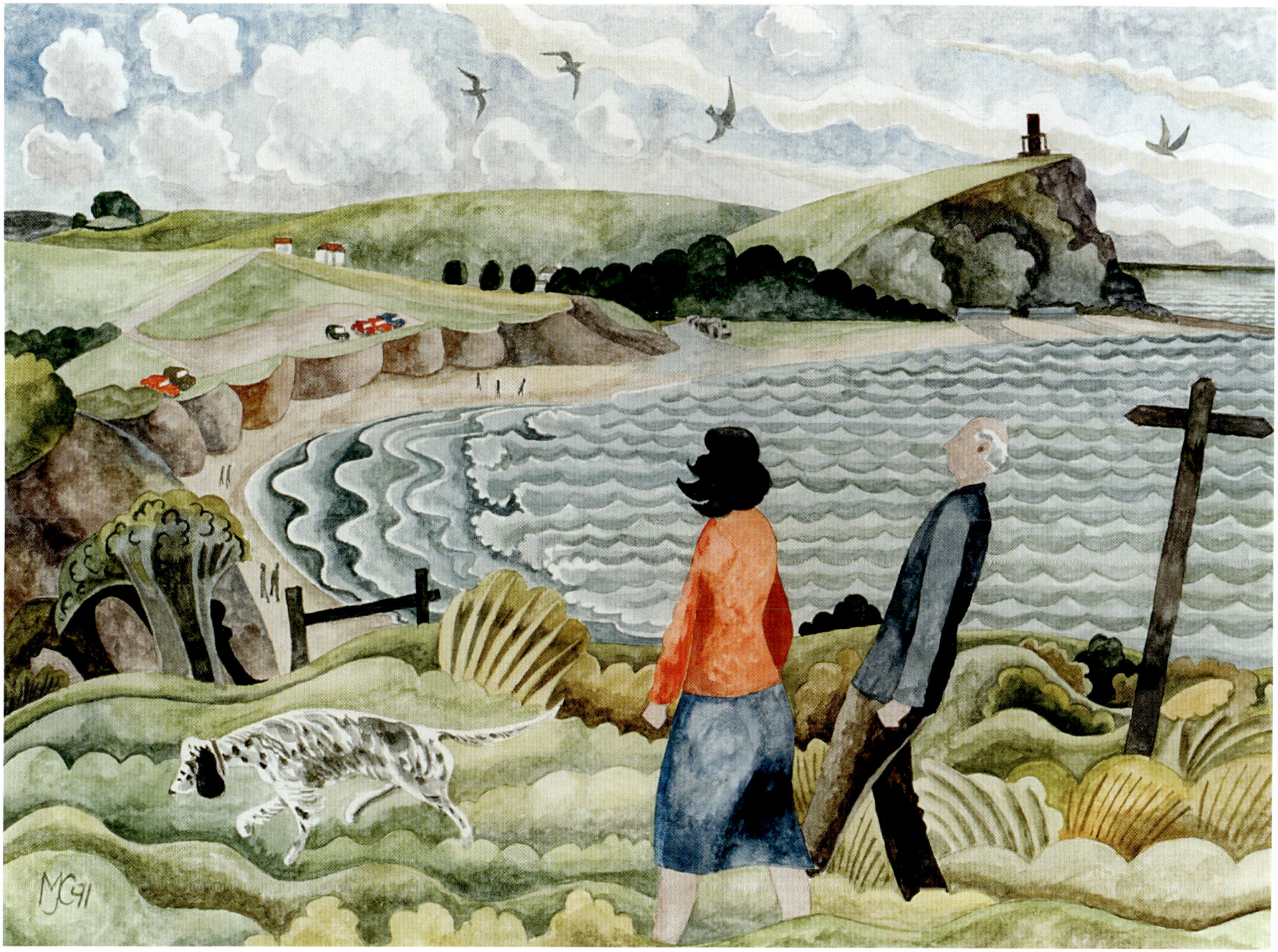

'Kimmeridge Bay' (1991) "The couple walking on the cliff are dear friends who owned the Peter Hedley Gallery in Wareham. I exhibited there for many years. Peter saw my work in the Royal Academy Summer Show in 1986 and invited me to put on a one-man show at his gallery in August 1987. This went on to become a very happy relationship. There followed several one-man shows. I was frequently invited to Dorset, often staying with Peter and his wife Jenny while I researched pictures for these exhibitions."

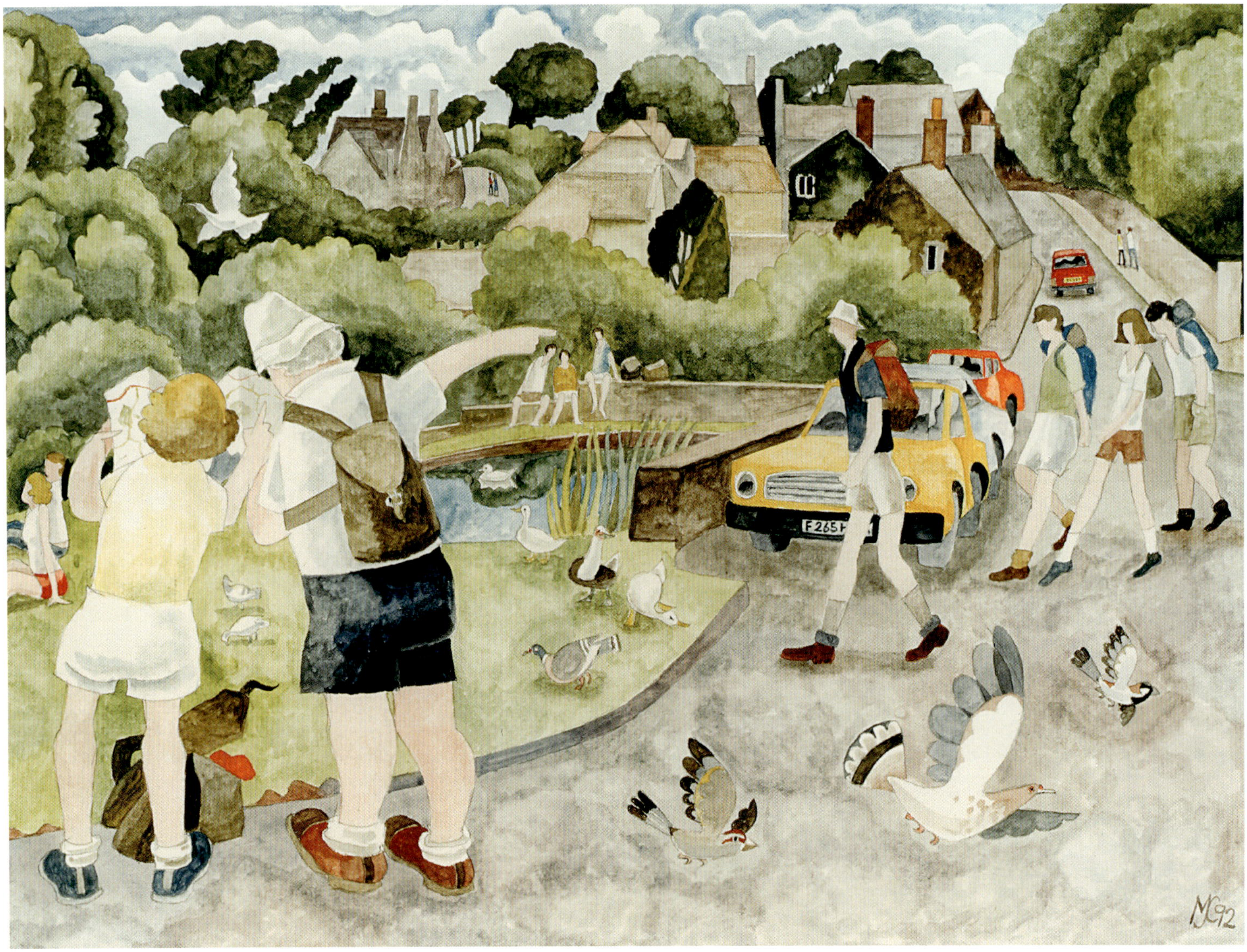

'Walkers in Worth Matravers' (1992) Worth Matravers is a village in Dorset, situated on the cliffs west of Swanage that once were the site of a Chain Home radar station during World War II and instrumental in the development of radar. "An interesting historical village famous for smuggling and caves. Purbeck stone is quarried near here. The East Indiaman 'Halsewell' was shipwrecked just offshore in 1786, inspiring Charles Dickens to write a short story about it."

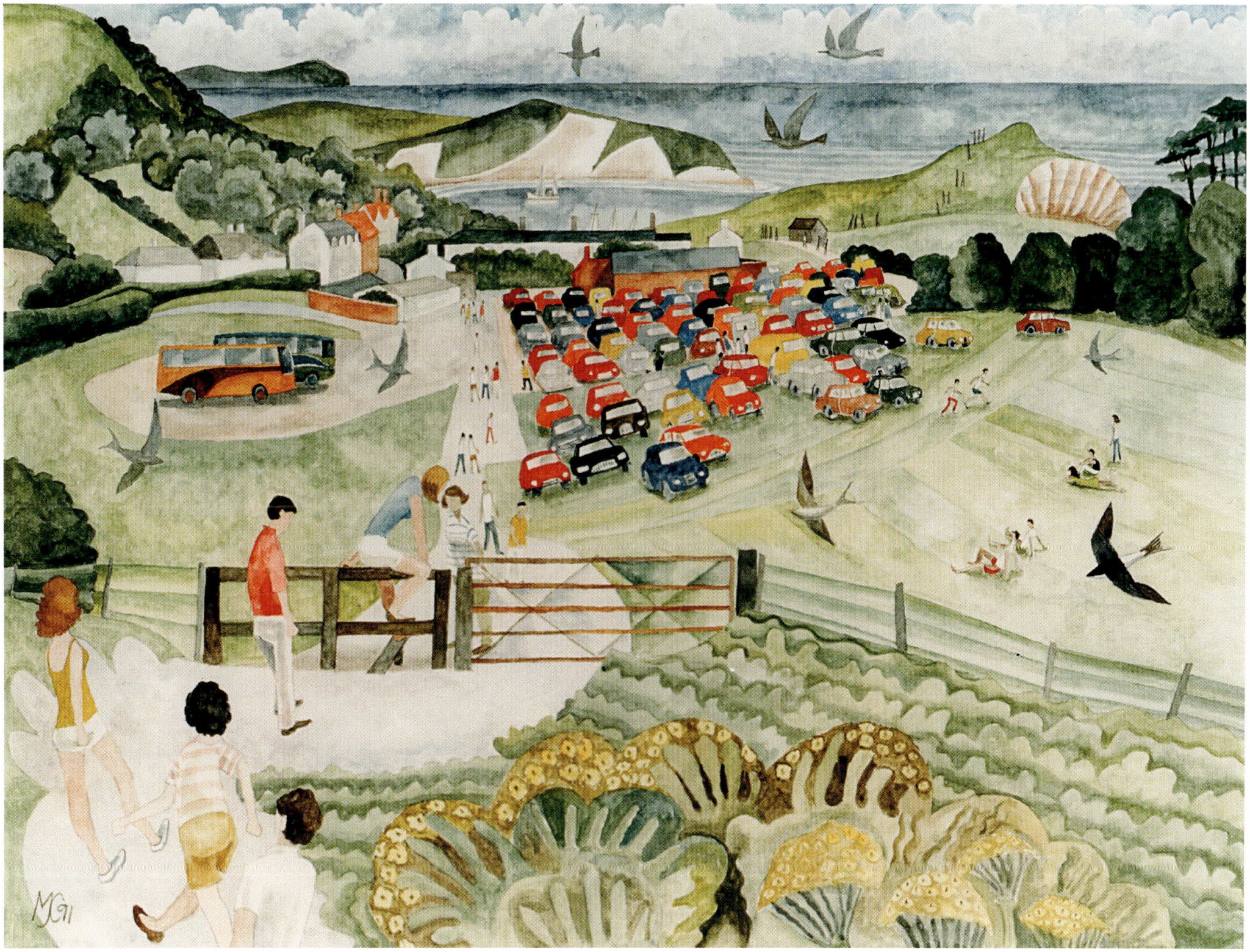

'Lulworth Cove, Dorset' (1991) Lulworth Cove is near the village of West Lulworth on the Jurassic Coast. This unusual geological feature is one of the world's finest examples of such a landform. It is located close to the rock arch of Durdle Door, and to the east there is a fossilised forest. Lulworth is also near Kimmeridge, famous for its rocky shore and fossils. The artist included the packed car park that is typical of the site, although not many coaches were in that day!

'Lyme Regis' (1991) Previewed earlier in this section, Michael's painting shows the sea wall known as The Cobb that was a feature of Jane Austen's 'Persuasion' as well as of the John Fowles novel 'The French Lieutenant's Woman'.

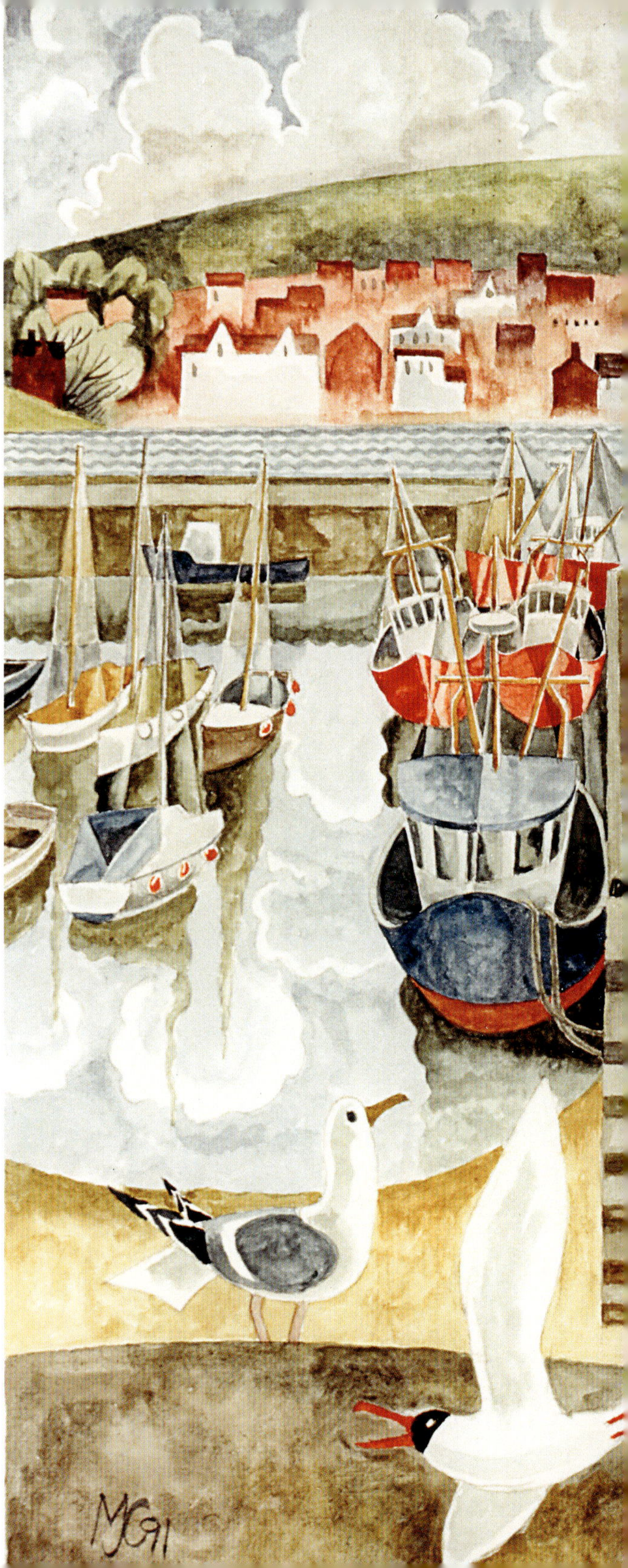

'The Swanage Railway' (1992)

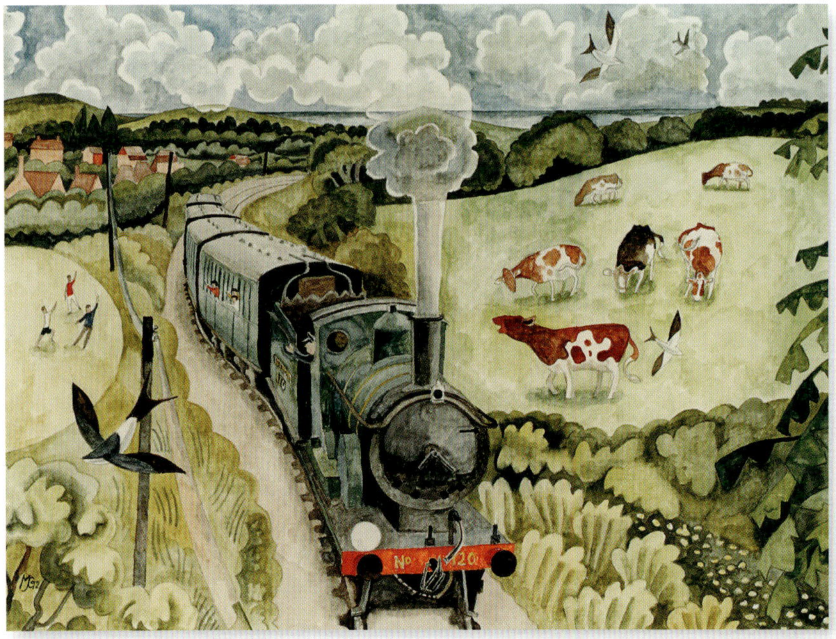

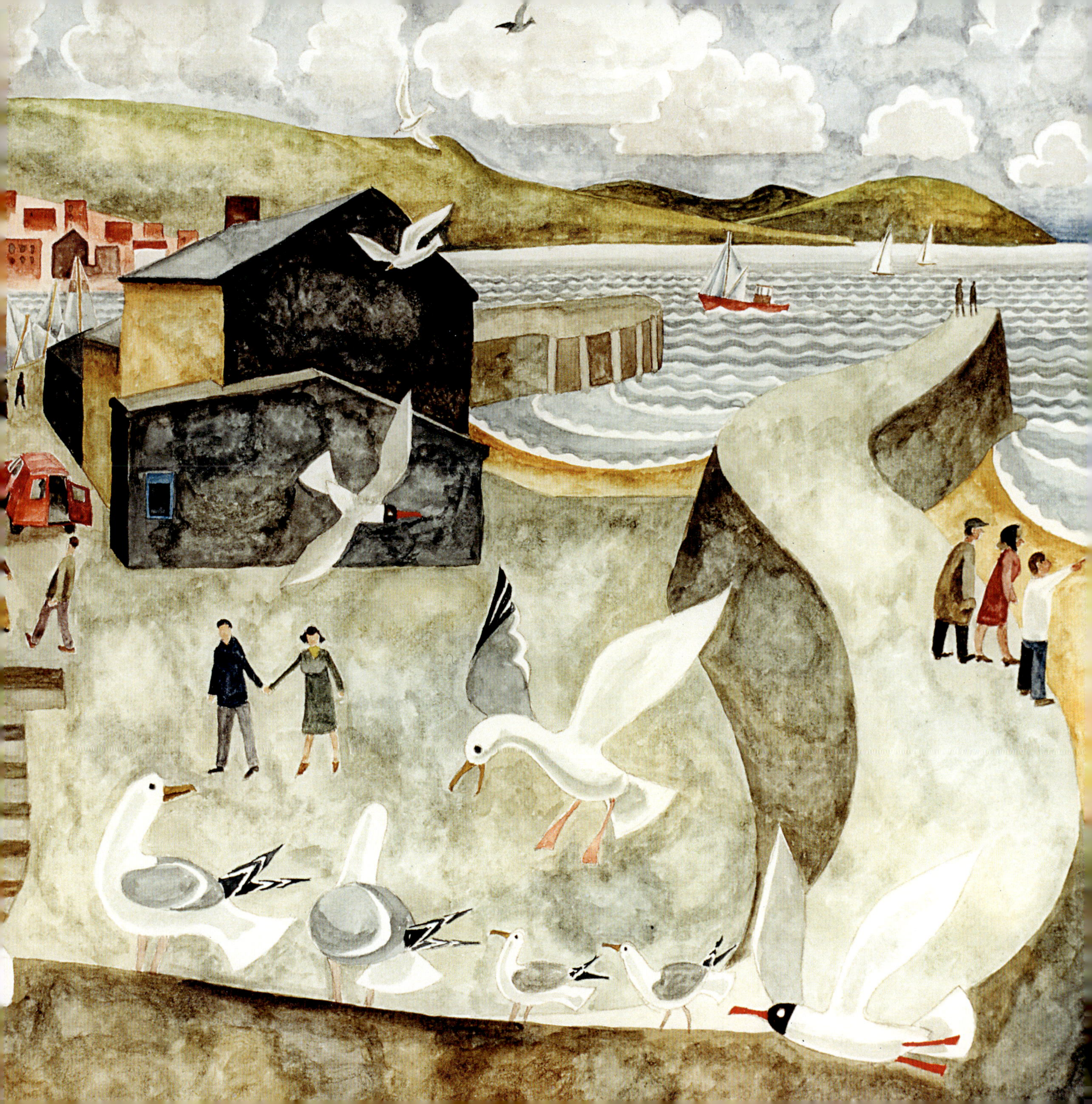

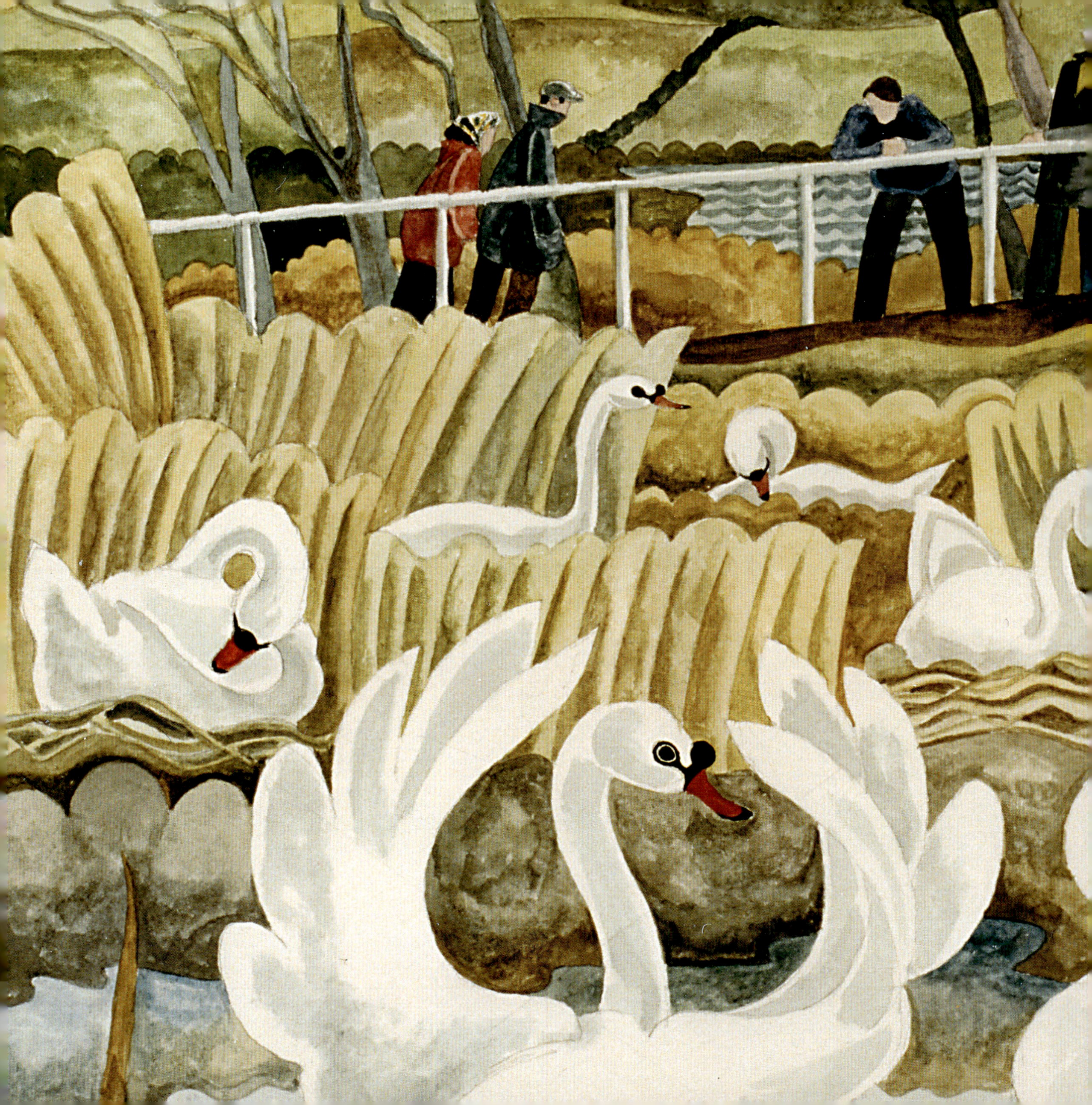

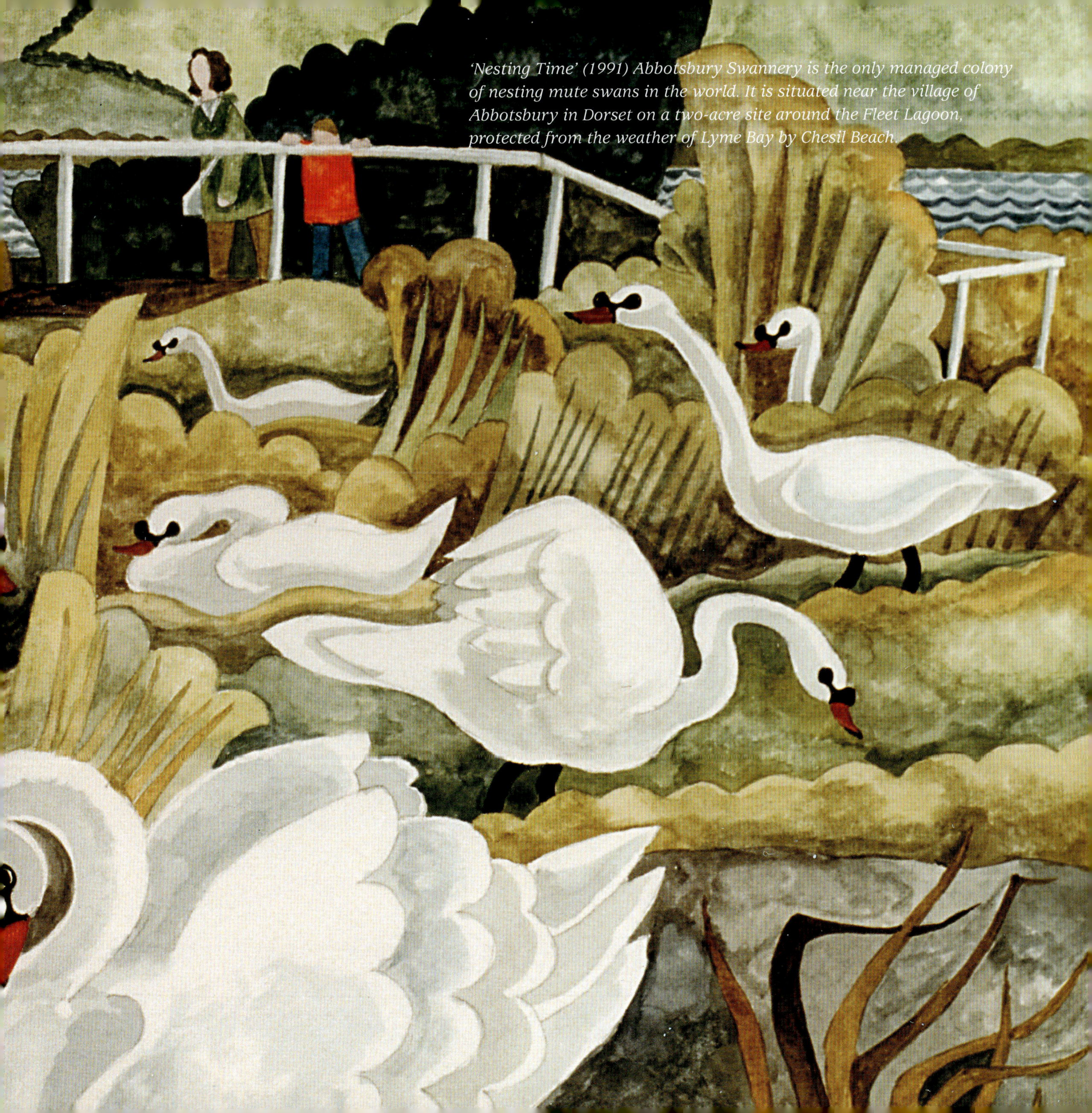

'Nesting Time' (1991) Abbotsbury Swannery is the only managed colony of nesting mute swans in the world. It is situated near the village of Abbotsbury in Dorset on a two-acre site around the Fleet Lagoon, protected from the weather of Lyme Bay by Chesil Beach.

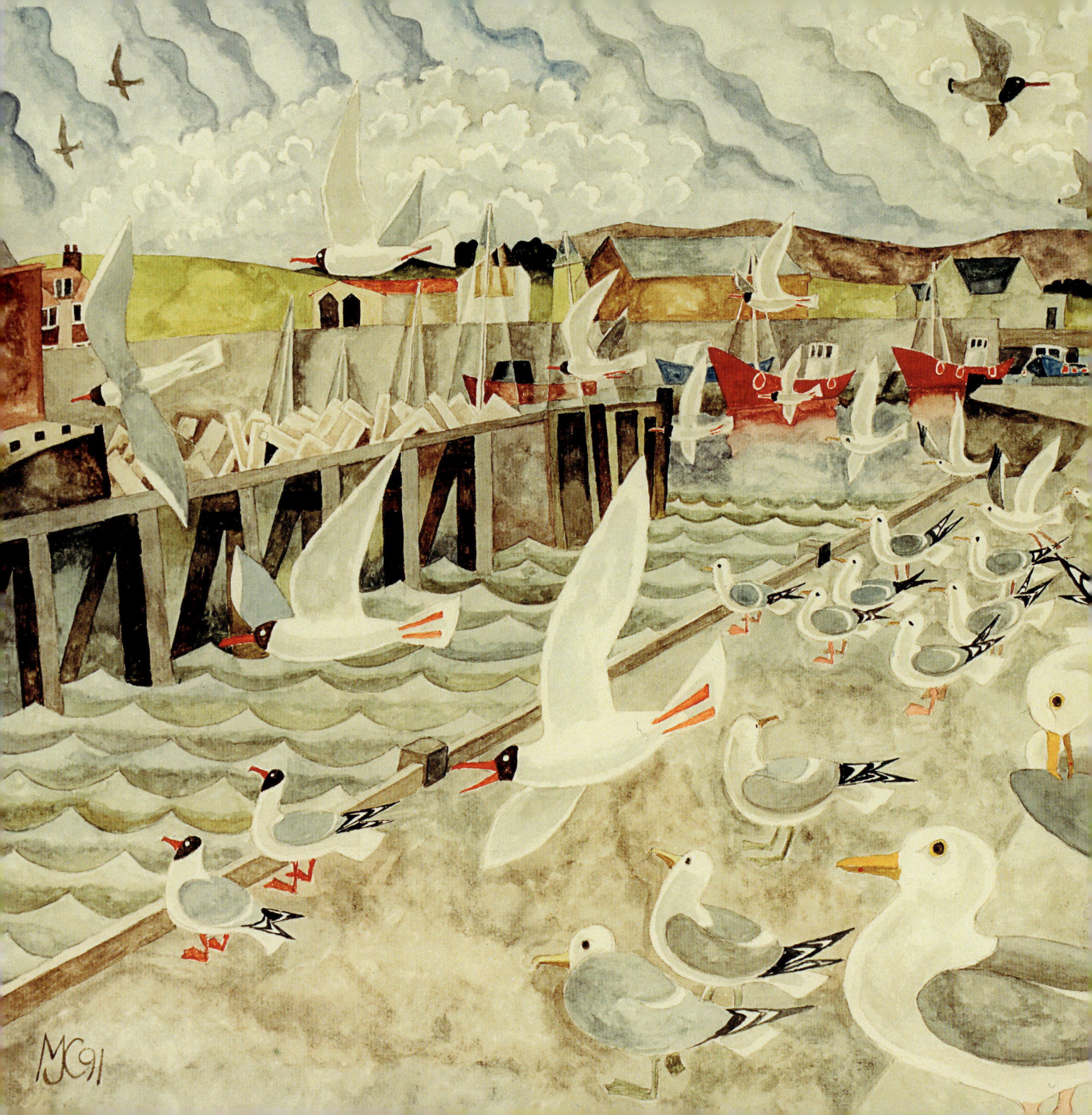
MJC91

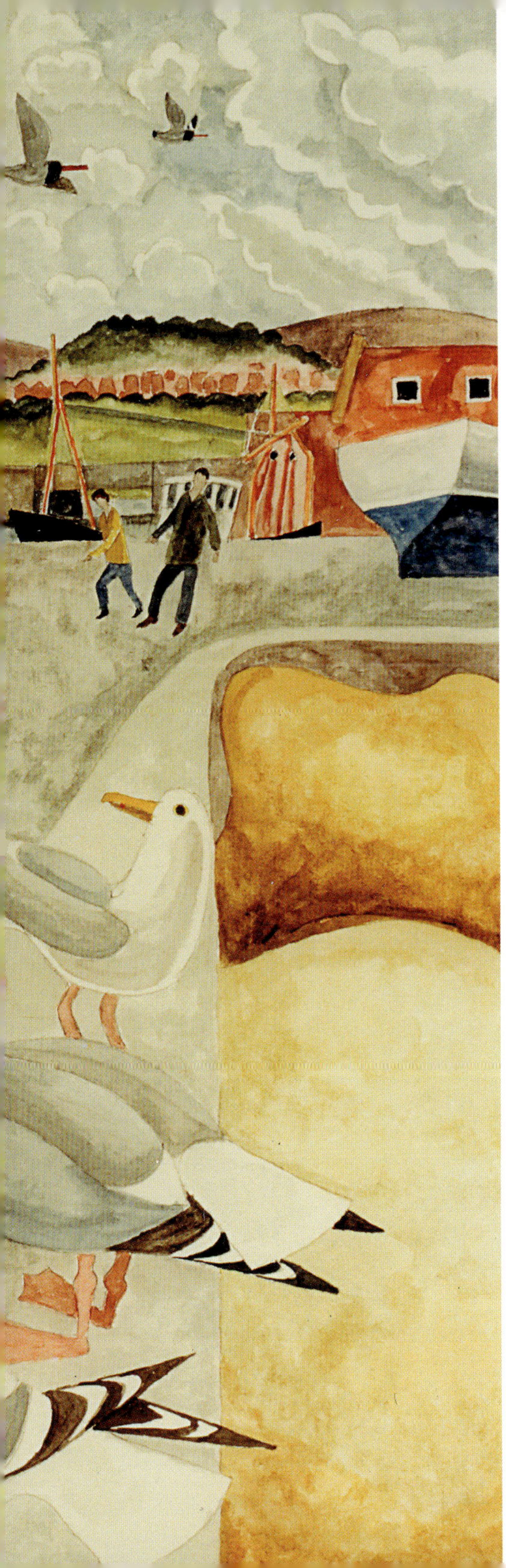

'West Bay' (1991) Also known as Bridport Harbour, this is a small Dorset coastal settlement sited at the mouth of the River Brit approximately 2.4km south of Bridport. The harbour at West Bay is not a natural landscape feature and it has a long history of having been silted up, blocked by shingle and damaged by storms. On each occasion, repairs, improvements and enlargements have been made. The harbour has been moved twice. It was originally 1.6km inland, then was moved to the coast beside the East Cliff. A later move saw it shift 270 metres to its current position.

'Coastal Path' (1992)

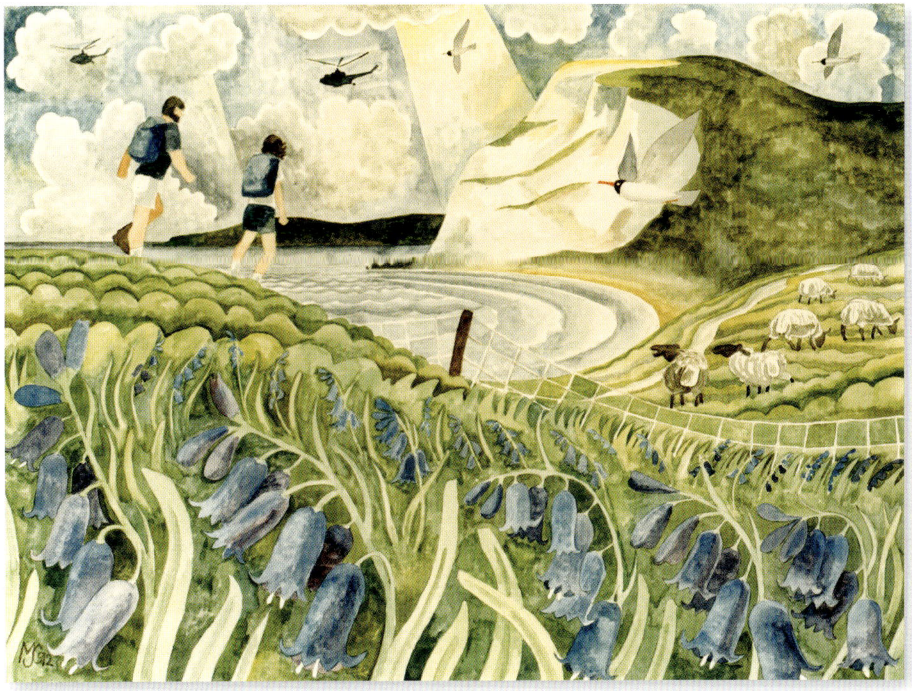

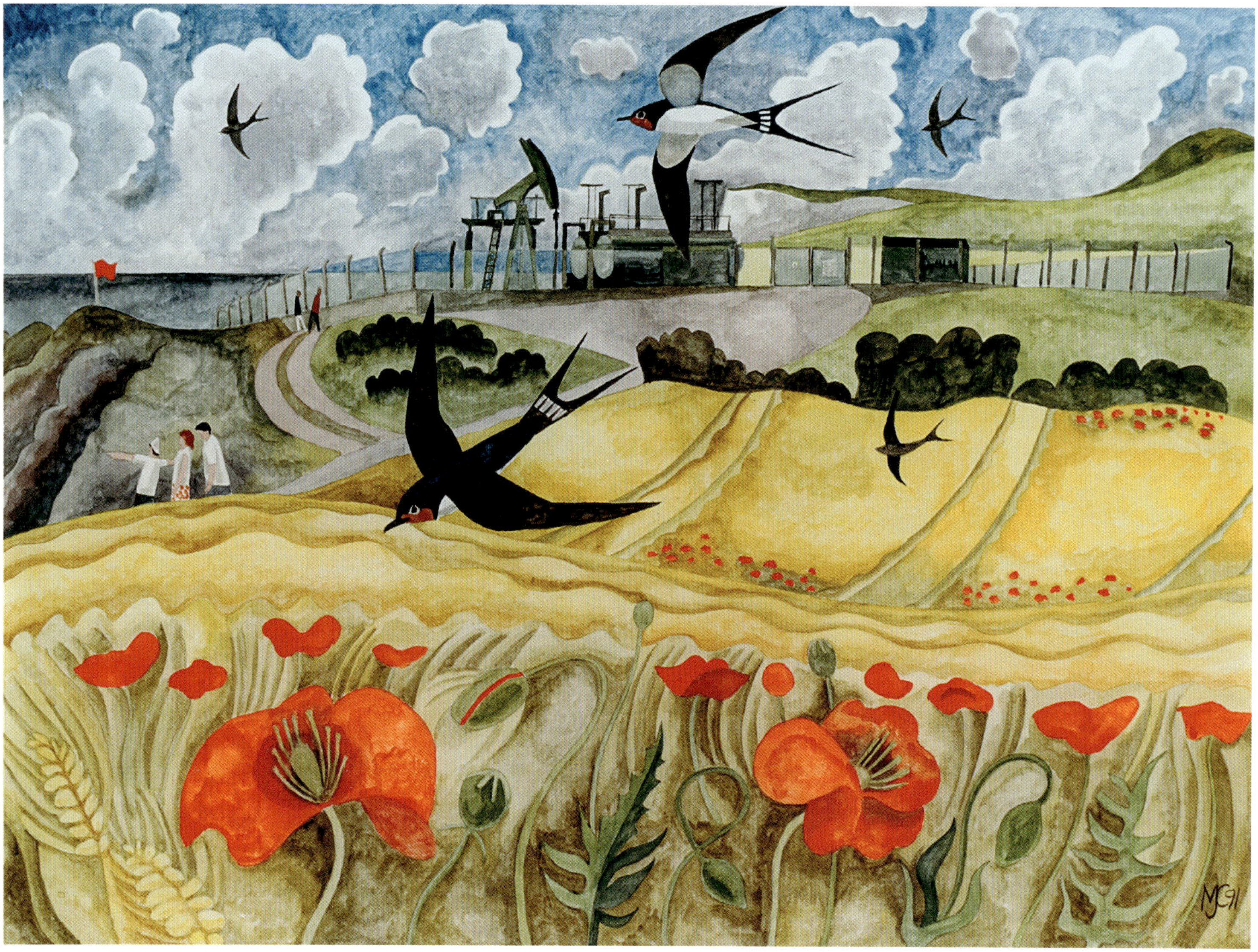

'Nodding Donkey, Kimmeridge Bay' (1991) These two facing pictures are linked by oil, a seam of which runs under parts of mainland Dorset, Poole Harbour and its islands. Kimmeridge Bay forms part of the Jurassic Coast. Kimmeridge is the type locality for Kimmeridge clay, the geological formation that covers most of the area. An oil well (known as a nodding donkey) has operated on the shore of Kimmeridge Bay since 1959 – making it the oldest in Britain.

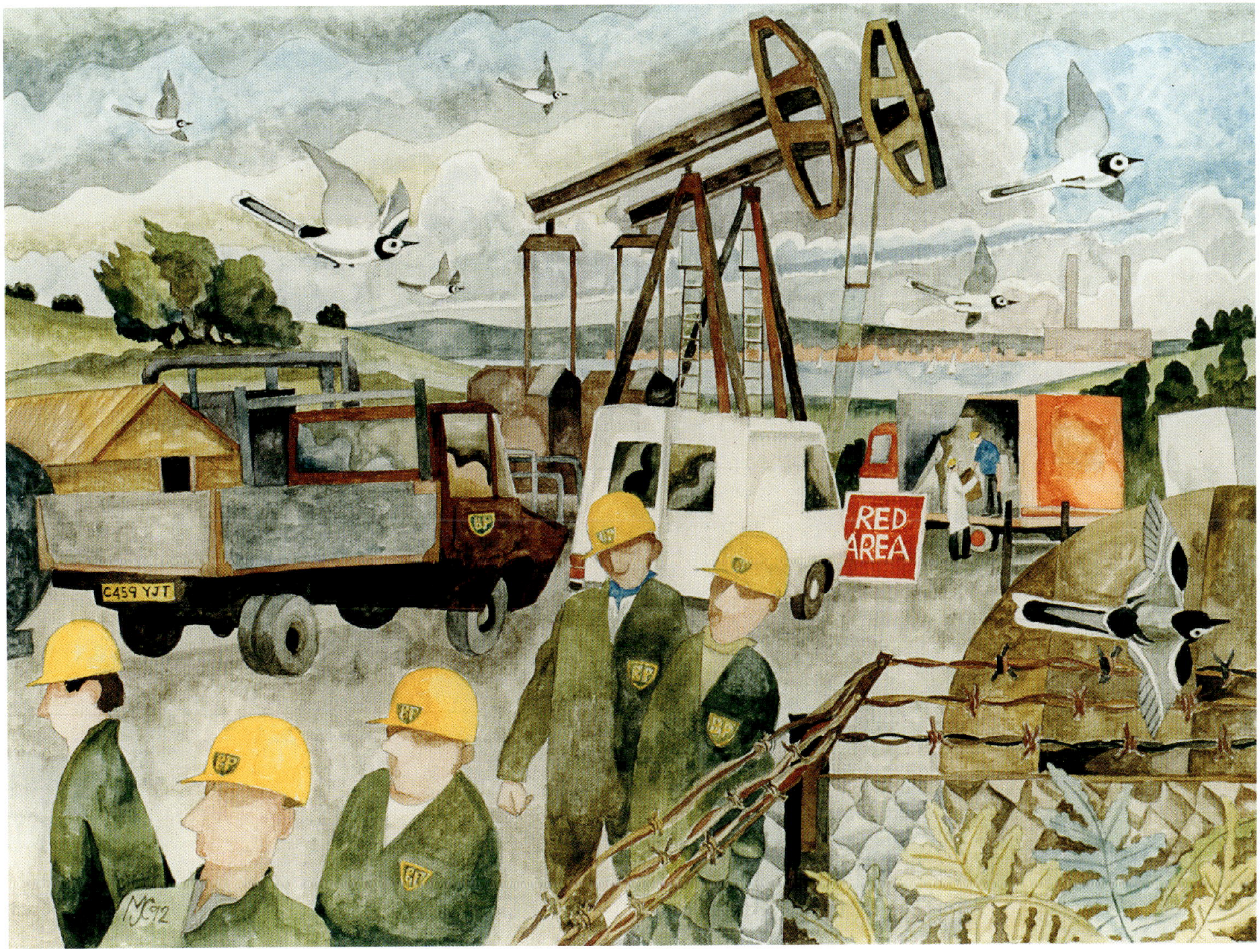

'On Wytch Heath' (1992) Wytch Farm in Dorset has long been the UK's biggest producing onshore oil field (with peak output of 110,000 barrels per day) and represented a technological challenge for the UK energy industry, thanks to the beautiful and fragile environment. The field extends out under Poole Harbour, and there are numerous drilling and production sites that are managed carefully to avoid uncecessary wildlife and landscape disruption.

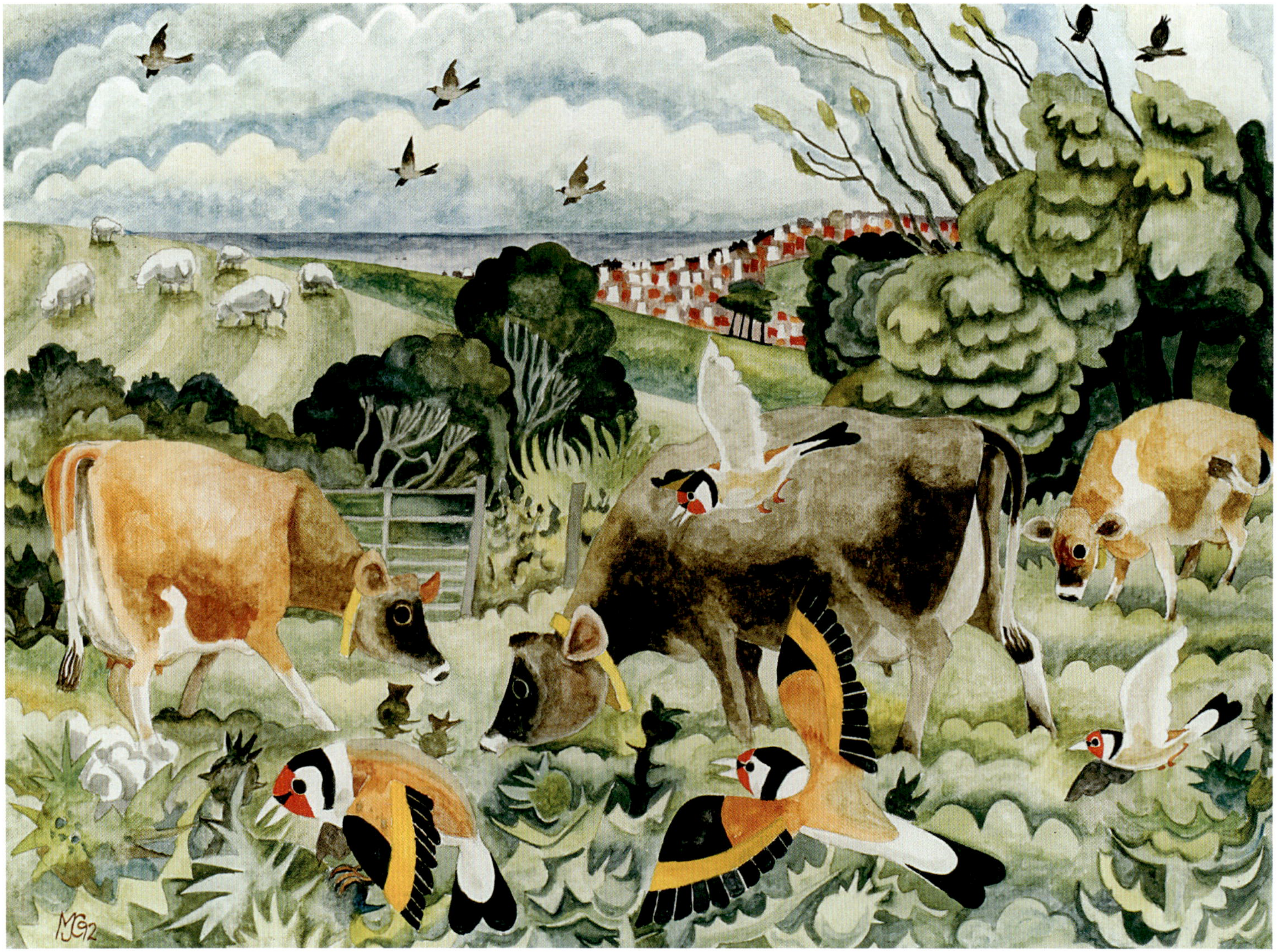

'On Knitson Farm' (1992) Knitson Farm is nowadays a campsite designed especially for modern self-contained touring caravans, tents and motor homes, with pitches over four acres of a busy working farm midway between Swanage and Corfe Castle. Footpaths and bridleways extend outwards from the farm, making it popular with walkers, while the Swanage steam railway is a short walk down the road. Visiting dogs have to negotiate the herds of cattle and flocks of sheep that live on the farm year round, enjoying spectacular views out to sea.

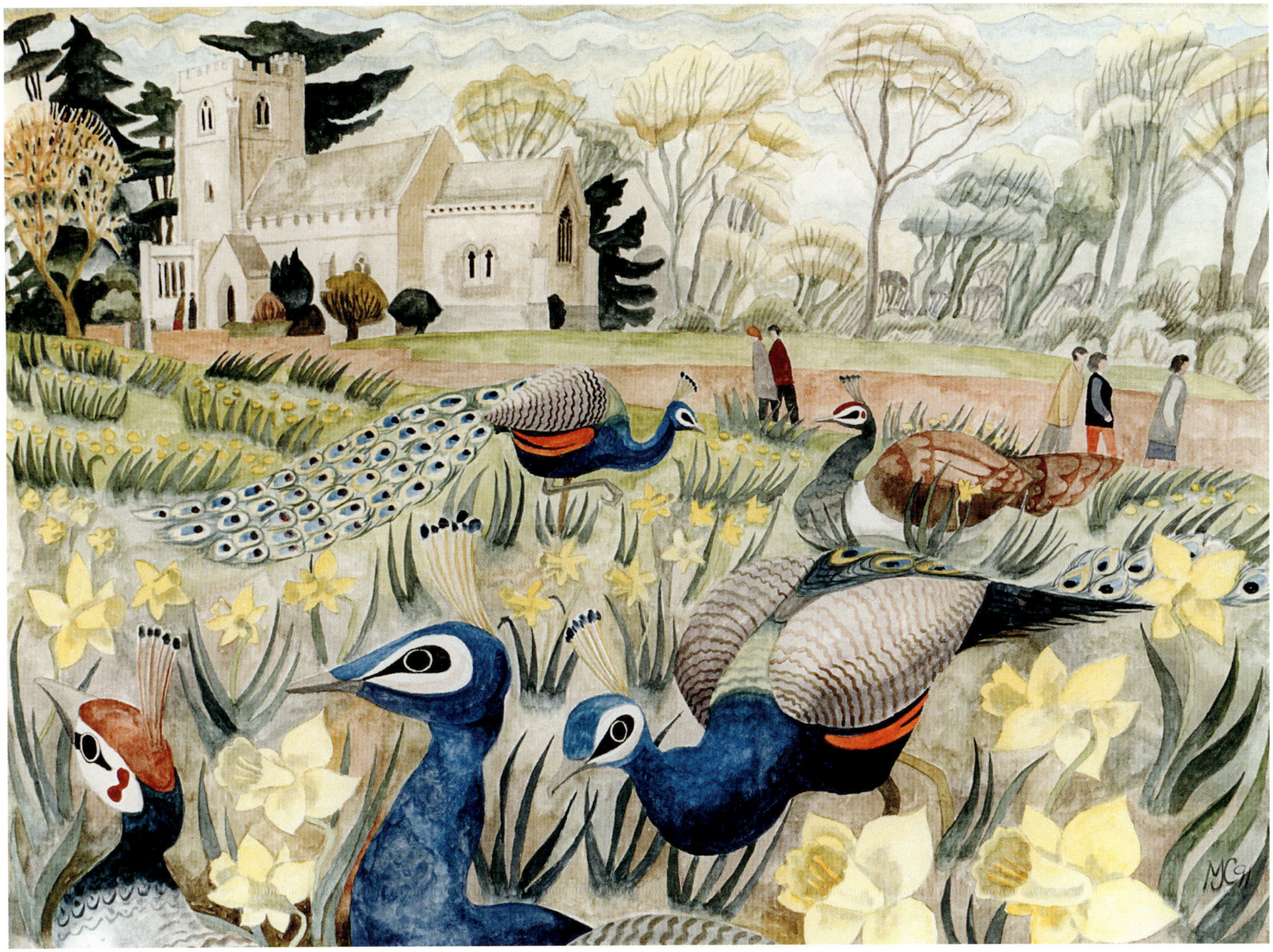

'Peacocks and Daffodils, Brownsea Island' (1991) Scouts, a castle, red squirrels and the John Lewis Partnership are long associated with this small island in Poole Harbour, which also boasts a population of peafowl and exotic species of pheasant. Red squirrels thrive and charm the tourists arriving by boat, or those staying at the castle – leased from The National Trust and managed as a hotel by John Lewis for its Partners. There are important wildlife sanctuaries on the island, and it has gone down in history as the first home of the Boy Scouts, founded in 1908 by Robert Baden-Powell.

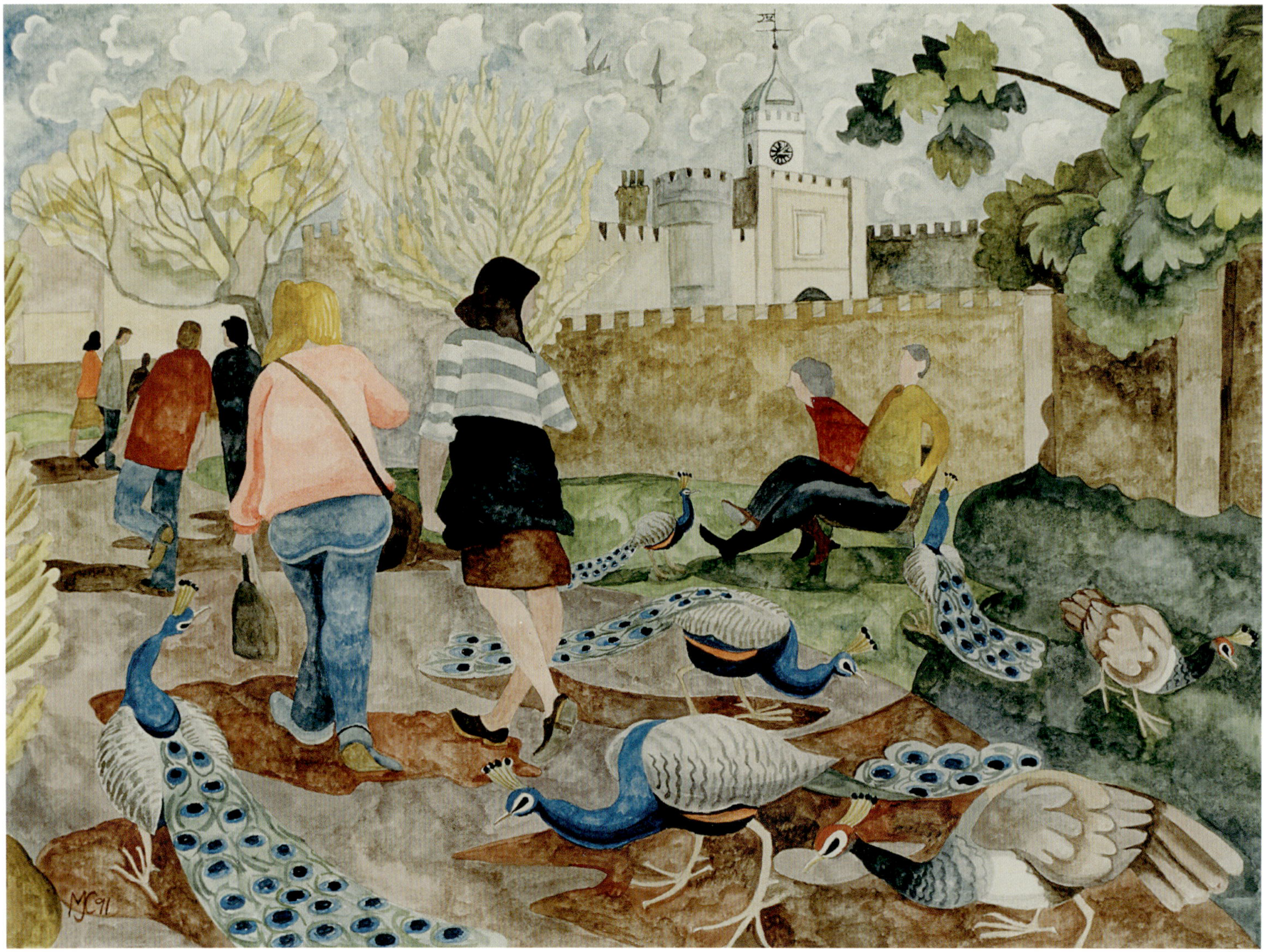

'People and Peacocks' (1991) Brownsea Island's nature reserve is leased from the National Trust by Dorset Wildlife Trust. This reserve includes a brackish lagoon and area of woodland. Other ecosystems on the island include saltmarsh, reedbed, two freshwater lakes, alder carr, coniferous woodland, deciduous woodland and arboretum. There is a small ornamental population of peacocks, and the island also has a heronry, in which both grey heron and little egret nest.

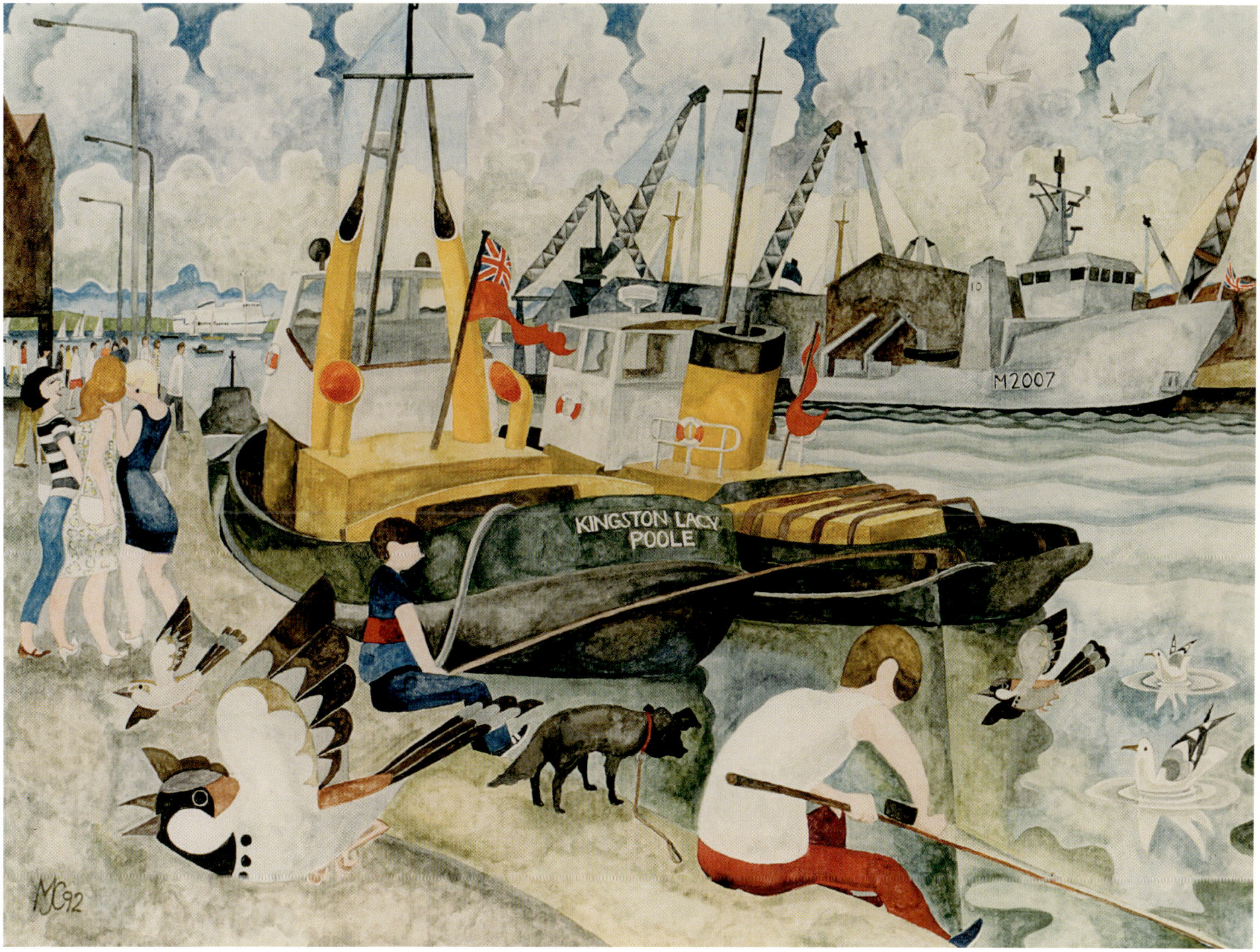

'Poole Quay' (1992) The quay at Poole has a very long history, being used for trade with the Roman Empire even before the Romans themselves arrived in AD43. The southern side of the quay is still dedicated to trade, and it is a lively port where coastal freighters are loaded and unloaded. High-cost luxury motor yachts are built, tested and sold here; while, on the quay, a statue of Robert Baden-Powell looks out towards Brownsea Island where he organised the first Scout camp.

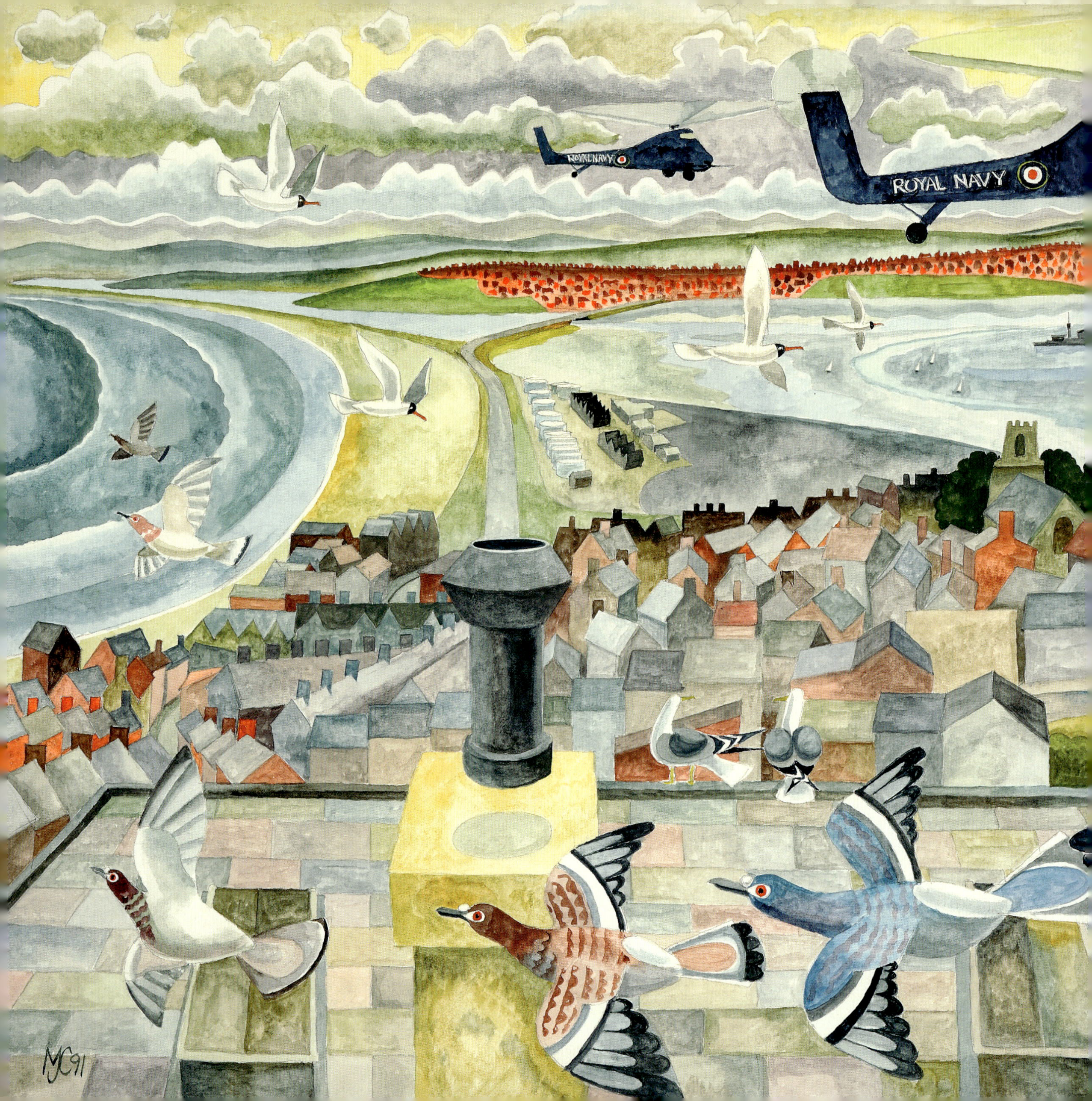
ROYAL NAVY
ROYAL NAVY
MJC91

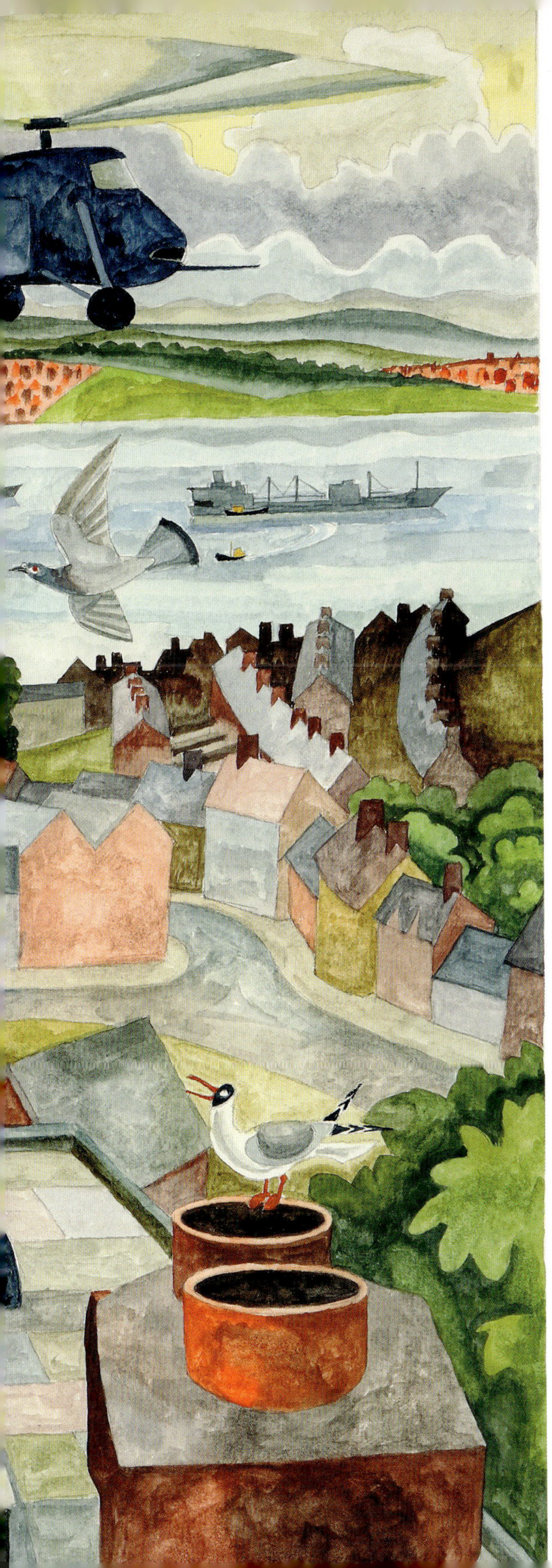

'Chesil Beach and Portland Harbour' (1991) One of three major shingle structures in Britain, Chesil Beach is 29km long, 200m wide and 15m high. The beach and The Fleet, a shallow tidal lagoon, are part of Dorset's Jurassic Coast. The beach curves sharply at the eastern end, near the village of Chiswell, and forms Chesil Cove against the cliffs of the Isle of Portland. This protects the low-lying village from flooding. Westwards, the shingle forms a straight line along the coast, enclosing The Fleet. Portland Harbour, when completed in 1872, became the largest manmade harbour in the world. It is protected naturally by Portland to the south, Chesil Beach to the west and mainland Dorset to the north. Portland Harbour was a Royal Navy base until 1995.

'Rowing Across the Harbour' (2008)

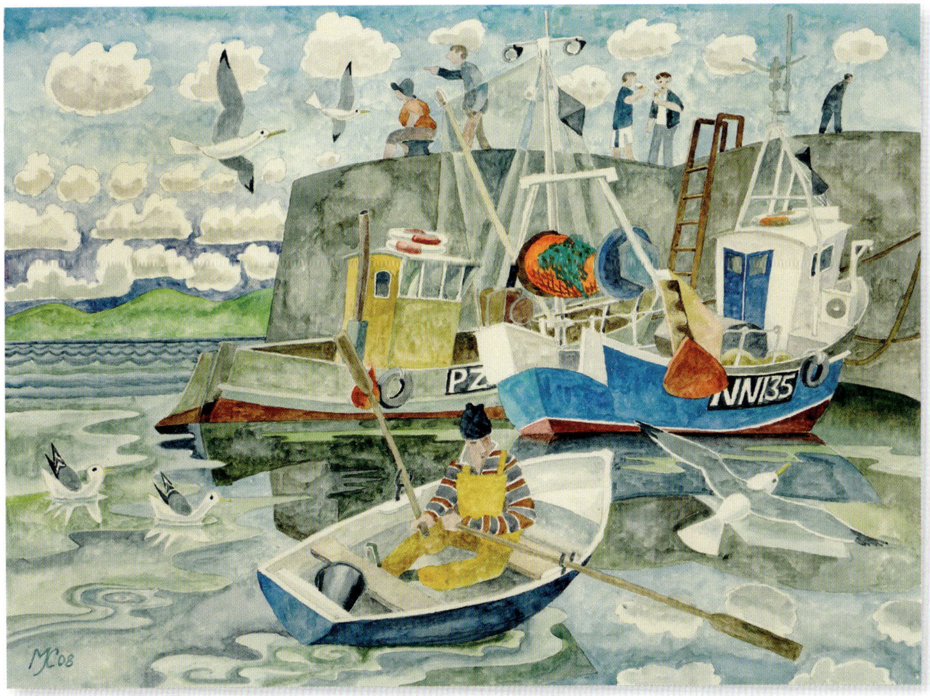

'Swan amongst the Daffodils' (1991) The Fleet lagoon provides an ideal environment for wildfowl. The Benedictine monastery of St Peter's was established on the site in the 11th century when King Cnut gave the land to his steward, Orc, and the monks managed the swans as a ready source of meat for their banquets. The swannery was used by the monks until 1539 when the monastery was dissolved by King Henry VIII. The ruined remains are still visible near the Church of St Nicholas, Abbotsbury.

'Two Minutes from the Sea' (1985)

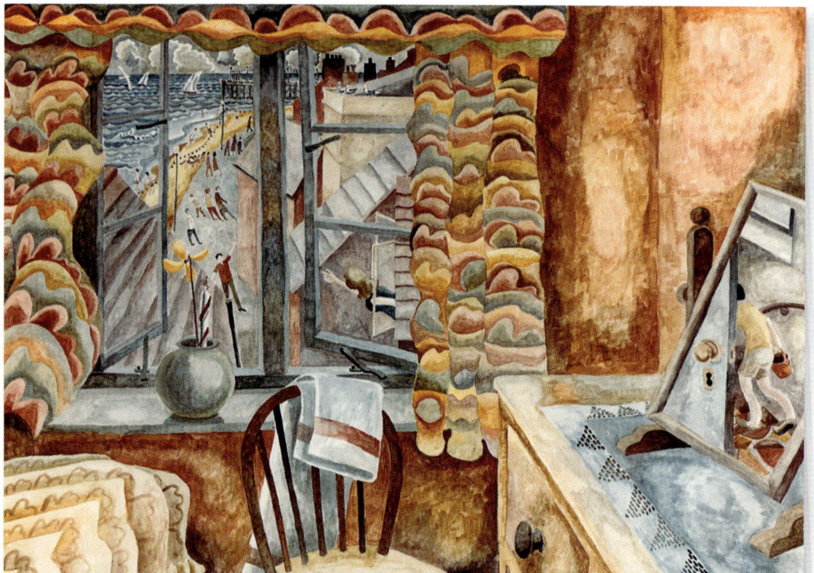

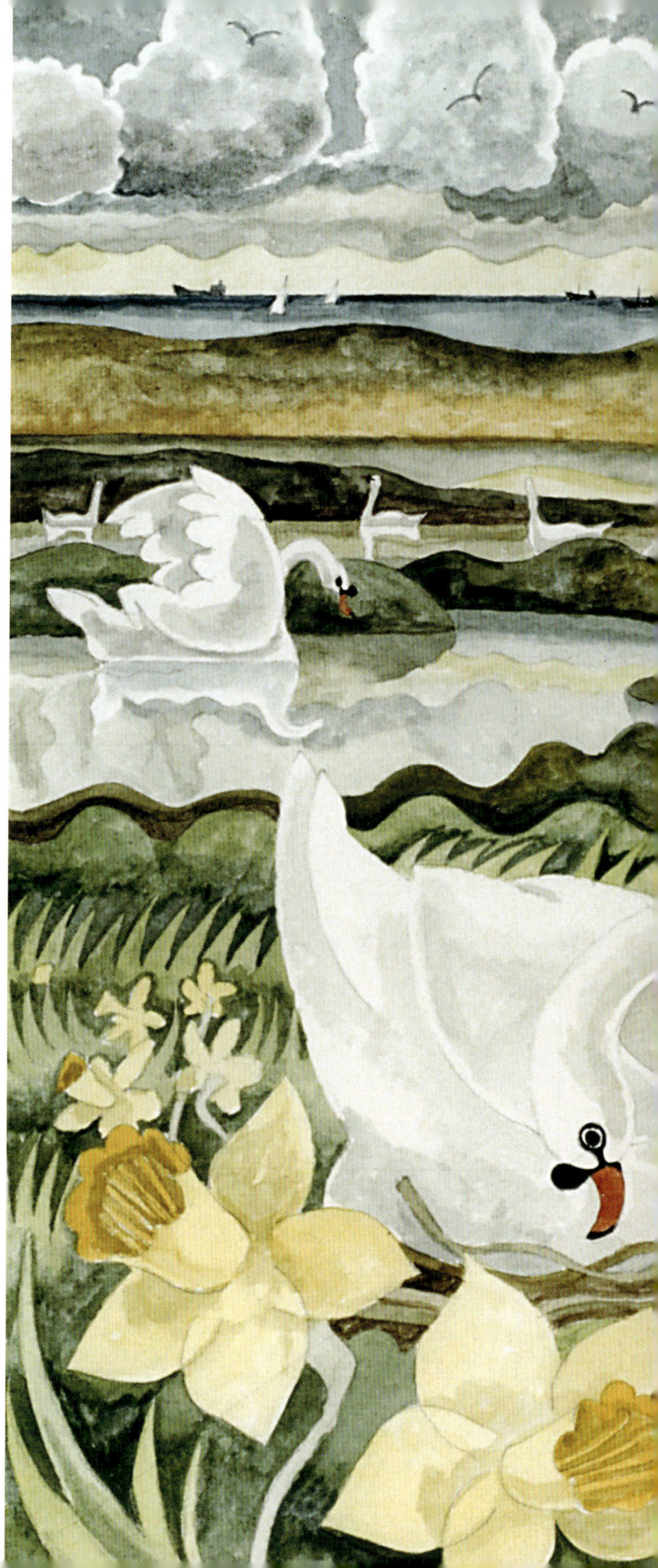

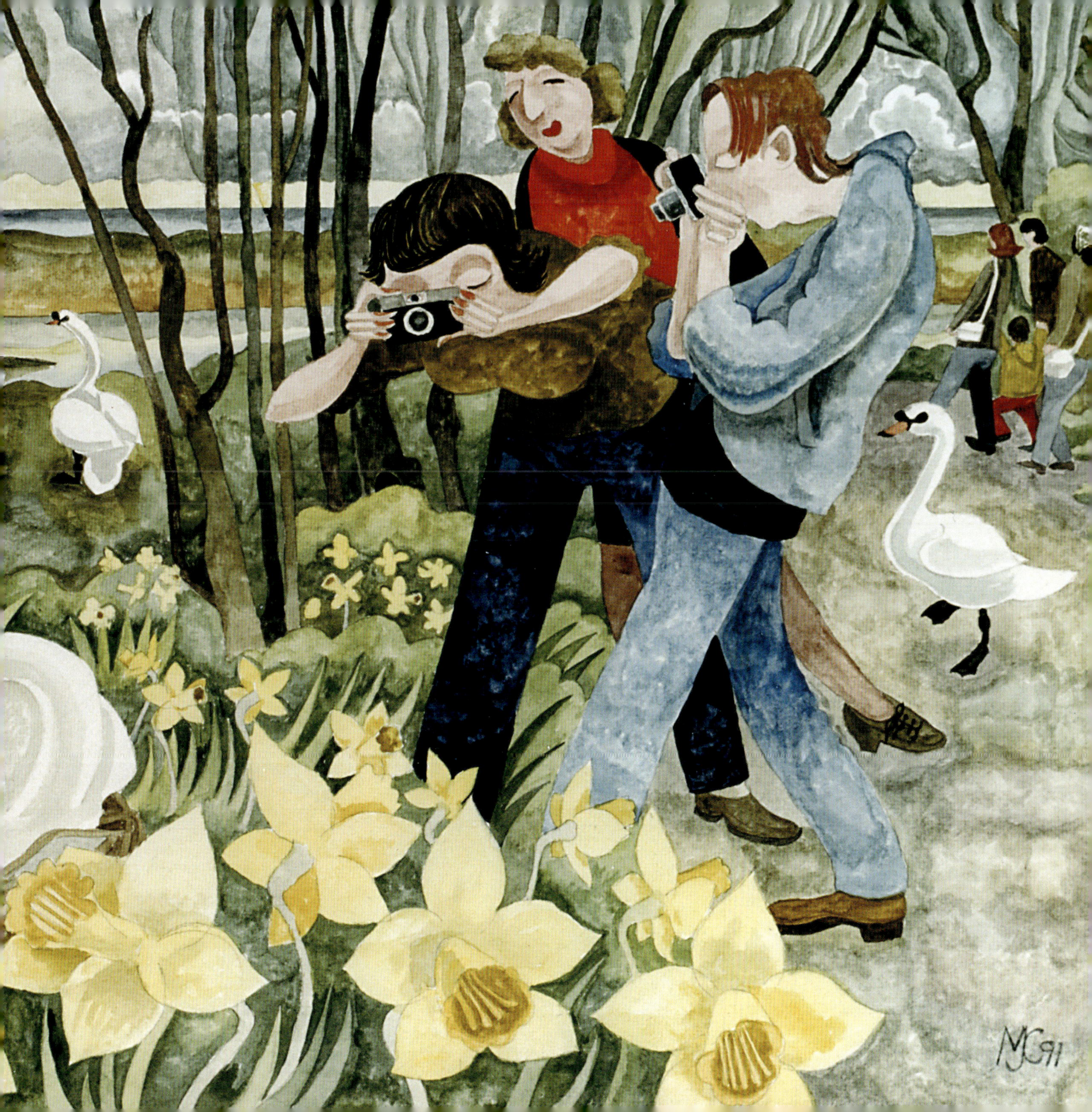
MJC91

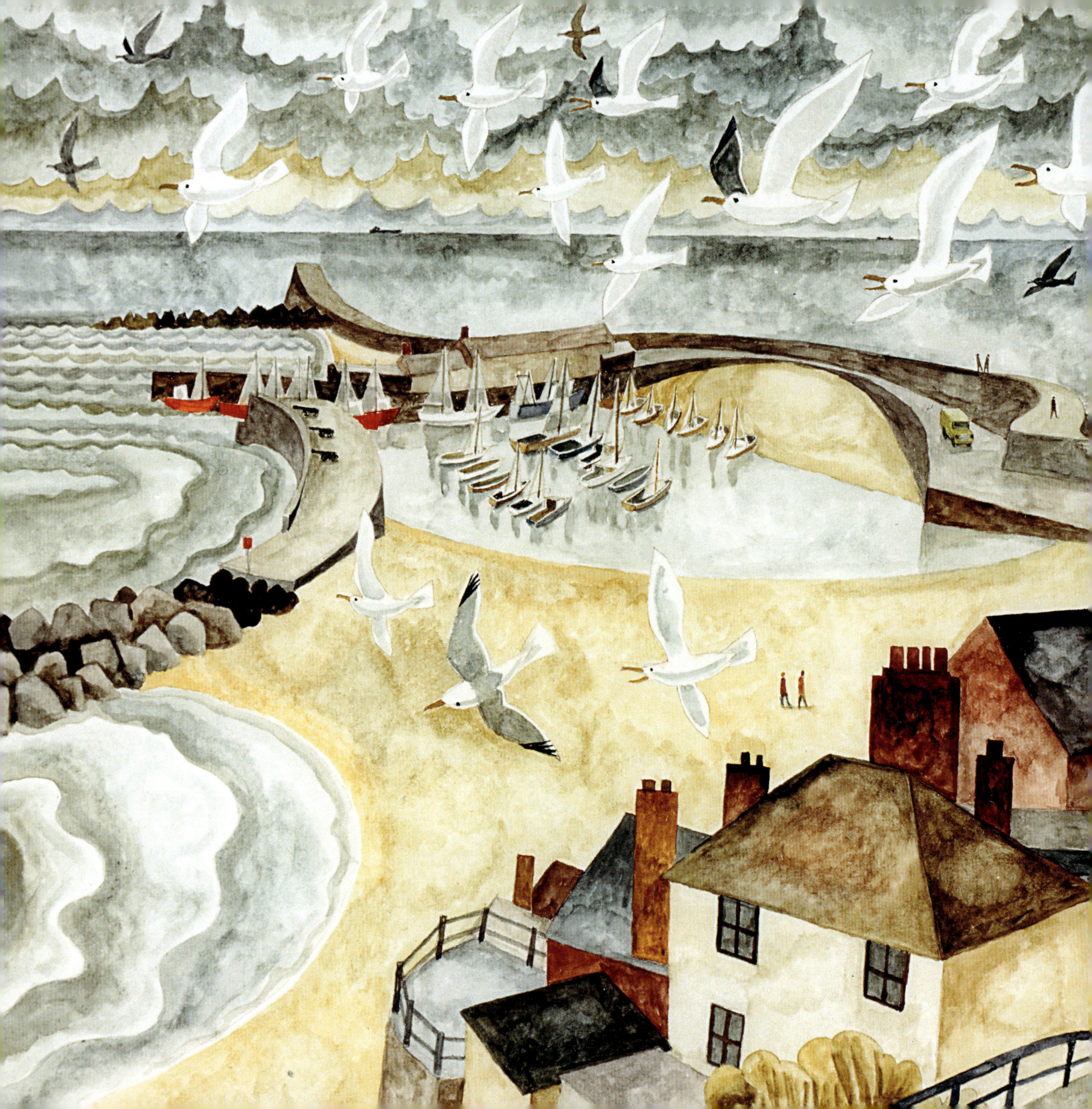

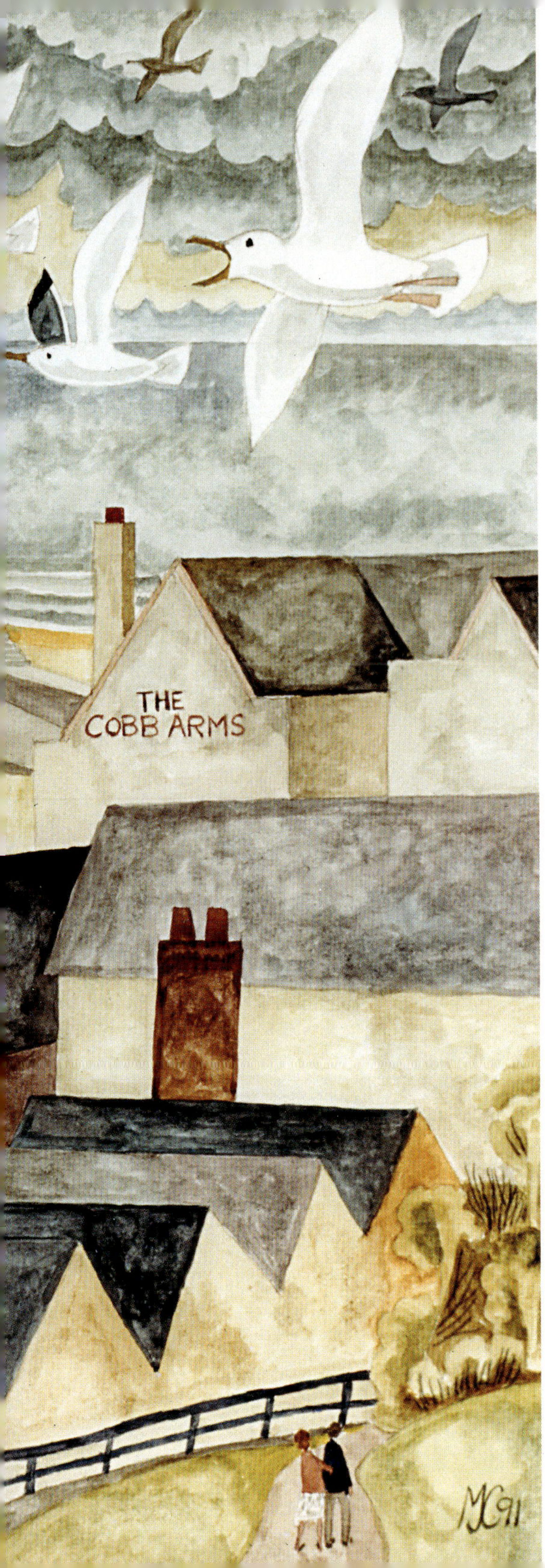

'The Cobb, Lyme Regis' (1991) The distinctive harbour wall for Lyme Regis is called the Cobb. No entirely plausible explanation for the name exists, but a manmade structure has served as a refuge since at least 1313. The major part of the current Cobb dates from the 1820s. A building on the Cobb has been converted to house an aquarium displaying local fish and marine life from the Jurassic Coast.

'Tank Ranges, Dorset' (1991)

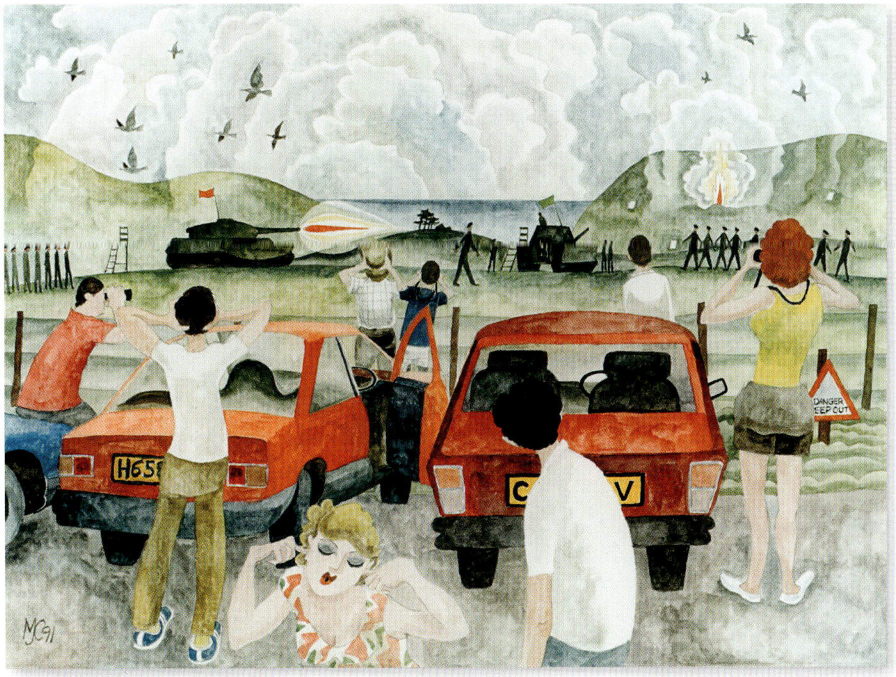

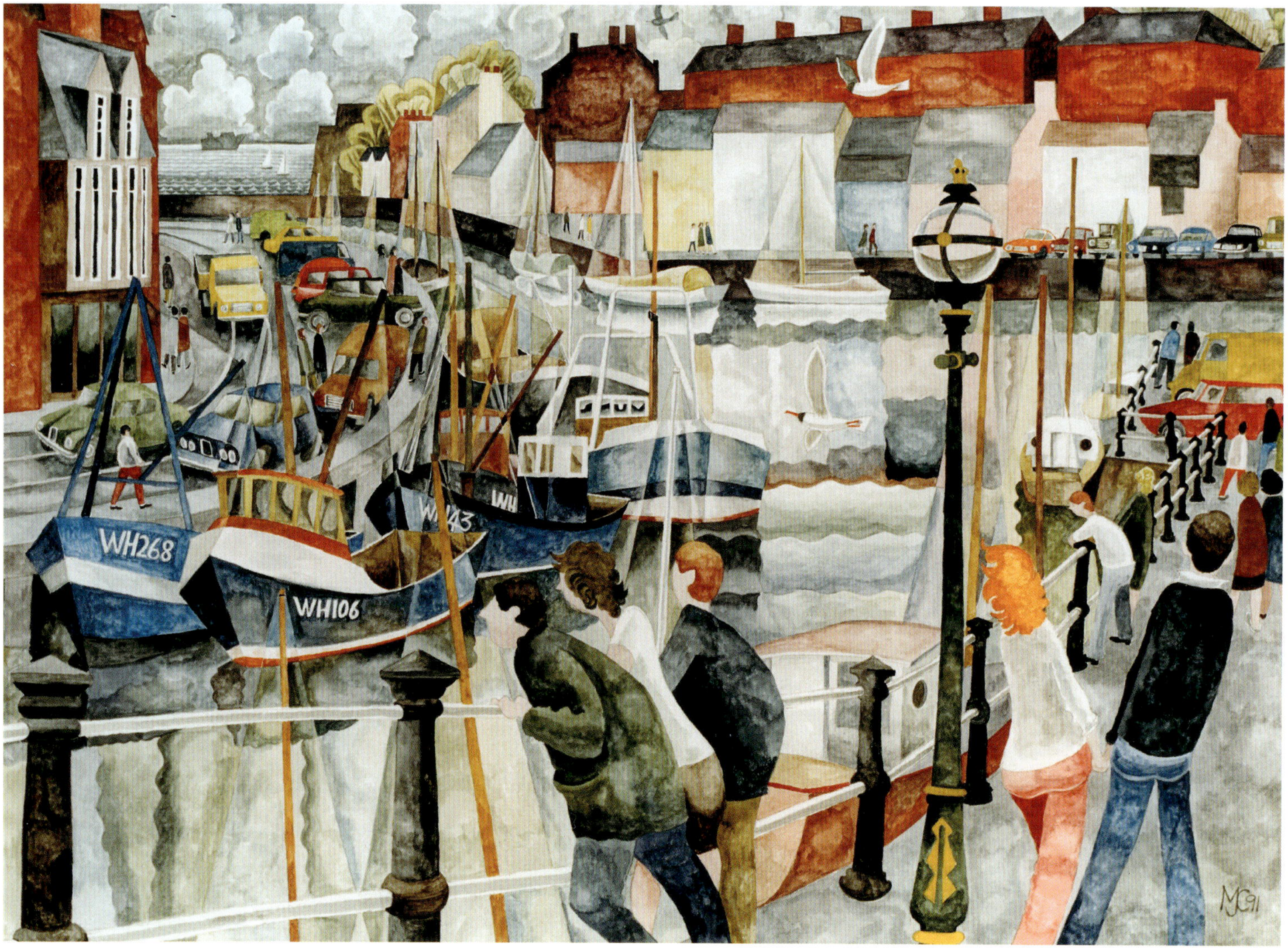

'Weymouth Harbour' (1991) Weymouth Harbour provides ferry services, and is also home to pleasure boats and private yachts. The disused Weymouth Harbour Tramway runs along the north side to the also disused Weymouth Quay railway station. To the north at the harbour entrance is Weymouth Pier, separating the harbour from Weymouth Beach and Weymouth Bay.

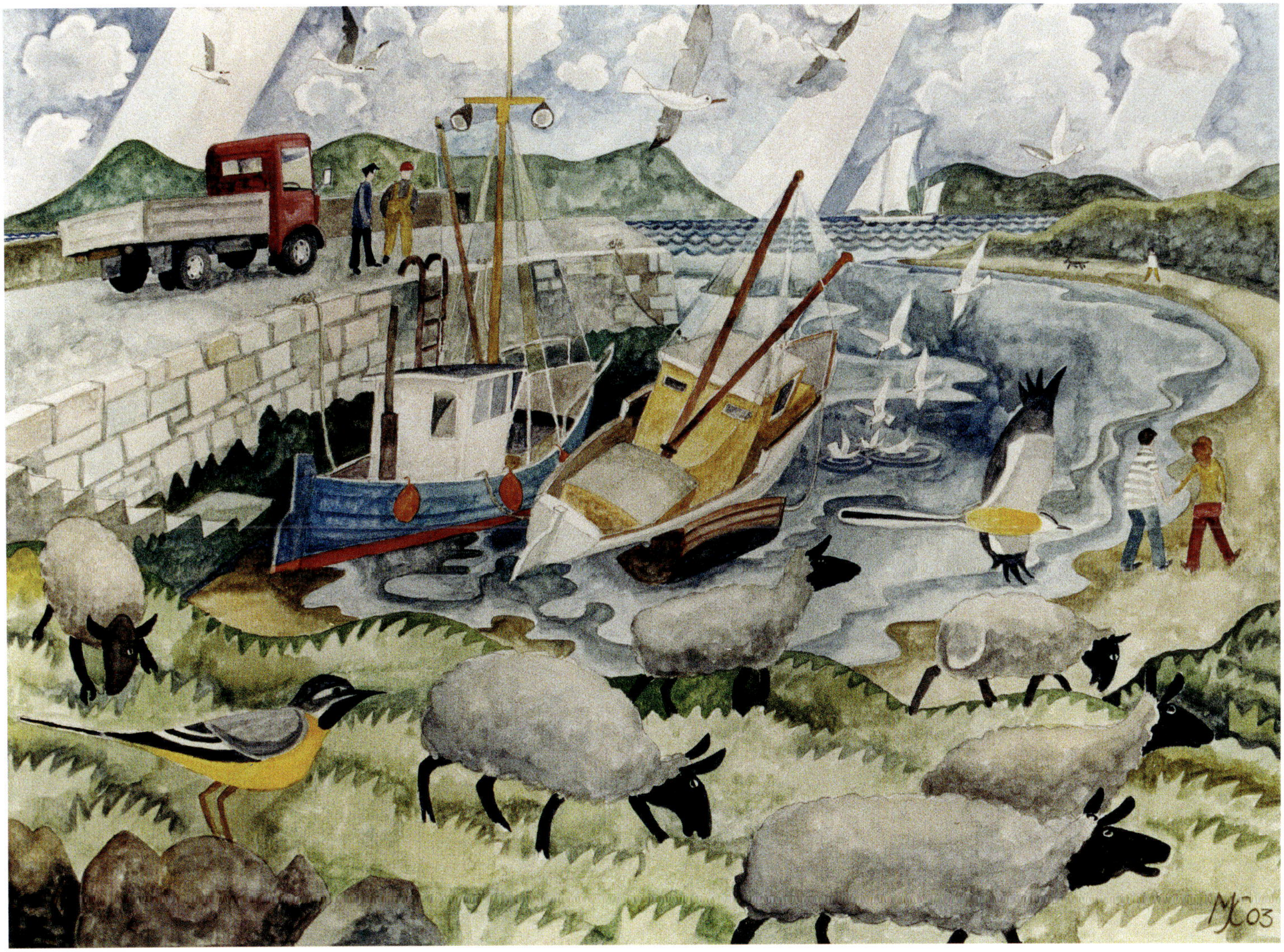

'Sheep and Fishing Boats' (2003) "Ireland is always full of surprise twists and turns when driving along by the sea. Small harbours and hamlets crop up on a journey along the south coast. The sheep were left alone to wander at will along the path and on to the sand. All very casual, Irish and willy-nilly."

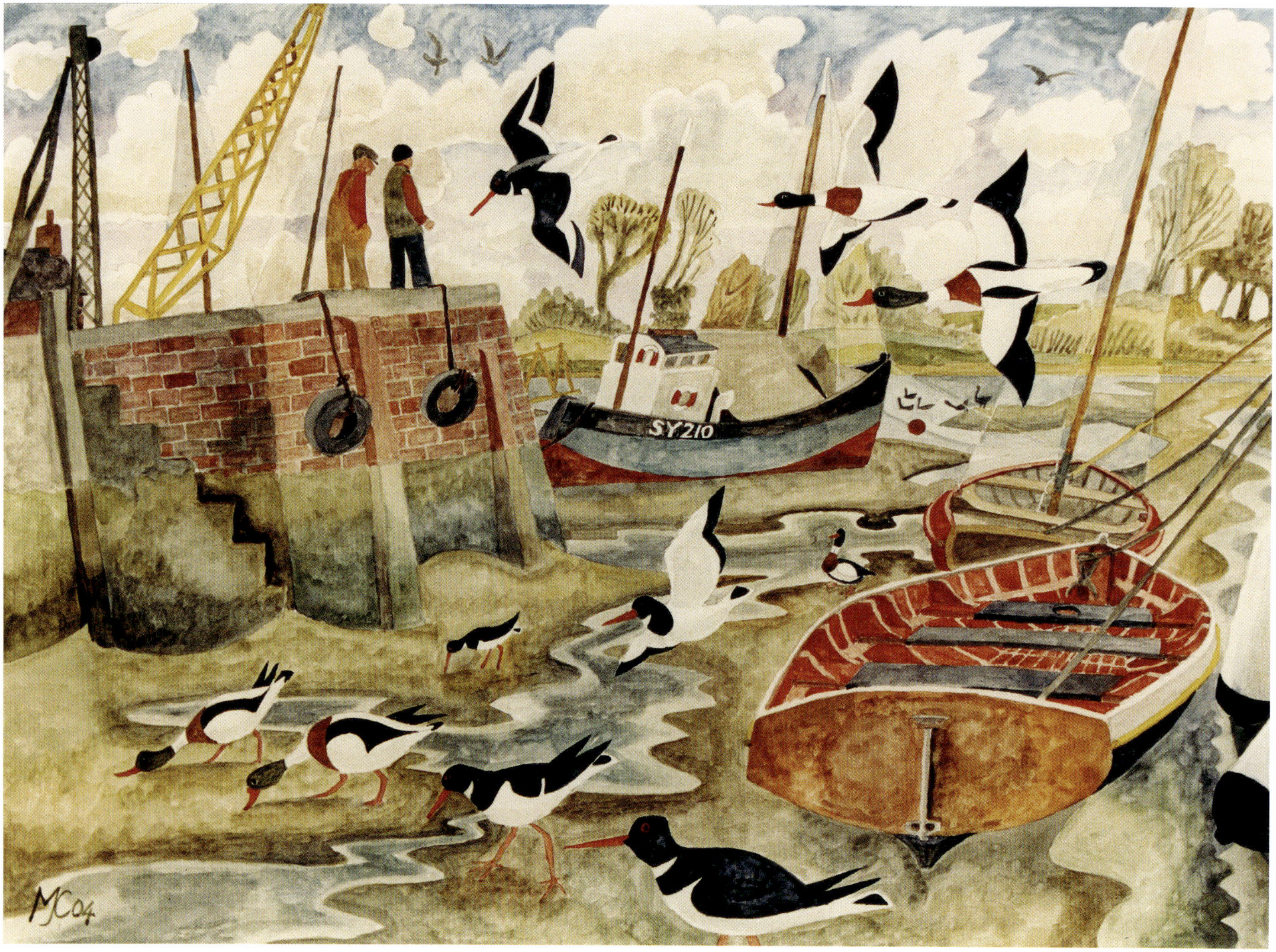

'Shelduck and Oystercatchers' (2004) "It always rains in Ireland – or so they say. This time, a week of sunshine with the roof down on the car gave us a magical holiday, touring the west coast. We made friends with a seal in a harbour. Birdwatched out at sea. Stayed in quaint villages and soaked up the Irish welcome in the local pubs. I think Ireland has become a gourmet destination; everywhere we stopped was a feast of delight. Cottages, once run-down and grey, now sparkle with every colour of the rainbow, row after row of them. Orange Montbretia covered the hills, and Fuchsia hedges brightened the roadside. A wonderful place."

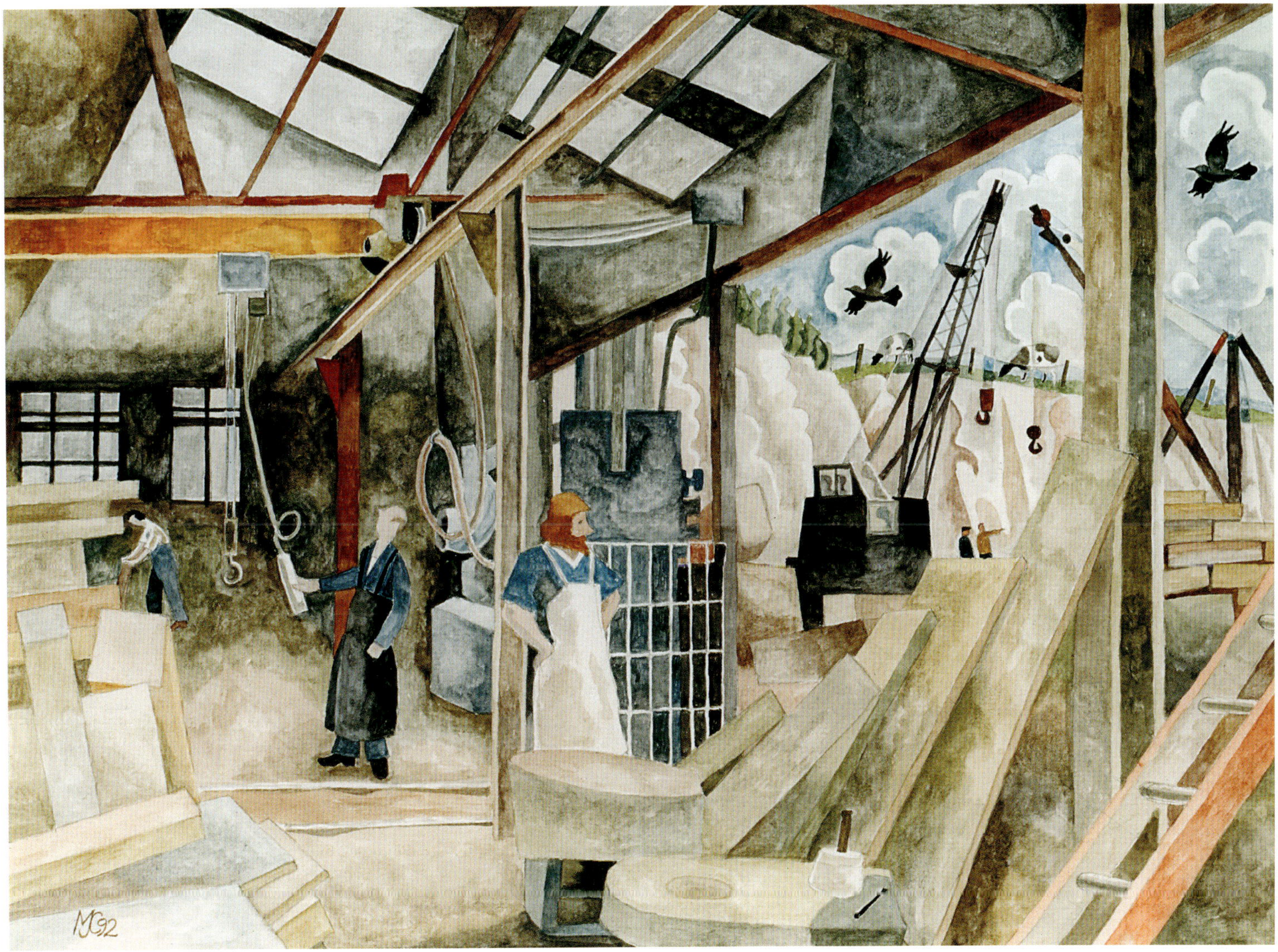

'St Aldhelm's Quarry' (1992) St Aldhelm's Head has a working quarry providing building stone used in Dorset and farther afield. This is the only working quarry where these stones are available for restoration work on historic buildings. Each bed of Purbeck stone is a different colour, ranging from grey/blue to cream/beige. The quarry's product is an excellent building material, as well as being ideal for internal and external paving. It is highly sought after in polished form for cladding, hearths, mantels and worktops, as well as being popular for all aspects of landscaping.

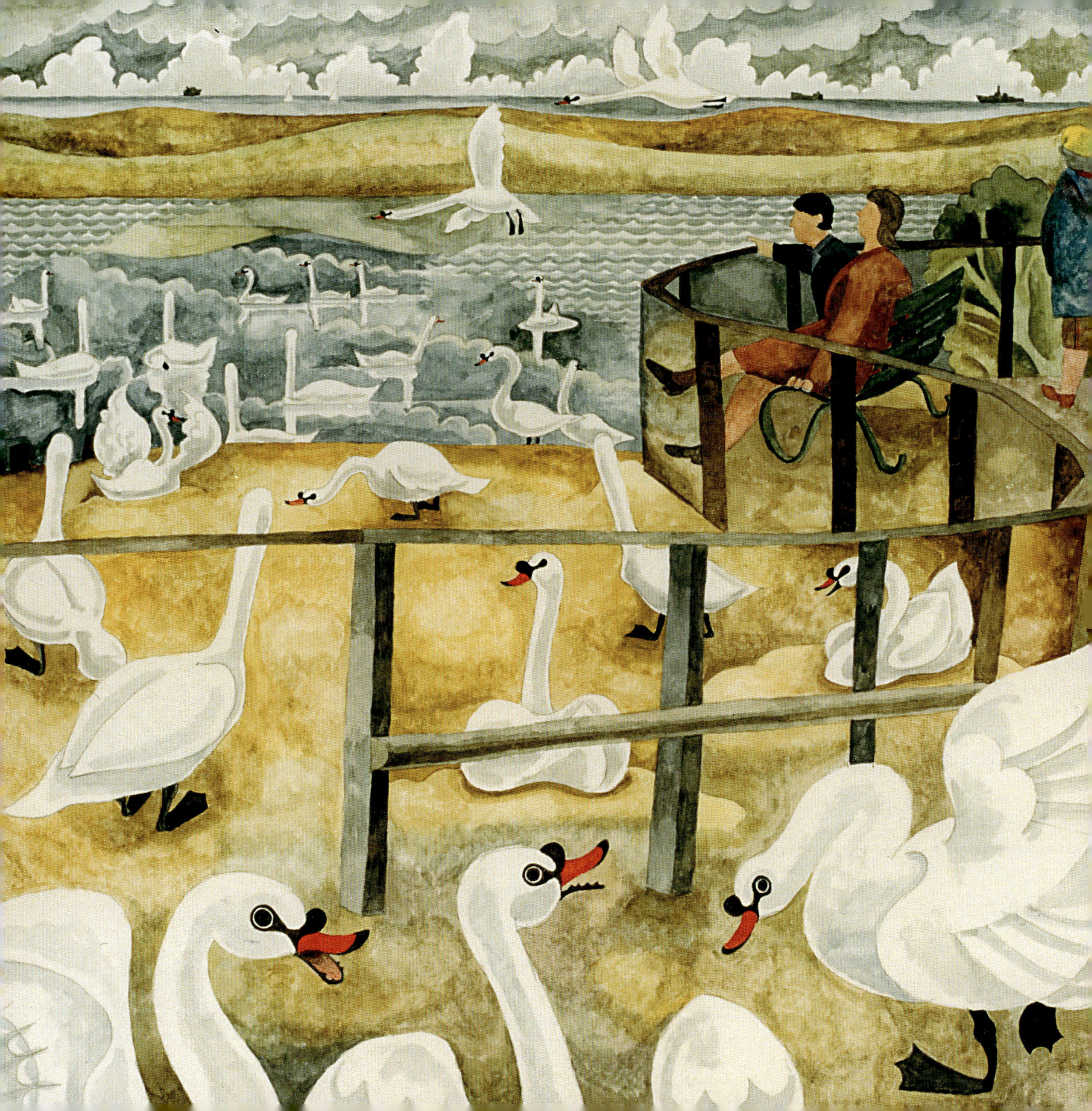

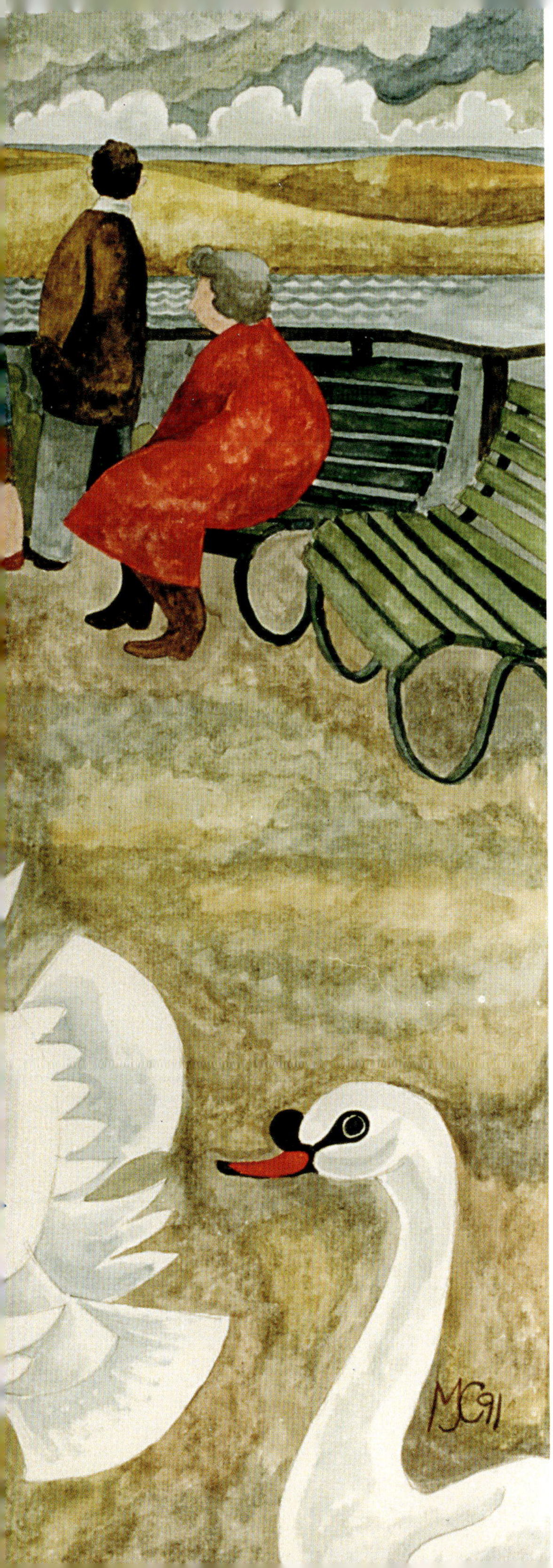

'Swan Watching' (1991) Abbotsbury Swannery is the only place in the world where people are able to walk through the heart of a colony of nesting Mute Swans, spread over a site of some 25 acres. Visitors can help hand-feed 600 swans at 12 noon and 4pm daily.

'Wareham Bridge' (1993)

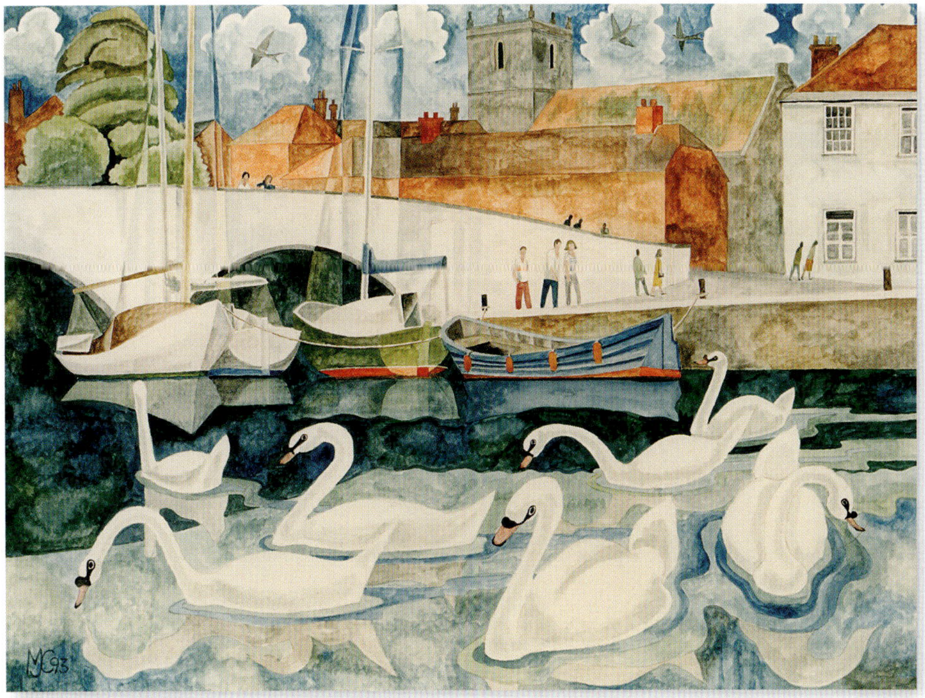

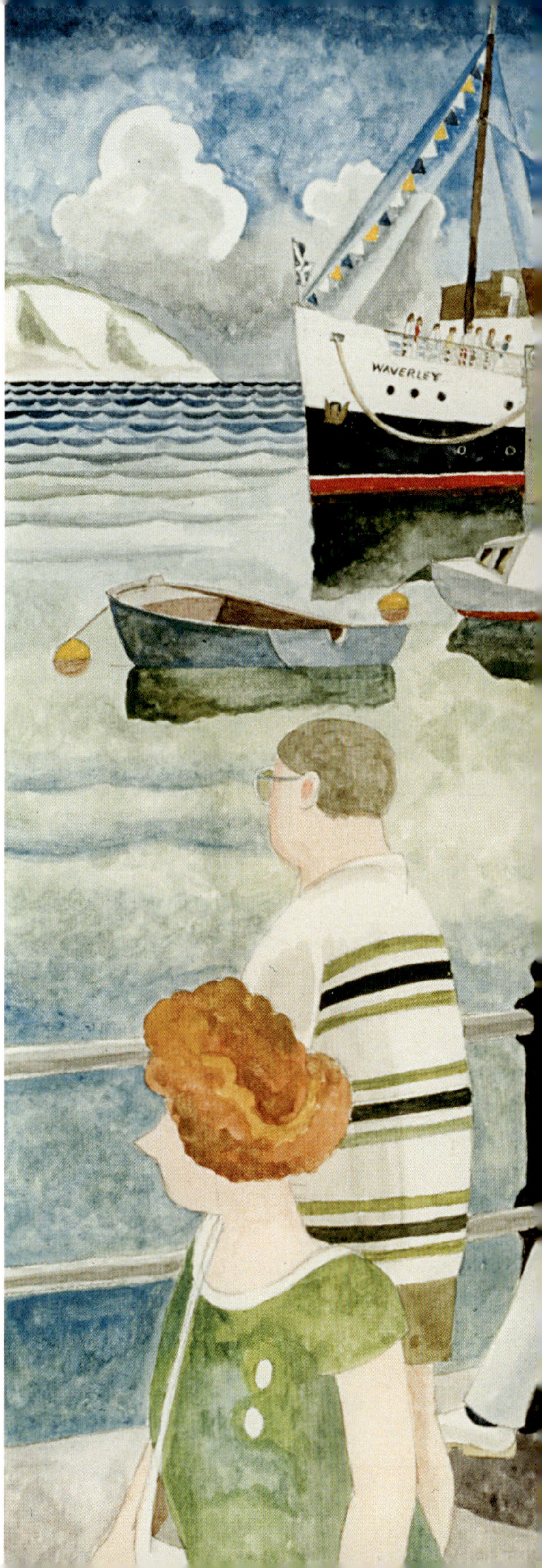

'Swanage Pier' (1992) Another appearance of the paddle steamer Waverley, built in 1946. This time the elderly vessel is moored alongside an elderly structure – the 120-year-old Swanage Pier on Dorset's Jurassic Coast. Time and tide have caused the structure to deteriorate, and in 2017 the go-ahead for restoration was announced after the receipt of £500,000 in funding. Swanage Pier was awarded government cash as part of a planned £2.2 million revamp that will secure its future as a visitor attraction. The project involves replacing pieces of the 120-year-old timber, and turning Marine Villas – which predates the main pier structure by 70 years – into a new visitor centre. There has been a pier at Swanage since 1859, but the current structure was opened in 1897.

'The Quay, Wareham' (1992)

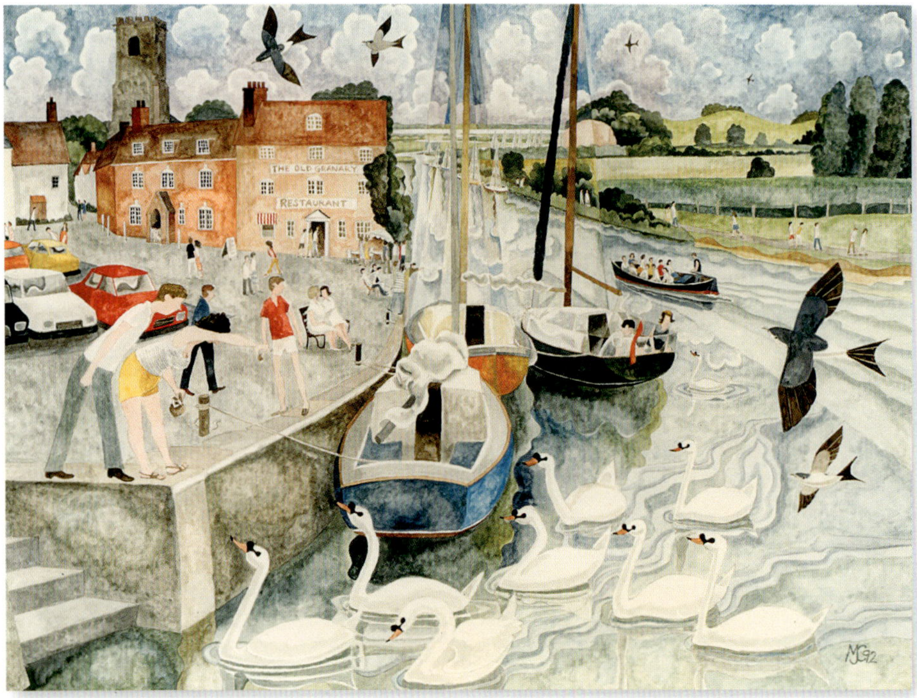

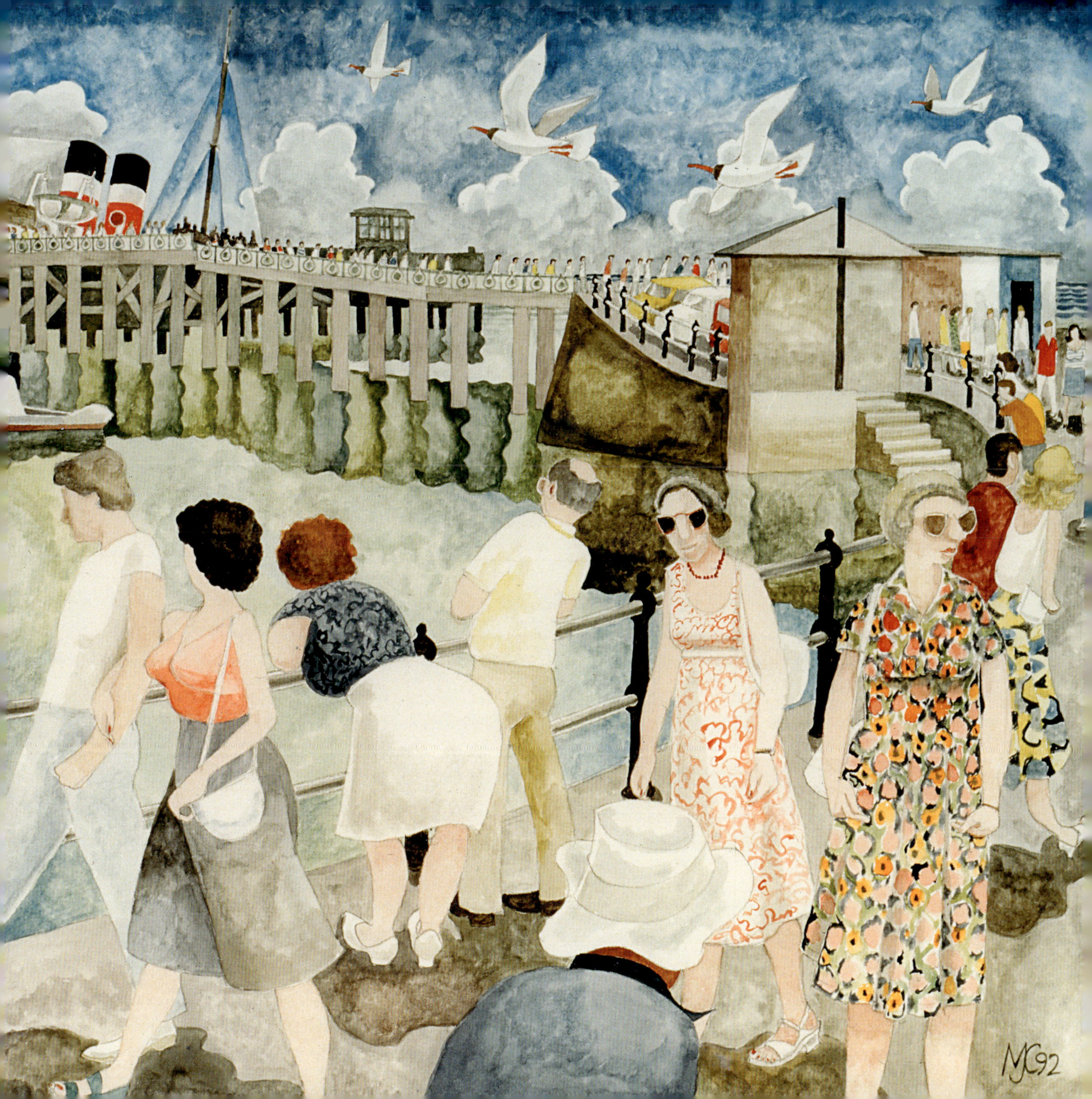
MJC92

INDEX OF PAINTINGS

'Picnic on Shore' (1986) – detail

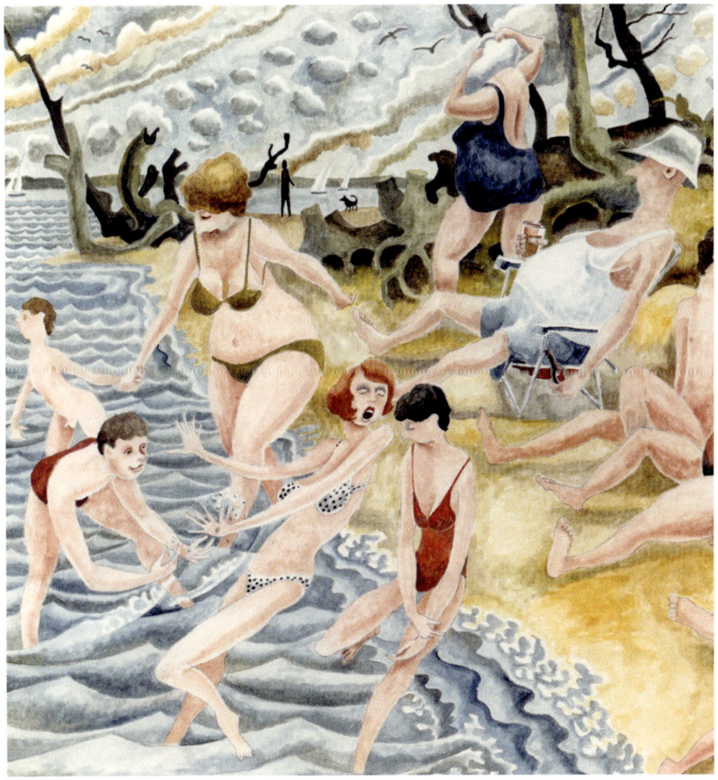

ACKNOWLEDGEMENTS

'Pub near the Docks' (1988) – detail

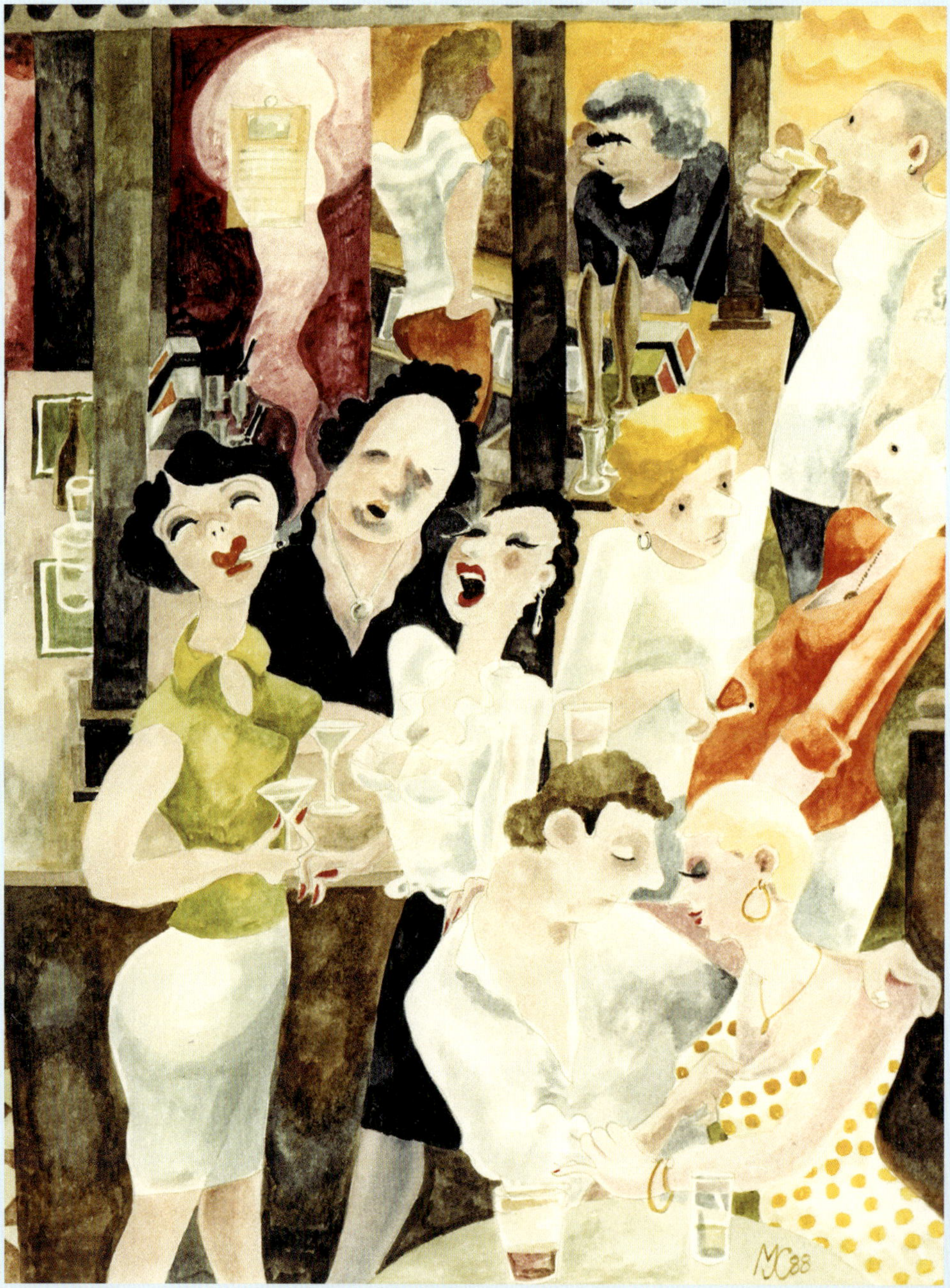

My thanks to my wife, Linda, for all her hard work and support, cataloguing, filing, managing *Coulter Cards* and sifting through more than 1,450 pictures for possible inclusion in my books.

Most of my paintings have been sold. I thank all those lovely people who have collected my work over the years.

To Alan and Marion Marshall (of Mascot Media) for having the confidence to invest in producing and publishing two books about me and my work.
Michael Coulter, Woodbridge, August 2018

Alan and Marion Marshall wish to thank Michael and Linda Coulter for their time and effort in providing material for this and our previous book on the artist. This new title has been conceived, designed, produced and printed in Norfolk by **Mascot Media**. Thanks to our friends at **Swallowtail Print** for another excellent job, printed in Norwich on 150gsm Essential Velvet.

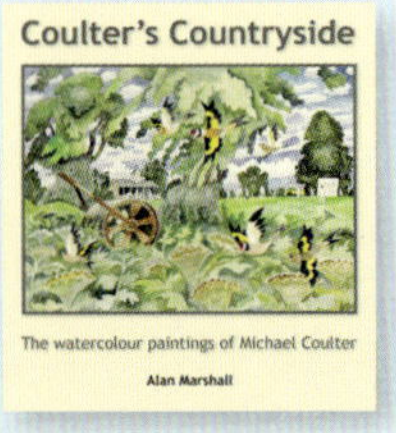